FAREWELL TO RUSSIA

FAREWELL TO RUSSIA

A JOURNEY THROUGH THE FORMER USSR

JOE LUC BARNES

Elliott&Thompson

First published 2026 by
Elliott and Thompson Limited
2 John Street
London WC1N 2ES
www.eandtbooks.com

Represented by:
Authorised Rep Compliance Ltd
Ground Floor, 71 Lower Baggot Street
Dublin, D02 P593
Ireland
www.arccompliance.com

ISBN: 978-1-78396-940-1

Copyright © Joe Luc Barnes 2026

The Author has asserted his rights under the Copyright, Designs and Patents Act, 1988, to be identified as Author of this Work.

All rights reserved. No part of this publication may be reproduced, stored in or introduced into a retrieval system, or transmitted, in any form, or by any means (electronic, mechanical, photocopying, recording or otherwise) without the prior written permission of the publisher. Any person who does any unauthorised act in relation to this publication may be liable to criminal prosecution and civil claims for damages.

Maps by JP Map Graphics Ltd

9 8 7 6 5 4 3 2 1

A catalogue record for this book is available from the British Library.

Typesetting: Marie Doherty

Printed by CPI Group (UK) Ltd, Croydon, CR0 4YY

To my parents

CONTENTS

	Introduction	ix
1	Russia: The Republic of Indifference	1

THE CAUCASUS

2	Armenia: The Republic of Survival	21
3	Azerbaijan: The Republic of Oil and Gas	47
4	Georgia: The Republic of Thorned Roses	63

CENTRAL ASIA

5	Kazakhstan: The Republic of Compromise	85
6	Kyrgyzstan: The Republic of Uprisings	107
7	Uzbekistan: The Republic of Islam	121
8	Tajikistan: The Republic of Emigration	141
9	Turkmenistan: The Republic of the Great Leader	165

EUROPE

10	Belarus: The Remainer Republic	189
11	The Baltic States: The Straight-A Republics	211
12	Moldova: The Republic of Reunions	233
13	Ukraine: The Republic of Resistance	249

| | Epilogue | 273 |

	Acknowledgements	279
	A Note on Names	283
	Notes	285
	Index	295

INTRODUCTION

Back in 2014, I landed a job as a kind of private tutor for an obscenely wealthy Russian boy. The Governor – that was my official title. It was sold to me as akin to something out of a Tolstoy novel: I would be playing the twenty-first-century role of the educated Frenchman, sent to civilise a young boyar.

I was matched with a whimsical six-year-old called Ivan, who lived just outside Moscow in a sprawling wooden country house that Russians call a dacha. For the first few months, I went resignedly into battle, armed with nothing but the threat that I might not let him play on my phone after dinner. He spoke no English and I no Russian, and he resented being forced to talk to me every day after school. Classes were a non-starter, but he occasionally consented to let me join in doing things he liked. We played Lego, rode bikes and, for an hour of each shift, I read him a story in an attempt to coax him towards the writing desk.

Sundays were the worst. That was when the cousins came round. Ivan's nanny, a stout, kindly woman named Zhenya, encouraged the children to 'play hide-and-seek with the Englishman'. I trod a lonely trail around the fairy-tale grounds, surrounded by ten-foot-high walls, combing the garages and checking under the fleet of cars for Vanya, Leonid and Anya. It was great fun for the kids, who asked the rest of the household staff for help. The drivers would point me in one direction, the armed guards in another. It was the cleaners who took pity on me, usually breaking the news that the kids had got bored ten minutes ago and gone back into the house, where the rest of the family was having a champagne lunch.

Champagne was just the start of it. The caviar and the private jets, they really were a thing. But the place to truly observe how much Russia had moved on from its proletarian past was on the roads.

With the dawn of the free market, those with a rouble or two to rub together rushed to the showrooms, and Moscow's neoclassical avenues became a place to display all kinds of pomp and chicanery. It wasn't just the brand of car that was important: wealth and power were demonstrated by the ease with which you navigated the apocalyptic traffic.

Those with deep enough pockets or good enough connections could attach a flashing blue light to their executive limousine. Locals dubbed these *blue buckets* and there was a special lane in the middle of the main avenues reserved for them to whizz to work, untroubled by the gridlock on either side. The little people were left to battle through the morass, each doing their best to claw back vital seconds. Some even resorted to tailgating ambulances as they scythed their way through the morning rush hour.

Ivan and I spent a lot of time on the road, chauffeured to his various extra-curricular activities by one of the family's many drivers. They tended to be ex-military types, perhaps because they were used to taking orders. Some had seen action in Afghanistan and Chechnya, but left the military unprepared for a world of ruthless landlords and insecure contracts. Work with this family at least provided steady employment.

Zhenya had been a nurse in the Soviet days. When she found she could earn three times more as Ivan's nanny, the decision to abandon a lifetime of public service was an easy one. The transition to capitalism in the 1990s saw her savings evaporate and she had her daughter's future to think of after all.

The Soviet Union, the world's first socialist state, spanned around one-sixth of the world's land surface. 'An unbreakable union of free republics', according to the first line of its national anthem, it was nevertheless given a firm steering from Moscow. In the late 1980s, Mikhail Gorbachev's attempts at economic and political reform, which began gradually, quickly spiralled out of control. Moscow's grip on the economy – and over the fifteen republics – slipped away as the state shrivelled into non-existence and the unbreakable union fell apart.

The new Russian Federation descended into a maelstrom. In 1992, inflation hit 2,500 per cent, and male life expectancy had collapsed to just fifty-seven years by 1994.[1] In Saint Petersburg, one KGB officer later claimed to have worked as a taxi driver to make ends meet.[2]

That's not to say there hadn't been winners. Those who moved fast and lived on their wits made millions – and some. Ivan's father remembered the period following the Soviet collapse as the most exciting of his life. On Sunday mornings, on family trips to the *banya* – a Russian take on the sauna – he would regale me with tales of high-stakes business deals in the far-flung Russian regions. With the pair of us stripped naked and getting whipped by birch leaves amid the scalding heat, he spoke with pride about the gold-plated pistol once gifted to him by a local mayor, or the redneck slang he'd learned from Texan oilmen eager for their cut of the communist carcass.

But by 2014, the former KGB cabbie was now running the country, and the days of Texan oilmen flying in to cut deals were over. Sanctions had taken hold, and the West was no longer a business partner but the enemy at the gates.

I had picked an inauspicious time to arrive. Not three months prior, Russian special forces had taken over Ukraine's Crimean Peninsula in an almost bloodless coup, and Moscow was still basking in the glory of conquest. Everyone I met loved discussing international affairs, and they did so with an alarming intensity. As soon as they knew they were talking to an Englishman, the subject of Crimea would rear its head.

The arguments in favour of Russia's actions, first alien to me, soon became predictable. There were three general lines of attack:

1. *Khrushchev's kickback:* this tended to be first port of call for the educated classes. Ivan's mother once cornered me with it over dinner in a luxury French ski resort. According to her, Crimea had always been part of Russia. However, Khrushchev* had transferred it as a sweetener to Ukraine when both were part of the Soviet Union. It was just a piece of administrative tinkering to get the Ukrainians to back his bid for Party leadership. Now that Ukraine and Russia were no longer part of the same country, Russia was 'simply taking back what is ours'.

---

* Nikita Khrushchev, leader of the Soviet Union from 1953 to 1964 (serving as First Secretary and later premier).

2. *Protecting the ethnic Russians:* a favourite of Zhenya and people who watched a lot of state television, this was the belief that the new government in Kyiv, installed after an illegal and anti-democratic coup in February 2014, was full of fascists who were forcing the Russian-speaking majority in Crimea to speak Ukrainian. Crimeans wanted no part of this, and it was Moscow's duty to protect them.
3. *Securing the Black Sea Fleet:* The Crimean naval base at Sevastopol is one of Russia's most storied ports – so strategically important that Moscow negotiated to lease part of the port from independent Ukraine and continued to base its Black Sea Fleet there. This third theory claimed that the new government in Kyiv and its Western allies planned to boot the Russians out and turn Sevastopol into a NATO base within weeks. Therefore, the president had no choice but to act. The drivers, as former military men, liked this one.

This triad – historical justice, linguistic determinism and national security – were employed again and again with varying levels of sophistication and pedantry. It was only when all three had failed to convince a sceptical foreigner that they would play their ace: 'The Americans invade whoever they want, so why can't we?' The usual suspects were then reeled off: Iraq, Afghanistan, Libya, Yugoslavia – they held a particular animus about Kosovo.

That is not to say there was no nuance, but there was remarkable unanimity on the merits of the military conquest of another country's territory, and Vladimir Putin's popularity rating had risen to a record high of 85 per cent.[3] The patriotic zeal reached fever pitch on 9 May, or Victory Day, held to celebrate the triumph of the Soviet Union over Nazi Germany in the Great Patriotic War of 1941–5. It was the day new Russia paid homage to its Soviet predecessor.

This wasn't the only echo of the USSR: in the media, the weeknight news show *Vremya* remained the same that had been broadcast since 1968. Every evening at the dacha, Ivan, Zhenya and I would watch it while we ate. As the summer wore on, images of the 'War in the Donbas' flashed across the screen. According to the channel, this area of Eastern Ukraine had been inspired by the example of Crimea and risen up to liberate itself from the 'fascists' in Kyiv.

For a bunch of apparently unaided freedom fighters, these separatists were doing remarkably well. There was much tutting from Zhenya as the news reports went into gratuitous detail about the atrocities committed by the Ukrainian army.

'We are one people,' she would tell me. 'The Russians and the Ukrainians. Why did they want to pull the whole thing apart? Was it worth it, their *independence*? Look at the state of their country now . . .' and she would stand, gazing despairingly at the screen, before Ivan would jerk her out of her nostalgic reverie by demanding more ice cream.

I decided the time was ripe for a weekend jaunt to Ukraine. In those days you could still fly from Moscow to Kyiv (you could also still call it Kiev), and in some ways it was difficult to tell the two cities apart. The Ukrainian capital had the same belligerent drivers, the same architecture and an eerily similar metro system, replete with glittering chandeliers and steely blue trains that hadn't changed since the 1980s. The food too was similar – the debate about who invented borscht, a traditional beetroot soup, went all the way to UNESCO in 2020; Ukraine won.[4] The two peoples even shared the same wicked sense of humour.

Yet there was something about Kyiv that felt more open. Perhaps because we weren't asked for documents every fifteen minutes, or that people weren't constantly primed for a political argument, but Ukrainians seemed a laid-back bunch compared to their northern cousins. There was no trace of these legendary fascists either. For all the huffing and puffing of the Kremlin's television channels, nobody had any problem with us speaking Russian. Many Kyivans were native speakers, and it was generally accepted as the language of business. Our guide, a warm, extremely patriotic young woman named Julia, did her best to teach us a few words of Ukrainian, but the only one I remembered was *budmo*, which meant 'cheers'.

Another difference was the attitude of people here towards the Soviet Union. Despite four out of its seven leaders having strong links to Ukraine,* the USSR was viewed in Kyiv as primarily a Russian colonial project and remembered mainly for its most evil acts.

At Chernobyl, for example, we were treated to a tirade about how the incompetence of the Soviets had cost thousands of lives, and how 'the Russians' had forced the people of Kyiv to participate in the Victory Day march of 1986 when the air was still thick with radioactive fallout. Meanwhile, at the Holodomor Museum, we were told about how Stalin had perpetrated a deliberate, genocidal famine against Ukrainians in the 1930s. Stalin also took a lot of flak from our hosts for destroying much of Kyiv's architectural heritage – the Red Army had mined the entire city as a welcome present for the Germans in September 1941.

While in Moscow Karl Marx's statue still stood opposite the Bolshoi, Lenin remained embalmed in Red Square and red stars adorned many public buildings, Ukrainians were busy toppling and defacing communist relics. One Lenin in Odessa was given a Darth Vader makeover, while in an East Ukrainian village a statue of Friedrich Engels was sawn in half.[5] In an unlikely victory for upcycling, it was later restored and now stands in Manchester city centre.

Given the loss of Crimea and a Russian-sponsored war in the east of the country, perhaps it's unsurprising that Ukrainians took every opportunity to scorn their Soviet heritage. But it intrigued me that two countries could view a shared history so differently.

Over the years that followed, I would travel to some of the other forgotten fragments of the Soviet empire, and there were a hundred different takes in each country on communist rule and the merits of independence. Later I would live in China, which has been ruled by its own Communist Party since 1949, and where the collapse of the Soviet Union is viewed as a salutary lesson from history. Slowly, the idea of this book began to

---

* Leonid Brezhnev preferred to consider himself Russian towards the end of his life, but his early passport shows him as Ukrainian; Nikita Khrushchev was born on the Russian border with Ukraine and raised in the Donbas; Konstantin Chernenko was born to a Ukrainian family in Siberia. Mikhail Gorbachev was also half-Ukrainian.

emerge: I would go back to Moscow and then journey across all fourteen of the other former Soviet states, exploring the varying paths they have taken since the red flag fell.

It's about time we went through the list of countries of the former Soviet Union that are the subject of this book, which I've grouped geographically:

The Caucasus: Armenia, Azerbaijan, Georgia
Crushed between Russia and Iran, the Black Sea and the Caspian, the Caucasus has long been a pilgrimage site for poets. Its towering peaks promise paradise, but uncompromising pride has all too often left its valleys stained with blood.

Central Asia: Kazakhstan, Kyrgyzstan, Uzbekistan,
Tajikistan, Turkmenistan
Something of the ancient khans endures in Central Asia's modern rulers, who reign with iron fists, their wild monuments rising from desert to steppe. As a slumbering giant awakes to the east, Russia's backyard is becoming China's front porch, breathing life into the bazaars of the old Silk Road. Meanwhile, the revival of Islam seems unstoppable, especially among the region's restless youth.

Europe: Belarus, Lithuania, Latvia, Estonia, Moldova, Ukraine
Brussels and Moscow vie for influence over the green fields and forests of the old continent. Its cobblestone streets and Soviet towers are rent by insecurity and an ever-present nostalgia – although for what, that varies.

And of course there's Russia.

Now, you might be asking yourself some obvious questions. What is it that actually connects these former Soviet countries today? The term post-Soviet is now widely criticised, with some arguing that, after thirty-five years apart, the only things these states now share are a tragic history and their use of the 1,520mm rail gauge. After all, how much do a Tajik Muslim on the border with China and an Estonian atheist committed to the EU really have in common?

But for me, the very fact that these republics became independent at the same time binds them together. Each has had to confront dilemmas that will face any country learning to stand on its own two feet: how to keep faith in independence when the promised benefits are not immediately realised; how to muzzle an old elite bent on turning back the clock; how to safeguard the rights of minorities in the new state, or those of mixed parentage who felt the former union gave them a sense of identity; and how to manage a fraught relationship with an old master too large to ignore.

They say it takes half the length of a relationship to get over it. The Soviet Union fell just short of its sixty-ninth birthday. So as its successor states enter their thirty-fifth year, now seems a good time to take stock of the lessons of independence. I also happen to be the same age as these countries, and, as I am constantly reminded, by thirty-five one should have got one's act together and started laying down some roots.

These fifteen coming-of-age stories could be viewed as a guidebook for Catalans and Celts, Kurds and Québécois, and all manner of peoples seeking a state to call their own. Equally, they might offer warnings. After all, not everything about independence is rosy. It's also difficult to come back once you've left – a collapsed empire tends to be something of a geopolitical Humpty Dumpty.

But whether this book gives secessionists encouragement or pause for thought, the former Soviet Union is a part of the world that deserves to be engaged with more. Whatever buzz issue it is in today's politics, be it climate change, the market versus the state, identity politics, migration, democracy, gay rights, radical Islam, nuclear weapons or genocide, these countries have seen it all and have something to teach us.

We all know the stereotypes that conspire to keep them off most people's travel itineraries: a cold, snowy land populated by hard, unsmiling people, where cities are a sea of identical, monochrome tower blocks and the countryside is infested with bears. Meanwhile the KGB (who are always watching you) enforce the compulsory rolling of all 'r's, as well as a blanket ban on the use of the indefinite and definite article. Violation of these laws, or indeed any other, will see you carted off to a Siberian labour camp in the back of a Black Maria.

I won't pretend that there are no tower blocks or that the winters are balmy, but I'd like to think that this book might inspire at least some readers to give these countries a chance. Nature lovers will find epic mountains; historians cobblestone old towns and storied Silk Road cities; and those partial to a tipple are spoiled by Georgian and Moldovan wines, Armenian brandy, and vodka in industrial supply. There is food to warm the soul – hearty soups, pilaf ladled straight from a bazaar cauldron, bread baked in clay ovens – and landscapes to stir the imagination: the endless Kazakh steppe, potholed mountain passes in the Caucasus, Tajikistan's 'Tunnel of Death', Turkmenistan's 'Gate to Hell', or a sunset over Ukraine's glowing wheatfields.

Thirty-five years after the Soviet Union fell, this book traces how these countries have emerged from the chaos, dusted themselves down, and set about building nations, identities and a future. In some places, the 'Farewell to Russia' has been hesitant and incomplete; in others, brusque and not so fond, though none has been able to dismiss it entirely. Stepping back, the question remains: has independence delivered what was promised?

1

RUSSIA
THE REPUBLIC OF INDIFFERENCE

Friday, 11 February 2022

You know it's a cold day when the snow squeaks as you tread on it. You know it's a very cold day when your snot starts to freeze in your nostrils. Today is a very cold day. The sort of dazzling winter day when the low-angled sun reflects off the icy roads, when Muscovites whip out a combination of sunglasses and long fur coats, only to sweat profusely as the latter prove far too warm when packed onto public transport.

It's been four years since I was last in the Russian capital, but I receive a reassuring static shock of welcome from the door handle to the metro station. The architecture remains as imposing as ever, and the gaggle of bored, puffy-hatted police officers still mill around the station entrance. A Central Asian commuter in front of me is pulled aside for questioning – evidently the shameless racial profiling hasn't changed either.

But an undeniable air of sleekness has slithered in. The officers don shinier armour, and sophisticated CCTV cameras stare blankly down from the ornate ceiling. I buy a pre-loaded metro card as usual from the sullen-faced babushka in the ticket office, but it seems I'm the only one still doing this; everyone else is using Apple Pay.

One minute and thirty-five seconds are showing on the platform timer when a quiet, modern engine appears where the rattling tin can should have been. Slightly unnerved, I board to find a spacious carriage with digital screens and USB chargers under each seat. Meanwhile, beneath each Cyrillic station name is a neat Latin transliteration. No one is reading books any more; the furrowed brows are now flicking aimlessly through their phones.

As I exit the station onto the vast, snowy square, I'm confronted by a bus pulling silently up to the traffic lights. Emblazoned in large letters on its side are the words 'This is an Electrobus'. Even Russia, the oil-belching, gas-guzzling heir to Stalin's five-year plans, is going green.

An antidote to all this aspirational globalism arrives in the form of lunch. I'm meeting an old friend at Café Pushkin, which, as Moscow restaurants go, is the closest you can come to cliché. The suffocating warmth of the air conditioning blasts me as I step inside, and I'm immediately ushered to the cloakroom. A quick note in praise of Soviet civilisation: in every restaurant, bar or nightclub there is *always* a cloakroom and it's *always* free. Feeling considerably lighter, I spot Yegor in a corner, dressed very formally as usual. I befriended Yegor long ago at a language exchange; I never quite found out what he does, but he's always been a reliable drinking companion.

'Good to be back?' he asks, after grabbing me in a bearhug. I tell him of the jarring feeling of unfamiliarity I'd experienced that morning.

'A lot can change in four years,' he beams. 'The good life has finally arrived here. Moscow has become super-liveable. I never thought I'd say this, but the city is now a bit of a foodie paradise. In fact, you know what really kick-started all this change? It was your sanctions back in 2014. Before that, the only foreign food we had here was pizza and sushi!'

I sigh. We're on to geopolitics already. 'I think they were *your* sanctions actually,' I point out.

'Hmm,' Yegor grunts, 'they were in response to Western sanctions though, remember?'

I remember only too well. Back in August 2014, Russia banned fresh food imports from the EU and USA as part of the sanctions warfare that followed the annexation of Crimea.[1]

'It made us self-sufficient,' Yegor continues proudly. 'Now we grow our own food, or get it brought in from friendly countries.'

A waiter floats over, smartly dressed and addressing us politely in thinly accented English. We start with traditional cabbage soup called *shchi* (pronounced she), along with a plate of appetisers: black bread, boiled potatoes, raw onion and herring.

'Lots of dill please,' adds Yegor. 'We want to sate this man's desire for authenticity.'

I wince. Russians treat dill like most countries treat salt and pepper. I've seen it on pizza more than once.

'And to drink?' asks the waiter.

Yegor turns to me, reddening slightly. 'I was thinking we could lay off the vodka. I'm trying to slow down a little at my age. Plus, we've got some great craft breweries here now . . .'

'Lay off the . . .' I splutter. This was not the Yegor I remembered. 'I haven't come all this way to try local craft beer!'

It wasn't until 2011 that beer was even classified as alcohol in Russia.[2] This sounds more reckless than it is: beer was never that popular until marketing moguls began to promote it as a 'healthy alternative' to vodka in the early 2000s, and it has soared in popularity since. The marketers might have been on to something: according to the World Health Organization, alcohol-related deaths in Russia fell by 43 per cent between 2003 and 2019.[3] But that does not concern me now; at this moment I need something to chase down the taste of raw herring and boiled potatoes covered in dill. The waiter moves to de-escalate matters. 'If you are looking for something traditional, might I suggest some *kvass*?' he suggests, referring to a drink made from fermented rye bread. It isn't the worst idea.

'This is another thing I don't like,' I confide to Yegor as the waiter departs. 'The service is actually good these days. People are friendly. This guy even *smiled*!'

Yegor laughs. 'Like I said, Moscow has come a long way. You only came here a few years ago though; you missed the really mad days. People need to understand how bad it really was, especially in the nineties: chaos, the mafia ran things; everything was for sale and only about one per cent of people knew how to do business. They made billions, literally billions, while most people couldn't even get basic stuff! And this was in Moscow, imagine what it was like in other cities! My wife grew up in a village where there was so little money that they used vodka as currency. We'd been brought up to believe that we were the greatest country in the world, but all we could see was violence, alcoholism, shootings, bombs, poverty, and then the war in Chechnya. It was a shitshow.'

I start to note some of this on my phone. The war in Chechnya, which began in the mid-1990s, was meant to crush a separatist movement but dragged on for years, leaving tens of thousands of civilians dead and exposing the weakness and brutality of the Russian army – a humiliation that scarred the country as much as the violence itself.

'Ah, I see you're writing down all the bad stuff!' he smirks. 'I suppose modern Moscow isn't very useful for your book, is it? You came here to write about the Wild East and all you find are iPhones, flat whites and craft beer! Well, maybe this is the price we pay for a bit of normality. We want a quiet life for a change.'

I try to protest. 'I'm trying to go everywhere without any preconceptions . . .'

'Yeah, right. The Westerner with no preconceptions, that'll be the day. At least you're not writing about the "Crisis in Ukraine" that your media have been fantasising about for the past six months.'

I wondered how long it would take for this to come up. For all the modernity, for all the improvements in people's spoken English, for all the global food, Russian foreign policy remains steadfastly opposed to the West. The feeling is mutual, and for the past six months Western newspapers and intelligence agencies have been watching a Russian military build-up on the Ukrainian border with growing alarm, predicting the worst. I decide to say nothing, but Yegor is determined to have this conversation.

'There will be no war,' he presses on.

I take the bait: 'What about all the troops on the border?'

'You mean the *Russian* troops that are stationed on *Russian* territory?' he says, leaning forward. 'We can place our soldiers wherever we like in our own country! We're not like the Americans, who have soldiers all around the world. If you ask me, the West is trying to goad us into a conflict. Only Washington benefits from a war, they want Europe to stop buying gas from us so the Americans can sell it to them instead. Why would we want a war with Ukraine? Give me one good reason!' He doesn't wait for an answer. 'The bigger problem is NATO. Why does it keep expanding east? Poland, Romania, the Baltics . . . You promised you would never take those lands! It's a military alliance, and you keep moving towards us. What are we supposed to think?'

He seems to notice his voice rising, but his face softens suddenly. 'Maybe we should get some vodka,' he mutters.

'*Za mir*,' says Yegor, intoning the old Soviet toast once the drinks arrive.

'To peace,' I agree.

The raw herring suddenly tastes a lot better.

Friday, 18 February

US intelligence had stated boldly that the Russian invasion of Ukraine would begin on 16 February. This day has come and gone, and Russian diplomats are struggling to hide their glee.[4] Muscovites appear convinced that the CIA is having hallucinations.

Then the evacuation of the Donbas region of Eastern Ukraine is announced, due to an apparent 'genocide' that has been uncovered there.

Who could have committed the genocide, while it's been under the occupation of Moscow's proxies for the past eight years, is not explained. The TV footage switches to images of women and children being loaded onto buses and brought across the border to the safety of Russia, where cameras are waiting to capture the heart-warming scenes of food and blankets being given out to the refugees. I switch off; it's Friday night and I've been invited to some karaoke.

In the days before the introduction of ride-hailing apps you had to do the dirty work yourself, standing by the road trying to flag down a taxi, or approaching a group of men who loitered around metro stations, cigarettes lit and gold teeth flashing. Most of these drivers were non-Slavic, and whether they were Uzbek, Georgian or Chechen, you were always in for a tough negotiation. Their cars bore no hint of a seatbelt, nor a meter, and, it goes without saying, you were paying in cash.

Today, though, there is Yandex, Russia's equivalent of Uber and Google rolled into one. It drops me at the karaoke venue where Steve, another old friend, has hired a private salon for his girlfriend Julia's birthday. Most of the party are already there, and one glance around the room has me feeling rather self-conscious in just a T-shirt and jeans. As a rule, Russians don't do smart casual: it's either slumdog or Cinderella; sweatpants or Chanel. Admittedly, the super-rich do wear Chanel sweatpants.

Great wafts of perfume rushing at me, I skirt around the forest of heels and dresses to the back of the room where Steve is standing in a crisp shirt.

'Barnesy, good to see you, pal!' Steve has lived in Moscow for the past twelve years; he's half-English, half-Russian, not that you could tell from his broad south London accent.

'You could have told me to dress up,' I mutter by way of greeting.

Before long, I meet a couple from Saint Petersburg, Leo and Maria. I tell them about the book I'm writing.

'Oho,' says Maria. 'Will you go to all the republics?'

'That's the plan.'

'And Ukraine?'

'That's one of the republics, yep.' I try to keep my voice casual, but I know what's coming.

'Do you still think we're going to invade Ukraine?' She's smiling dangerously now.

I shrug.

'It's the fault of that Zelensky,' Maria snaps. 'He's a coward, he came to power promising peace, but he's too scared to go against the fascists who have taken over Ukraine's army. They're not interested in peace; this war has been going on for nearly ten years! The Ukrainians are still sending rockets into towns and cities in the Donbas, all they want is to dominate the people there, force them to speak Ukrainian and cut them off from Russia.'

'With the entire Russian army on their doorstep, you really think Ukraine is going to launch an attack to provoke them?' I ask.

'Maybe it's not Zelensky's plan; but how much control does the Ukrainian government have over its own army? Everyone knows that they are fascist mercenary battalions who act independently of the government. Many of them benefit from war. Who knows what they will do? Ukraine is a mess.'

'But what about *Russia*?' I'm determined to get to the bottom of this. 'Why do you think over a hundred thousand Russian troops are on the border?'

'How do we even know there are one hundred thousand troops there? Where has that figure come from?' she asks (no people love a rhetorical question quite as much as the Russians). 'I'll tell you where: from the same Western media that said Russia would invade Ukraine two days ago!'

'Let's have a drink,' says Leo, standing up. 'This war talk is stressing me out. I've got a sales meeting in London next week.'

Monday, 21 February

On Monday morning Putin convenes the Security Council, which agrees unanimously that the two breakaway Ukrainian regions of Luhansk and Donetsk should be recognised as independent states.

The president addresses the nation that evening – a long, potted-history lesson that smears the idea of Ukrainian statehood, claiming that modern Ukraine was a creation of Lenin, and which had generously and needlessly been showered with territory by Stalin and Khrushchev. There's venom in his voice as he discusses the Ukrainian authorities, whom he paints as fascists and criminals. The speech ends with Putin announcing that he will recognise the 'People's Republics' in Donetsk and Luhansk.*

Tuesday, 22 February

The financial markets are presaging the worst, with the value of the rouble falling steeply overnight. But there is still little sense of panic or urgency. I go ice-skating in Gorky Park with Oksana, a second-generation immigrant who is part of the large Armenian diaspora in Moscow. My fears make no headway with her on this crisp winter's evening. As we glide past trees

---

* The full speech is worth reading in full to get a sense of Russia's many well-worn geopolitical grievances: http://en.kremlin.ru/events/president/news/67828

wreathed in fairy lights and little wooden cabins selling mulled wine, I ask if she has at least begun stockpiling dollars.

'There is no need, the rouble will rise again once this hysteria is over,' she assures me, giving that laconic Russian shrug, the I've-seen-worse expression that I've encountered so often.

Wednesday, 23 February

I go to a bar to meet Steve again. Crystal Palace are playing and he's determined to keep it light. He's laughing more loudly than usual and keeping up a storm of bravado. However, at half time he turns to me and lowers his voice. 'I've just got this message from my brother, he's into international politics and all that. He thinks things are about to get a bit hairy around here. Told me to get out as soon as possible. "Reboot and reassess," he says. What do you reckon?'

I admit I'm having similar thoughts.

'Pff, it's easy for you. You've only been here a couple of weeks. I've got skin in the game here: a girlfriend, a life. I can't just leave.'

That night I message Julia, the guide we befriended in Kyiv. I'm not really sure why. After all, what do you say to someone preparing to face the Russian army? 'Good luck?' 'Break a leg?' I reach for the homely comfort of the cliché, saying that my thoughts are with her and everyone else in the country. Thoughts that will offer little protection against inbound missiles. Her reply is short but epic:

'Thank you for your care and support. We are united as never before. Let's go make history.'

Thursday, 24 February

Thursday dawns uncharacteristically warm in Moscow, the sky grey and unassuming. But the only sky anyone sees is the black Ukrainian night, illuminated by iridescent flashes on screens across the country as the invasion begins.

The scale of it is breathtaking – Kharkiv, Odessa, Ivano-Frankivsk

– cities and military bases across the country are pounded from above. I lie in bed; the fresh images uploaded every minute have a horrifying magnetism: helicopters prowl over the snowy countryside blazing anti-missile flares; a convoy of tanks rolls down the highway towards the capital, a Soviet flag fluttering from one of them. Paratroopers have seized the airport beside the city – the Antonov An-225, the largest aeroplane in the world, with its iconic six engines, lies destroyed. I notice the female reporter embedded with the Russian troops. I'd met her five years before at an academic conference. She had been charming and erudite, there to present her research on the Middle East. Now she's at the vanguard of an invasion force.

I go to a café, just to get out of the oppressive atmosphere of the flat. The snowy hush is magnified this morning. It seems everyone is operating on autopilot: the metro continues to run, the gyms and schools and cinemas are all open, but conversations are subdued, there is little laughter.

The waitress tries to hitch up a smile as I enter. As she busies herself with the coffee, she and her colleague discuss her son's birthday party that weekend. Their conversation is monotonous, forced. I take a seat, fighting the urge to return to the war on my phone. One woman in the corner is reading a Russian translation of Richard Osman's *Thursday Murder Club*. It amazes me that people can still read books, go to work, talk about birthday parties, when bombs are falling in Kyiv.

The first protesters gather in Pushkin Square that evening. They are few in number and their plaintive shouts of '*Nyet Voine! Nyet Voine!*' – No to War – echo hollowly in the uncaring night. Just a thousand or so members of the castrated middle class make their voices heard in a city of 15 million. There are more journalists than protesters in the end, and the riot police outnumber both. Anyone without a fluorescent 'PRESS' jacket risks being arrested arbitrarily, and often violently.

Friday, 25 February

The police are taking no chances. An abnormal number of military vehicles, riot vans and police buses with metal grates on their windows lurk at intersections. The Garden Ring, Moscow's inner ring road and not as pleasant as its name might suggest, has been closed off in large stretches. The main squares are manned by officers in full body armour, their heads helmeted and faces obscured by opaque, mirrored visors. Locals call them cosmonauts.

I order a Yandex. The driver scrolls through his Instagram as we wait in the long queues. I see more snatches of orange fires lighting up the night sky, helicopter strikes on villages, MiG dogfights.

He glances round and sees me watching. 'Awful,' he mutters.

I'm unsure what to say. We don't know each other. We don't know who might report on whom. The society is so atomised, the media so strident, that any public utterance on the war seems subversive. The word *war* itself has been proscribed: according to the authorities this is no war, it's a *special military operation*.*

'Terrible situation,' I say, rather pointlessly, but with poor enough pronunciation for him to notice I'm not Russian. Fortunately this gets me into his good graces. It turns out he's from Chechnya.

'You see this?' he says, gesticulating to a rubble-strewn house on somebody's Instagram story. 'This is what Putin did to my village fifteen years ago.'

'Why did you come to Moscow?' I ask.

'For work. There's nowhere else,' he shrugs, and goes back to Instagram, where the explosions jostle for his attention between MMA fights and scantily clad models.

We eventually pull up at Simach, an upmarket restaurant-cum-nightclub where I'm meeting some of the gang from last week. The clientele waiting outside are stylish and beautiful, but with that vacuous, disinterested hauteur that possesses most of the sons and daughters of the post-Soviet elite – an aloofness that can apparently only be cured by cocaine. The queue for entry is unusually short.

---

* This piece of semantic skulduggery is not uniquely Russian: the USA also used the term 'police action' to describe its involvement in the Korean War, as well as its early military presence in Vietnam.

'Why's it so quiet tonight?' the silicone-lipped girl in front of me enquires of her friend.

'No idea,' shrugs the other.

I think of Julia, sheltering in the metro deep below Kyiv to avoid the bombs falling out of the night sky. I feel a dull rage at this pair's obliviousness. But am I any better? I'm in the same line after all. I tell myself I need a drink, to be around people.

Maria is waiting inside, along with her friend Kristina. She's no longer the confident, playful young woman from the karaoke. She seems immensely stressed, though not necessarily about people dying in Ukraine.

'Have you heard from Leo?' she asks me. 'He's not answering his phone.'

I haven't been able to get hold of him either.

Her hand trembles as she takes a sip of her cocktail. 'All my friends abroad are messaging me saying "What the fuck are Russians doing? Why are you not out protesting?" What do I say to them?'

'I guess you didn't join the protests then?'

'Yeah, right,' she laughs hollowly.

'People only protest on Instagram,' says Kristina softly.

'Can you blame them?' says Maria. 'What can we achieve by going out there except getting arrested? What good will it do? You saw what happened last year.'

In January 2021, almost 10,000 people were detained across two weekends of protest that followed the arrest of opposition figurehead Alexei Navalny.[5]

'Brave people, those that protest,' says Kristina.

'Stupid people,' mutters Maria.

We slump into silence. At last, Leo arrives; he too looks shaky.

'The police stopped me in the street on my way here,' he says thickly, picking up the first drink he can find and necking it.

'They *did*?' says Maria, alarmed. 'What did they do?'

'They wanted to look through my phone.'

There's a general shudder around the group.

'What did they look at?' asks Maria.

'Which apps I had. Which Telegram channels I was following. So you should be careful, make sure you're not following anyone linked to the opposition, and nothing Ukrainian. They wanted to know why I had a Ukrainian channel – they made me unfollow it in front of them.'

Maria and Kristina go to get more drinks, leaving Leo and me sitting in silence.

'You think it will end quickly?' he asks.

'Who knows?'

'Maybe if Ukraine accepts neutrality, not joining NATO, and accepts that Crimea and the Donbas are Russian?' he asks, before continuing to gabble as though it's a tech problem that needs solving. 'I don't think anyone expected this. How do we get out of this? Do you think they'll negotiate?'

'They don't look like they're in the mood for negotiations. Did you see the guys on Snake Island?' An audio clip has emerged of a group of Ukrainian soldiers, surrounded by the Russian Black Sea Fleet, without any prospect of rescue, being asked to hand over the island peacefully:

'Snake Island, this is Russian warship. I suggest you lay down your arms and surrender, otherwise you will be hit. Do you copy?'

The response was emphatic: *'Russian warship – go fuck yourself.'*[6]

'That audio is fake,' snaps Leo. 'It's Ukrainian propaganda.'

Despite being anti-war, now that it's started, I have a feeling that Leo is rather keen for Russia to win.

I end up talking to Kristina. She's one of those mixtures that the Soviet imperium has thrown up – her father is Belarusian, her mother Ukrainian, she grew up in Crimea and is now in Moscow for work. I ask where her parents are.

'In Kyiv.'

'Oh.'

'Yeah.'

'Are they OK?'

'For now.'

A few hours later, Kristina and I are having a smoke outside. We're both very drunk.

'Why aren't you helping us?' she shouts suddenly.

'Me?'

'You, Britain, America, Europe! You're just standing there and letting us die. You have planes, why aren't you stopping them? Have you seen what they're doing to our cities? Why don't you *do* something?'

I try to look her in the eye and explain, explain about the lack of public will, the fear of nuclear war. There are no words.

Monday, 27 February

The collective West does muster some kind of reaction. Flight sanctions are the first things to come in: Britain, the EU, USA, Japan, Canada and even neutral Switzerland have blocked Russian airlines from their airspace, with the Kremlin quickly reciprocating. Before long, Air Serbia is the only airline permitted to fly between Russia and Europe. Flight prices to Belgrade, as well as Turkey, Dubai and former Soviet countries, have spiked. While I was prepared for a run on the rouble, it's unsettling to suddenly see the escape routes disappearing one by one.

Then come the financial sanctions. Visa, Mastercard and Apple Pay are blocked, which makes for long queues at the ticket barriers in metro stations as confused Muscovites are forced to become reacquainted with prehistoric forms of payment. I, with my trusty pre-loaded card in hand, speed straight to the front. I feel like Ivan's father.

These aren't the only queues. Russia's well-developed digital banking sector allows people to search on their phones for cash machines that contain dollars and euros, and belatedly lines have begun forming behind them – orderly, but dozens deep. One stock market analyst drinks a toast to the death of the Russian stock market live on state TV, to the horror of the presenter.[7] Another diktat is passed limiting foreign currency bank withdrawals to $10,000.

Fortunately, I have my dollars stockpiled, and funnily enough my old Chinese bank card has not been affected by the sanctions. Some other dark arts picked up in China are starting to come in handy too: as the Russian censor scrambles to limit access to the bad news coming out of Ukraine,

I'm forced to boot up my VPN to bypass the hastily erected internet firewalls. The lightning assault involving Russian airborne troops has begun to flounder as the Ukrainians put up stiffer than anticipated resistance. Twitter has been blocked,[8] independent Russian media such as Ekho Moskvy (or Echo of Moscow) radio station and TV Rain have been closed down, and foreign news sources are going the same way – even Facebook and YouTube are being considered for bans.* A law is passed condemning people to up to fifteen years in prison for distributing 'fake' news or 'discrediting the use of Russian armed forces to protect the interests of Russia'.[9] In addition to jail time, anyone found guilty will also be slapped with a million-rouble fine.

Leo tries to look on the bright side. 'Well, at least they're only fining us a couple of dollars.'

Bars and restaurants are noticeably quieter. The initial moral outrage has dissipated, and the economic panic is now a bigger topic of conversation than the war itself. There's still occasional dissent, particularly from people within the cultural sector, but I'm under no illusions that my small group of middle-class Muscovite friends are a minority in the country.[10] Proof of that is offered when I try to speak to Yegor about the whole affair.

'This is what happens when you push us,' he messages me. 'Russia has been given no option. We've tried for years to negotiate, and you never took us seriously. This is not a war between Russia and Ukraine, it's between Russia and America. I think it's better if we don't speak until this is over.'

Many are heading for the exits. Leo and Maria have decided to leave for Latvia. 'Leo's company have asked him to move. They don't want to operate in Russia any more. I'm going to take holiday from my job for a bit, maybe retrain to do marketing or coding,' Maria tells me in a listless tone.

'Masha's not too happy about it,' says Leo. 'But she's worried about me being called up to serve. They say they're stopping men of serving age from leaving.'

---

* Facebook and Instagram were officially banned in late March with their parent company Meta being branded a terrorist organisation in October.

Steve, however, remains as resolute as he was last week. 'How do you expect this place to change for the better if all the principled people leave? If you ask me, leaving is the coward's way out.'

My own decision is reasonably easy; these dollars are only going to sustain me for so long, and, depressing as it is, the past weeks have already given me enough material for one chapter. I find the first flight I can to Armenia, counting on the crisp Caucasus air to provide an antidote to the madness of Moscow. I'm not the only one with this idea, normally a flight to Yerevan sells for around $50; tickets on this plane went for ten times that.

Thursday, 3 March

The two-and-a-half-hour flight south is packed with émigrés. The check-in queue crawls along as people try to bring as many suitcases as possible. Most of them are young couples; some have even brought their dogs. Despite the courteous passport control officers wishing me well on my journey with a smile, my nerves remain until we're out of Russian airspace. I'm not alone in feeling this way. The man next to me visibly relaxes as the in-flight map shows that we've cleared the mountains of southern Russia and are now cruising over Georgia. I ask him where he's headed.

'The first bar I can find,' he mumbles. 'I just booked the flight this morning when I saw there was a seat available. I've got no hotel, no plan. I think I just quit my job.'

'You think?'

'I'm a journalist. I work for one of the state news agencies. They wanted to send me out to Ukraine this morning to cover the war. Let's say I've gone missing in action.'

'When will you go back?' I ask.

'I don't know if I can.'

The air hostess brushes past our aisle. It's only 10 a.m., but I could do with another beer already.

'Good idea,' says the journalist, ordering a coke for himself. Once the air hostess heads off, he reaches into his bag and pulls out some duty-free whisky, which he adds to his drink. He gives me a sly, slurry wink.

THE CAUCASUS

2

ARMENIA
THE REPUBLIC OF SURVIVAL

'Sign here,' says the stern-faced matriarch stationed at reception. I'm surprised to find my hand is steady. I sign.

'And here.' Another form is shoved under my nose. The world swims once more. I force myself to remain upright. Once refocused, my eyes are confronted by a sea of Armenian text. If you've ever seen Armenian writing, you'll know that it is not a cure for nausea. Great curly snakes writhe on the page, twisting themselves round each other to form words so alien it makes Russian Cyrillic look like Times New Roman. I scrawl another hasty signature beneath the orderly ranks of squiggle.

'Is that it?'

'Yes. Now we can proceed.'

I sense the gentle pressure of two hands grasping the wheelchair before I'm rolled slowly forward towards the operating room. Save for the sound of heeled shoes slapping the terracotta-tiled corridor, the silence is foreboding.

Down another corridor, then a right, signs in squiggle give me little chance to get my bearings. At last we reach a blue door with a silver plaque attached. On it, beneath the serpentine hieroglyphs, is a name written in English: Dr Tumasyan.

'Here's the soldier!' says the doctor as I'm wheeled in. 'Let's have a look at you.'

I'm shifted, belly down, onto a stretcher bed.

'Hmm, not the worst I've seen,' he says absently, peering down at my cranium. He calls out something in Armenian to the assistant, who returns with a pair of scissors. Hands clamp round my ears, holding the head in position. This is followed by a distinctive snipping noise; a lock of hair drops to the floor by my side.

'Yes, yes. Not so bad,' says the doctor as he leans in closer. 'It's a deep one, but it should heal up fine. Now, why don't you tell me how you got yourself such a mighty wound while we get you sewn back together?'

I sigh into the stretcher bed. The hollow, self-flagellating sigh that every medical professional hears in the wee hours of a Saturday morning, followed by those timeless words: 'I got quite drunk . . .'

'Go on,' the voice above says wearily.

'We lost a game of table football to some girls. And then my friend – he's Russian, he's had to leave his home – he insisted on more shots. Then I got back to the hotel and tripped over my suitcase.'

'And?'

'Oh, well, I just fell and banged my head on the table. I must have been out for a bit. Woke up a bit later and there was blood everywhere.'

'Hmm,' comes the voice above my head. Was there doubt in there? Maybe he was just busy reconciling the two estranged pieces of scalp.

Twenty minutes later, bandaged tightly, I'm wheeled back to reception.

'Another form?' I sigh, correctly interpreting the babushka's expectant look. She nods, unsmiling. I scan the squiggle and sign.

'Now you must make payment.'

Fortunately, some semblance of socialism still exists in Armenia, and the whole service comes to the princely sum of 15,000 dram, which to my relief is only about £30. The old lady hands about £5 of this to the ambulance drivers who brought me here. They grasp it eagerly and shuffle into the night. Surely they hadn't spent the past half-hour hanging around just to get paid? I can't be the only patient in Yerevan this evening. I'm distracted from these musings by the stamp of feet, and half a dozen policemen stride into the room.

'Mister Bar-nez?'

'Yes?'

'Is this your passport?' the lead officer asks, picking it off the desk. It's already been blitzed so many times in the photocopier I'm surprised it isn't radioactive. He rifles through it for a moment or two.

'We have a few questions for you, Mister Bar-nez. We have just received a call from Doctor Tumasyan, he says you sustained a head injury this evening.'

'Yes, but—'

'Would you be so kind as to tell us who did this to you?'

'No one. I just tripped.'

'You tripped?'

'Over my suitcase.'

'You tripped over your suitcase?' repeats the policeman in his slow, accented Russian, eyeing my bandaged head disbelievingly. He leans forward conspiratorially. 'It's OK Mister Bar-nez, you can tell us . . .'

'I *am* telling you.'

Unfortunately, I'm in a part of the world where people who get on the wrong side of power have a nasty habit of sustaining fatal injuries from banal causes – *falling from windows, involved in a car crash* . . . that sort of thing. So it's hardly surprising that a man with a hole in his skull who's told the doctor that he *tripped over his suitcase* has set this sleuth's snout aquiver.

The policeman sighs. 'The doctor said you'd been out drinking. Where?'

'Lots of places – Dargett Bar, Beatles Pub . . .'

'Beatles Pub!' smiles one of his younger colleagues. 'I like that place.' There's a general murmur of agreement from the others. The lead officer hisses at him before rounding on me.

'What is your address in Armenia, Mister Bar-nez?'

'I don't have one, I'm staying at a hotel.'

'You have a Moscow registration inside your passport. Do you live in Moscow?'

'No. Well, I did. And then—'

'And then?'

'And then the war happened, I came here. To escape the war.'

'You came to Armenia to escape war?'

His voice has changed, in my blurry state I can't quite define how. I look up and the policeman has turned to his colleagues, his arms outstretched.

'He came to Armenia to escape war!' They all laugh uproariously.

I join in, my head giddy. I can kind of see what's funny here. Over the din I hear the police chief's voice.

'You came to the wrong place, Mister Bar-nez! War beat you here by about thirty years.'

Some days later, the sun is sinking in the spring sky. The late-afternoon light catches the pink, tuff stone buildings arranged around Yerevan's Republic Square, which is beginning to fill with people. It's a mixed, intergenerational crowd; many hold Armenian flags and their babble mixes with the rushing fountains. There's an air of expectation; even the stray dogs seem interested.

As night creeps closer, lights flicker into life in the arched canopies of the surrounding buildings, their auburn glow mirrored in the pools of water around the fountains. A speaker enters the stage; he toys with the assembled masses, addressing them in low sepulchral tones that slowly build in emotion. The crowd grows restless.

He pauses for a rendition of the national anthem; I feel rather exposed as the only one not singing. His speech resumes with a new tone of urgency. There's a definite Middle Eastern character to his fiery zealotry. A few words come up repeatedly – Turkey, Azerbaijan, Erdoğan – all greeted with a hiss from his audience. And then comes an English word, said slowly, and then with more passion.

Boycott.

The cry is echoed by his audience. 'Boycott!' People shout. 'Boycott!!'

Soon the whole crowd has taken up the cry of 'Boy-cott! Boy-cott! Boy-cott!'

Then, from near the stage, torches spring to life, first a dozen, then hundreds are raised aloft to the dark heavens.

'Boy-cott! Boy-cott!' continue the roars.

Behind the speaker, two giant flags are unfurled. The first is red; the second a tricolour – blue, red and green. On each is the star and crescent of Islam. The preacher takes up his own torch and lights first the flag of Turkey, then that of Azerbaijan.

Savage cheers echo into the night.

When it comes to the Caucasus, it's probably best to begin with the cross and the crescent. At Khor Virap monastery, just south of Yerevan, King Tiridates the Great converted to Christianity in 301 CE. This makes Armenia, by some measures, the world's oldest Christian country. It was rather larger in those days as well. Armenians often speak nostalgically of a time when their territory spanned from the Mediterranean to the Caspian. Today, however, it is a landlocked state ringed by rocky mountains, with few natural resources and fewer friends. Relations with Georgia to the north and Iran to the south are at least cordial. To the east and west, however, lies only trouble. And this brings us back to the flag-burning.

The ceremony I have just witnessed takes place on 23 April every year: speeches are made, torches are lit, and people march to Tsitsernakaberd (the Swallow's Fortress), a lonely outcrop overlooking the capital. Atop this hill is another flame, an eternal flame that burns restlessly to commemorate events that took place at the start of the twentieth century.

Armenians sometimes refer to these events as *Medz Yeghern*, which literally translates as the Great Crime. More often, they are simply called the Armenian Genocide.

Armenia has long straddled the borders of empires, from the Romans to the Arabs, the Mongols to the Persians. By the early twentieth century, their ancient kingdom having long been digested by larger powers, Armenians found themselves living in lands that were contested between the Ottomans and the increasingly assertive Russians. Armenians integrated well into both empires and were renowned as traders and merchants. However, when Moscow and Constantinople lined up on opposite sides in the First World War, the Ottomans began to consider the Armenians living among them as a potential fifth column who might side with the tsar's fellow-Christian armies.

Turkish nationalism was on the rise and anti-Armenian pogroms had already taken place around the turn of the century. The war gave these nationalists the excuse they needed to answer the so-called 'Armenian Question' once and for all. Between 1915 and 1922, an estimated 600,000 to 1.5 million Armenians were slaughtered by the Turks, who rounded them up and drove them to face starvation in the Syrian desert. Millions more fled into exile.

By the time the Treaty of Kars was signed in 1921 between the Soviet Union and the Republic of Turkey, the Armenian people had been almost wholly purged from the lands west of the Aras River, which would mark the border between Lenin's and Atatürk's new states. Lands to the east of the river became the Armenian Soviet Socialist Republic, within the USSR.

Ten miles beyond the Aras on the Turkish side is Mount Ararat, the Armenians' holiest mountain. The ancient, dormant volcano, where Noah is supposed to have been marooned by the receding flood, is depicted on every Armenian bank note; brandies and hotels bear its name; and its twin, snow-capped humps can be seen from almost anywhere in the country. Ararat remains tantalisingly in sight, but untouchable, a constant reminder of the lands and lives the Armenians have lost.

These days, the border with Turkey is closed. All that is exchanged across the Aras are the sounds of religious posturing: the call to prayer and the clanging of church bells.

'Check,' says Oksana, moving her pawn forward and flashing the same sly smile she wore on the ice at Gorky Park. Luckily, I've got a bishop handy to scythe the critter down.

Her grin fades as she drifts into thought. She has a habit of taking a long time between turns.

We're sitting in the leafy shade beside Yerevan's classical opera house. There's a light spring breeze, waiters stroll to and fro bringing coffees or fresh pomegranate juice; it's not yet noon, but one old boy is already cradling a brandy. There's little chatter, instead there's a frowning, fervent buzz of concentration and the occasional muffled knocking as pieces shuffle across the board. Chess is a national pastime in Armenia; in fact, it's the only country in the world where the game is compulsory at school. Bars will often have a chess set that you can hire for a pittance, although many players prefer to use their own pieces.

Oksana begins another assault on the crown, sliding her castle into a menacing position. Gleefully my bishop pounces again; I'm just considering promoting him to inquisitor when she springs the trap, her knight making a bloody mess of the overzealous clergyman.

'Check,' she says again, this time allowing herself a grin. The game doesn't last much longer after that.

'So, how've you been?' asks Oksana, having mopped up. She was so keen to get a game in that we've barely had a chance to say hello.

In the wake of the Ukraine invasion, Oksana was one of the hundreds of thousands of Russian citizens who decided that they couldn't remain in the country in good conscience. The wave of nationalism that swept Russia left her feeling more Armenian than ever before. Having waited for a month or so to be able to withdraw foreign currency from her bank account, she's arrived in Yerevan with the intention of getting more in touch with her roots.

'You told me you wanted to chat about the diaspora?' she prompts me.

The Armenians that survived the genocide were scattered around the world. While some came east to join their brethren in what would become the Soviet Union, others went to France and America, to Iran, Syria and Lebanon.

They weren't always welcome. Armenians have historically been portrayed as sneaky, conniving and untrustworthy – an attitude I've seen frequently articulated in Moscow.

Oksana experienced this first-hand after her parents moved to Siberia in the early 1990s. 'Back then you had a lot of neo-Nazis and skinheads in Russia; people always assumed that we had money, because we were Armenian. My parents wanted their kids to integrate, that's why they gave us all Russian names.'

In some ways, Oksana is a classic second-generation immigrant, assimilating so well that you would never guess her heritage were it not for her surname (almost every Armenian surname ends in -yan or -ian). Indeed, whenever she speaks with her mother, it's always in Russian.

'Is there not a risk that after one hundred years, Armenians might integrate too well and lose touch with their roots?' I ask her.

She smiles. 'In Siberia I was actually monolingual. I understood Armenian, but I wouldn't be able to articulate well, just a few words with a heavy Russian accent. When we moved to Moscow there was a larger diaspora, who were unhappy that we could not speak Armenian. So when I was nine I started attending an Armenian Sunday school run by the embassy. We learned to read, write, sing, dance . . . they taught us about the culture too. We learned prayers there, even though it wasn't a religious school, and also the national anthem.'

It's estimated that there are around 10 million Armenians around the world, far more than the 3 million that reside in the republic itself. The government has made efforts to lure the diaspora home, but far more people have flowed in the opposite direction. Armenia's population has fallen from 3.6 million to just 2.9 million over the past thirty years.

Those that have heeded the call of the motherland tend to settle in the capital. My local watering hole has been a place called Jack's, whose owner, Garun, is a former lawyer from Los Angeles who gave it all up to move back to his roots.

'My parents were Armenians living in Iran,' he tells me, 'but then they had the revolution there [in 1979]. After that Iran wasn't considered that safe for Christians, so the family moved to the US. But during the pandemic, and especially after the war with Azerbaijan in 2020, I started to feel more of a pull from back here.'

It's the kind of roundabout tale of life on the move that I've grown accustomed to hearing. His business partner, Rami, is a Lebanese Armenian who has spent long periods in Switzerland.

'In my bar, you can easily spot a diasporan from a local,' Garun tells me. 'First, they speak a different dialect, but also locals order the foreign lagers, whereas the diasporans prefer the local stuff.' This tends to be Kilikia, Armenia's biggest beer brand.

Diaspora Armenians settling in Yerevan have given the city a vibrancy – American whiskey bars, French cinema, Lebanese cuisine and Russian music all mix on the city's streets. I even bump into an Australian Armenian who has opened one of the city's first vegan restaurants. For many of the diasporan Armenians who have arrived in Yerevan over the past three decades, Armenia's Soviet experience has little relevance.

'Post-Soviet country?!' scoffs Roubina, a local journalist, when I tell her about my book. 'Armenia is not a post-Soviet country; it's a post-genocide country. The Soviet period is nothing to what we went through at the start of the twentieth century.'

Since my accident-prone arrival in the country, Dr Tumasyan has ordered me to spend the month convalescing. I begin my days with a coffee. In Armenia, the go-to is what we might call Turkish coffee, but, given the history with the Turks, here it goes by a different name. On English menus it generally gets translated as 'Eastern coffee'. In Armenian it's simply *sursch*. Most people take it strong, preferably outside, along with a cigarette.

Locals generally speak good Russian but derive enormous pleasure from hearing even basic Armenian uttered by a foreign tongue. The Armenian for 'hi' is *barev*, and simply saying '*Barev, sursch*' after rocking up to a café seems to make people's day. Not all words come so easily. I initially attempted to get my head round the Armenian for thank you, which is *shnorhakalutyun*, but gave up when I realised that most people just say *merci*.

The city's broad, tree-lined avenues make it an ideal people-watching haunt while *sursch*-sipping. Armenians are on the whole shorter than people in northern Europe, with dark hair and deep black eyes to match. Women dress conservatively with baggy jeans – the crop-tops that have taken over Moscow have yet to venture south. Young men, meanwhile, have a predilection for tight black tees, jeans and plimsolls, although you'll see the occasional pair of cheap snakeskin shoes – the hallmark of what Armenians call a *qyartu* (and what in Britain we would call a chav).

After concluding my coffee and mumbling my *merci*s, it's time for a wander. The city celebrated its 2,800th birthday in 2018. Yerevaners will proudly tell you that their city is twenty-nine years older than Rome. Sadly, successive waves of invaders have done a far better job than the Goths and Vandals of destroying that heritage.

The modern city is a product of idealistic Soviet planning from the 1920s. Cafés spill onto the pavement and there are fountains of fresh, cool drinking water on every street. Its wide avenues, flanked by smart, salmon-hued buildings, converge on the central opera house. Behind this rises the Yerevan Cascade, a grand series of staircases and art installations that was supposed to connect the lower part of the city with the higher northern plateau where many of the richer citizens live. Unfortunately, the Cascade's summit represents a mouldering, long-forgotten building site, perhaps a fitting testament to modern Armenia's wealth divide.

Not all construction in the city is so incomplete. In fact, the post-independence years have seen the slow death of the 'Pink City', abetted by a political system that existed on paper but frequently served the interests of a narrow elite. The rather chaotic democracy of the 1990s gave way to a corrupt authoritarianism following the assassination of Prime Minister Vazgen Sargsyan and other key leaders in 1999.[1] The 2018 Velvet Revolution marked a step towards some measure of democratic accountability but has failed to stop the pressures of wealth and speculation. The collapse of public land ownership has led to opportunistic redevelopment, with large parts of the centre now dominated by faceless glass and steel towers, many owned by affluent members of the diaspora. Locals lament the destruction of the city's architectural heritage and look up at the cranes dotting the skyline, worried that the speculators might only be getting started.[2]

On the ground, the city's infrastructure has struggled to keep pace. The streets are lamentably lit by tired lamps; tufts of grass push through cracks in the uneven pavements, which are prowled by innumerable stray dogs; having roamed the city with impunity for so long, these canine residents even halt obediently at pedestrian crossings until the lights turn green. Cars throng the roads, filling the air with the cloying smell of propane gas, which many use as an alternative to petrol.* Public transport options

---

* Should you find yourself in one of these propane taxis when the driver needs to fill up, you will be told to exit the vehicle and wait at the edge of the gas station while it's refuelled – all very reassuring . . .

are scant: there's the odd trolleybus and an infrequent metro with only one line.

'We used to have trams,' a guide at the city museum tells me. 'But the rails were ripped up and sold for scrap steel by some unscrupulous mayor looking for a quick buck.'

Still, enough of the old city hangs on to give it a sense of character. There's a pleasant hum of human energy that was absent in Moscow. There are more smiles, more markets and a general feeling of life lived outdoors.

Yerevan would look decidedly Middle Eastern were it not for one omnipresent, arresting feature: I gave the Armenian script short shrift earlier, and as much as it doesn't make life easier, these squiggles have demonstrated immense staying power.

The Armenian writing system was devised in 405 CE by Mesrop Mashtots, a monk. One of the capital's central boulevards, once called Lenin Avenue, is now named after him. It stretches from the south of the city right up to the rock face at the northern end. Carved into this rock face is one of Yerevan's more remarkable museums, the Matenadaran, which houses the Armenian language's most important texts and manuscripts. This includes the twelfth-century, 28-kilo Msho Charentir. Each incoming president in the modern Armenian Republic takes his oath of office on this vintage tome, the only time it is permitted to leave the walls of the building. The first of these presidents, Levon Ter-Petrosyan, was a senior researcher at the Matenadaran before making the jump into politics.

This is not the only literary tinge to the city: several of Yerevan's major thoroughfares are named after famous authors. There's even a street named after Lord Byron, who took the time to study Armenian while holed up in Venice. 'I found that my mind wanted something craggy to break upon,' he wrote to a friend, '[and found Armenian] the most difficult thing I could discover here for an amusement.'[3]

My sense is that their script has helped the Armenians survive. Plenty of peoples have inhabited this part of Eurasia and been wiped off the map, not necessarily by force, but merely by being assimilated into a larger culture. All around them, huge tracts of land were homogenised by Arab, Persian, Latin and Cyrillic writing systems. The Armenian script, as well as the Church, has acted as a refuge for a people who have spent long periods without a state, and more recently in exile around the world. Even the Bolsheviks, who were in no way sentimental folk and imposed Cyrillic on half of Eurasia, knew better than to tamper too much with the script of Mesrop Mashtots.[4]

One reason why the centre of Yerevan is such an ideal spot for a quiet game of chess is that, during my time here, it's become a car-free zone. The roads around the opera house have been blocked by protesters, and a tent city has emerged on the square out front. The squatters are predominantly scraggy-bearded males, forty or fifty years old, milling around in worn-out military garb, drinking tea, playing chess or just roasting in the sun.

'They're the Karabakh veterans,' Oksana informs me. 'Many of them fought in two wars – in the nineties, and the recent one in 2020. They're worried the government is going to sell them out.'

We come at last to the reason for the policemen's amusement.

I mentioned that Armenia has problems to its east and west. We've discussed the Turkish issue, but, amazingly, Armenia has even worse relations with Azerbaijan, its neighbour to the east. The latter conflict is very much a post-Soviet problem, with the USSR's break-up leading directly to a thirty-year dispute over a region known to most of the world as Nagorno-Karabakh.*

The area, predominantly populated by ethnic Armenians, was part of Azerbaijan during the Soviet period. When the USSR began to break up, these Karabakh Armenians attempted to claim independence with a view to joining Armenia proper, resulting in full-scale war between the two nascent states between 1991 and 1994.

Armenia won the initial conflict, taking the Karabakh and the region around it, and forcing around 800,000 Azerbaijanis to flee. Tension simmered for thirty years, before battle was renewed in 2020.

---

* Although Armenians tend to refer to Nagorno-Karabakh as Artsakh, one of the territory's historical names.

This time, the roles were reversed: the Armenian military was routed from many of its positions by the rampant Azerbaijani army. After forty-four days of intense fighting, Moscow stepped in to broker a deal. While I'm visiting, Russian peacekeepers patrol the Karabakh, and talks continue over its future status. Logic dictates that Armenia will have to renounce its claim to the territory, and it is this prospect that has brought the veterans out onto the streets for their sit-in.

Defeat has rocked the whole country. Some of the protesters I talk to are defiant, wishing to fight on, but mainly they seek someone to blame. Media owned by opposition oligarchs are keen to lay responsibility at the feet of Prime Minister Nikol Pashinyan for being weak and naive; others feel that there's little he could have done.

'We're all pawns in a much larger game,' one sunburnt greybeard tells me. 'Turkey sent their fighter jets, the Azeris bought rockets from Israel, and they could afford to hire Syrian mercenaries. We never had much chance.'

An old friend living in the Karabakh has invited me to visit, but getting there has been almost impossible for foreigners since the 2020 war. The closest I can get is Goris, about ten miles from the border. That's where Arayik has agreed to meet me.

You might be wondering how people get around a mountainous country like Armenia. The short answer is: with difficulty. There are only a couple of rail routes, most airports have now been given over to military use, and the roads are a state. I decide to make the best of a bad job and hitchhike.

Having taken a bus to a petrol station at the edge of the city (note to aspiring hitchers: petrol station exits are usually the best place to grab a ride), I stick my thumb out and prepare for a long wait. The sun is already sizzling, and Mount Ararat is smiling down from on high. A stork has laid its nest in the pylon above my head, casting the scantiest of shadows provided I don't move too much.

But I'm in luck. After a statuesque five minutes in the shade, a truck screeches to a halt in front of me. It's an ancient Mercedes, a crane perched on the back and music blaring loudly.

The trucker offers to take me to Areni, about halfway to Goris. There's only one seat in his ancient cab, so I'm forced to perch on an empty wine crate. Any heavy braking and my face is getting very closely acquainted with the windscreen.

The main risk of hitchhiking, especially in this part of the world, is that you never know how reckless your driver is going to be. Road safety is not the Caucasus's strong suit. In Yerevan, crossing the road as a pedestrian requires precise timing, like a striker bending his run to avoid the offside trap. Cars bear down on you with alarming speed, a prospect made all the more terrifying as many of them have been relieved of their front bumpers in previous incidents, giving them the impression of dogs with their teeth bared.

Outside the capital, things are even worse. The landscape around us is dry, flat and hostile, while the road becomes increasingly potholed and clogged with heavy lorries, which are responsible for most of the damage as well as most of the danger. They crawl along, goading the drivers behind them into risky overtakes. Mine is only too keen to oblige. The cab shakes as he guns the accelerator. I can't hear the engine, the music is deafening. He's playing *rabiz*, a genre of kitsch love songs to an electro-beat that became popular in Armenia in the late 1970s and still hasn't died the death it deserves. My precarious perch is becoming sticky in the heat, and the smoke of the driver's cigarette curls around the cab. All this may have been worth it if I'd had the chance to chat, but the rancid music is all-consuming. A load of *rabiz*, you might say.

I'm relieved to part ways at Areni, where I take ten minutes or so to revel in the silence. Feeling restored, I stock up on water and take up the hitching position once more. This time I hit the jackpot. I'm picked up by Artur ('Like your King Arthur!' he grins), who's behind the wheel of a white Ford Transit. Goris is on his way home.

Artur immediately puts me at ease. He speaks Russian in a kind, melodic accent; nothing he does is rushed; his gear changes caress the engine. Even the road feels smoother.

Clad in a blue denim jacket and maroon T-shirt, Artur's dark eyes stay fixed on the road. As we climb away from the thirsty Ararat Plain into the equally parched Lesser Caucasus Mountains that form the spine of Armenia, he embarks, unprompted, on his life story.

'I was born in Leninakan,' he begins. 'Of course, it's not called Leninakan any more; these days it's called Gyumri. You must have heard about what happened there? The earthquake?'

In 1989, just as a political earthquake was shaking Eastern Europe, the real thing struck the Armenian city of Leninakan. Half the town was levelled by the 6.8-magnitude shock, with around 30,000 people losing their lives and many more made homeless.[5] By the time of the 2015 census, the pre-quake population of 260,000 had dropped to a mere 118,000.

'I was doing my service in the Soviet Army out in Ukraine at the time. I came home to find everything had changed – my home was gone, the USSR was gone, and Armenia was at war with Azerbaijan.'

Genocide. Communism. Earthquakes. Social collapse. And then war . . . these people don't seem to catch a break.

'It must have been hard to adapt,' I suggest.

Artur shrugs. 'Yes and no. Life can be simple if you want it to be. My wife is a teacher at the local school; and I'm a driver. I deliver meat around the country – you're currently sitting in my office,' he laughs. 'Every month, I earn three hundred dollars and my wife about two hundred dollars – that's enough for us. What else do we need? We have a house; our children are educated. Why would I need the latest iPhone?' he snorts, eyeing my model mistrustfully. 'The problems have come with opportunity. If you love money or you're very ambitious, now is the time for you. That's the new system we've got here: a system that runs on jealousy and greed.'

We pull over at a roadside café staffed by a group of shawled women. They all seem to know Artur, who orders lunch for us both and insists on paying.

'You've already given me a free lift!' I protest.

'You are in my country, I pay here. When I come to England, you can pay.'

After a quick lunch of bread and some milky, lemony soup called *spas* – an Armenian staple – we're on the road again, heading east. For the first time, I can no longer see Mount Ararat. We're now rolling through windswept highlands covered in wild grasses, occasionally slowing to overtake ancient Soviet lorries, or flocks of sheep that shepherds coax along the road. Every time we pass a church, Artur crosses himself. The country is grimly beautiful in its understated way. I remark on this, and Artur nods approvingly. 'You need at least three years to really get to know Armenia, you have not only to see the land, but to touch it, feel it. Karabakh is more beautiful still – the air is clean there, so pure.'

Before long, Goris comes into view. Artur drops me on the edge of town. I hitch my bag onto my back. 'Thank you so mu—' I begin, but he cuts across me.

'Don't mention it. You made it an interesting journey! I just ask one thing in return – that you come and visit my family. We live nearby in Kapan. We will do a barbecue for you there. You can try the wine that I have started to grow!'

Goris is a sleepy town. People sit on benches smoking cigarettes, watching an articulated lorry inch along a worn-out road. The only other sign of movement is a man thrashing his turkeys with a cane. In the valley, cows graze on the local football pitch. These bovine groundsmen are unlikely to win any awards; in fact, there's no longer much grass left.

As I wait for Arayik, who is taking the bus here from Stepanakert, it's worth spending time discussing the Nagorno-Karabakh conflict in more detail, as it contains themes that will come up repeatedly over the following pages.

The Union of Soviet Socialist Republics was not a unitary state with no devolved powers – few countries are. It's best to think of the USSR as something like the UK or the USA – painted the same colour on the map but with fissures that are very obvious once you do a bit of digging. I'd go so far as to say that any country with the name United or Union in its title is more than likely built upon some form of wobbly constitutional compromise.

From the outset, the Soviet Union was a dizzying mosaic of ethnic groups wrought from the ashes of the Russian Empire. Ruled from Saint Petersburg by the Romanov dynasty, this empire collapsed during the First World War, succumbing first to the February and then the

October Revolutions. Its territories were plunged into what is generally known as the Russian Civil War (1917–22), although many modern states now view these years as their first wars of independence.[6] Having consolidated power over most of this territory, the Bolsheviks conducted their first census in 1926, counting as many as 169 different nationalities. It was a mark of the early idealism of the communist period that they not only ploughed enormous resources into each people's linguistic development – books were being printed in sixty-six languages by 1928[7] – but they actually had a stab at assigning territory to each ethnic group.

The result was a hierarchy of fabulously named territories, from the smaller *okrugs* and *oblasts* to the larger autonomous regions. Right at the top were the Soviet Socialist Republics (SSRs), each of which was named according to the majority group that lived there – the Ukrainian SSR was majority-Ukrainian, the Armenian SSR was majority-Armenian, and so on.*

Perhaps it's best to explain this complexity using the well-worn Russian doll metaphor. Nagorno-Karabakh was an Autonomous Oblast – one step down from being one of the fifteen fully fledged republics. Think of it as the little doll, slotting inside the medium doll – the Azerbaijani SSR – which itself sits inside the grandmother of all dolls, the Soviet Union.

The Karabakh was granted the status of Autonomous Oblast within Azerbaijan because its population was 77 per cent Armenian.[8] The arrangement may have rankled a little – many in the Karabakh wondered why the republican map could not have been drawn to allow the territory to be part of the Armenian SSR, which was only ten miles away after all. But during the seventy years of Soviet rule, the Azeris and the Armenians in the Karabakh rubbed along well enough. Besides, both Armenia and Azerbaijan were fairly multicultural republics in those days. Significant Armenian populations lived in Azerbaijan's major cities. There were also around 160,000 Azeris living in Armenia at the time of the 1979 census.

---

* The one exception to this was the Kazakh SSR, which from around 1940 to 1980 was majority-Russian.

Within a few years, however, almost all Armenians had left Azerbaijan and vice versa, and much of the Karabakh was a smouldering ruin. The conflict that began here is now seen as representing the first stones in a landslide that wiped away the entire apparatus of Soviet control. How did it happen?

Back in 1985, the newly appointed head of the Communist Party of the Soviet Union, Mikhail Gorbachev, had a problem. He had been elected to breathe life into the country after two decades of anaemic growth. His flagship policy of *perestroika*, or 'restructuring', sought to shake up the stagnating Soviet economy, making it more competitive and market-led. However, the multitude of vested interests, from the KGB to the army to the factory managers (the so-called Red Bosses) who had been doing very well from their positions within the state-run economy, had little interest in things changing and put the brakes on many reforms.

Gorbachev therefore formulated a new policy called *glasnost*, or 'openness'. He intended to bulldoze through his reforms by encouraging citizens and journalists to be more open, to expose cases of corruption and nepotism, thus fostering the competition that he viewed as essential to the survival of the state.

Openness was a novel concept in a country where a slip of the tongue could land you a twenty-year term in a labour camp, and it proved to be a Pandora's box. While people did use their new-found freedom of expression to uncover corruption and environmental mismanagement, long-dormant conversations about nationalism also began to reappear.

Ever since land in the Caucasus was divvied up by the Bolsheviks in the early 1920s, the Armenians had felt that they had been given a raw deal. The spirit of change ushered in by *glasnost* gave new momentum to these grievances, and the Armenian Supreme Soviet appealed to the Politburo in Moscow to transfer Nagorno-Karabakh Autonomous Oblast to the Armenian SSR. The Politburo would not hear of it, fearing the ethnic violence that would ensue if such a precedent were set. They were right to worry. Azeri nationalism was also on the rise during this period and the Karabakh issue acted as a lightning rod. A vicious anti-Armenian pogrom took place in Azerbaijan's industrial city of Sumgait in 1988. The Soviets struggled to keep a lid on the growing tension, and eventually sent tanks and 26,000 troops into Baku in 1990, killing 147 protesters – an event known in Azerbaijan as Black January.

Soon after independence was achieved in 1991, a full-scale war began over the Karabakh. The Armenians had the advantage of better organisation, greater funding and weapon supplies from the diaspora, as well as more officers (Muslims tended not to get promoted to the higher ranks in the Soviet military).

It was a crushing victory, and the Armenians were uncompromising in their triumph, seizing not only the Karabakh but also the surrounding provinces of Azerbaijan as a buffer zone. They subsequently refused all attempts to negotiate over the territory. The situation settled into an uneasy, unresolved peace – one of the many 'frozen conflicts' that would pepper the former Soviet Union.

At last Arayik makes it to Goris. His family were from Sumgait and fled to the Karabakh after the pogrom in 1988 when he was a small boy. It's been around five years since we saw each other last. Shaven-headed, with rounded specs perched on an aquiline nose, he looks a little ill, but otherwise pleased to see me. As a doctoral student studying for a PhD in Linguistics, he can be pedantic, a little cantankerous even. And in true Caucasus fashion, he doesn't tend to compromise in arguments. But for all that, he's also generous with his time and his manners.

We go for dinner, for which, like Artur, he insists on paying. Armenia has some rich culinary traditions, making ample use of grilled meat, chickpeas, walnuts and pomegranates. There is much dispute in the Caucasus over who invented which dish, but Armenians will claim – and UNESCO will back them up – that *dolma* (meat wrapped in vine leaves) and *lavash* (a type of flat bread) are very much theirs.

After ordering for us both, Arayik turns his beady eyes on me. 'So how are you? Better than me I guess. I've just been kicked off my PhD programme.'

'No!'

'Yep. Apparently, my supervisor cannot bear to work with someone who is pro-Russian.'

'Are you pro-Russian?'

'Not necessarily, but there is nuance to the situation,' he says earnestly. Arayik explains that, for him, the Russian peacekeepers are currently all that stand between the Karabakh Armenians and an Azeri takeover.

'It's not that I want war in Ukraine . . . I just wasn't prepared to badmouth an army that has done more to protect my people than anyone else! Obviously my supervisor took this completely the wrong way and said that I would need to find someone else to work with. Look, you can read his email . . .'

He pulls out his phone. It's a long email; I scan through it. The words 'problematic', 'unprovoked', 'war crimes', 'problematic', 'international law', 'innocent women and children', 'problematic' . . . jump off the page.

'So the Russian soldiers you've encountered have been OK?' I ask him.

'They made a big effort with hearts and minds when they first arrived. Remember that no one else is bothering to protect us, Armenia has shown it doesn't have the resources. Most Armenians only care about us for performative reasons, few of them have actually been to Karabakh. They see it as their land but never ask the people there for our opinion. We are very different to them. We have our own dialect, often people in Yerevan can't even understand me. It's easy for them to talk about fighting for the Karabakh, but few of them understand what it's like to live through war, especially people in the diaspora – they're completely disconnected. But I still remember it. Some of my first ever memories are of sleeping under the table at night as they were firing mortars down on the city. I must have been five years old at the time . . . so my generation, we have a different mentality maybe. Perhaps also because we're a Russian-speaking generation and grew up listening to Russian music, watching the films, so we're more positively inclined towards the Russians, but it's mainly because we have no one else to turn to.'

Around a year after our conversation, Baku began a months-long siege that prevented supplies entering the Karabakh from Armenia.

In October 2023, the Azerbaijan army launched a lightning assault to retake the remainder of the territory, causing over 100,000 Armenians living there to flee to Armenia proper. The Russian peacekeepers did not lift a finger.

Artur, my Good Samaritan from yesterday, is waiting for me in an ancient Nissan. 'We're taking an interesting route today,' he grins. 'In the last war, Azerbaijan captured part of the main highway to Kapan, so we'll be taking the high road.'

I wouldn't fancy being alongside anyone but Artur on this epic, winding route through the mountains. What makes it worse is the traffic: it's thronged with lorries, all sporting number plates written in Persian.

'This is now the main road to Iran,' laughs Artur. 'Quite a lot of our basic supplies, like petrol and steel, come into the country this way.'

It's nauseating, vertiginous, and the steep climbs play havoc with the freighters' engines. Even Artur gets bored after waiting for ten minutes for a chance to overtake a rusting wagon struggling against the upward camber. We're forced to pass on a blind bend. I shut my eyes – why look death in the eye before he slams into you? We survive, but no more than ten seconds later a petrol tanker comes rumbling down the hill. Artur doesn't try the same manoeuvre again.

'This is the *main* road into the country?' I ask.

'Yep. You must have seen the railway line running parallel to the road yesterday?' he asks. 'We haven't had a train pass along there since the late eighties as the line passes through Azerbaijan. Towards the end of the Soviet times, Azeris started kidnapping Armenians from the train and taking them hostage. Train travel pretty much ended after that.'

'If there was peace, would it open again?'

'Peace?' he laughs. 'We had peace for seventy years. You know, I used to work in Moscow, doing odd jobs here and there. I worked with Georgians, I worked with Azeris, we all got on fine, all friends. And then I come back here and there is all this nationalism, fighting over who owns what land . . .' he sighs. 'Maybe there's a driver like me in Azerbaijan who wants peace too. But I don't know; I think they want to press home their advantage. They smell blood, like an animal instinct . . .'

Every now and then we reach a flatter section where there are old women at the roadside, selling refreshments.

'It looks like they're selling Coca-Cola, doesn't it?' grins Artur. 'Well, not a bit of it. That's premium Armenian wine inside those bottles. Alcohol is banned in Iran, but who's going to stop a tired driver who has brought a bottle of Coke home from a trip abroad?'

I privately think that they'd be consuming most of the bottle's contents as a reward for surviving the journey.

We pull off on the outskirts of Kapan, following a gravel track for 200 yards before parking at an unassuming house, most of which is hidden by a stone wall. Inside, its grounds are spacious. The clucking of dozens of chickens fills the air. Artur is immensely proud to show it all to me: the apple and peach trees, the cucumbers and tomatoes; he even has two peacocks.

'*This*, Joe . . . this is what it means to be rich.'

An ancient bike is propped up against the house's stone wall, further along are rusting garden tools, caked in dried mud and worn with use. The electricity cables sprawl inelegantly over the roof's terracotta tiles. But I know what he means. The rooftop glows warmly in the sun, competing with the trees' dazzling lime-green leaves. In his own world, a man can be happy.

Inside, I'm immediately offered dates, apricots and dried fruit by his portly, kind-eyed wife, Ani. She takes me through to the kitchen and tries to introduce me to Artur's father, who is sitting in an armchair, engrossed in the boxing on the telly.

Ani soon realises this is a lost cause, but quickly makes up for it. 'Wine,' she says brightly, proffering a glass. It isn't a question. Then she chivvies me outside to join Artur, who's manning the barbecue with his brother, Abram, a beefy man with sharp, rather mistrustful eyes.

'So, what do you think of Armenia?' he asks, smiling wolfishly and launching right into his inquisition.

'It's lovely, really nice people.'

Abram doesn't trouble to hide his scorn. 'Nice people,' he laughs disbelievingly. 'You don't need to pretend; everyone here is a thief and a crook.'

'Abram,' says Artur warily.

'What? You know it's true! People don't know how to live well here.' He turns to me. 'In England people know how to live well.'

It's my turn to smirk. 'What do you mean?'

'Live well!' he says, as though talking to a child. 'As in a country where people don't steal; where if a person works hard, they can afford time off; they are respected by their employers; they have time to spend with their families. In England you have this. Here, honest people work hard and get paid nothing. Four hundred dollars a month. Maximum. This is not enough to live. It's nothing! In England salaries are much higher.'

I think about this. I'd read the British newspapers that morning, most of which bemoaned a cost-of-living crisis engulfing the country.

'What about your family, Joe, where do they live?' asks Artur.

I treat the pair of them to a potted history of how our family, originally from north-east England, was now spread across Britain and Europe.

'So strange,' says Artur contemplatively. 'To me, it doesn't make sense for you all to be in different places.'

'Of course it makes sense!' says Abram. 'They go where the money is. That's why England is a strong state: because people can earn money and pay taxes, so if something goes wrong, the government can afford to help them. Here, we rely on our families, we stay in the same place, we make no money, so the government has no tax revenue, they can't make the country any better, nor defend us from those Azeri fuckers.' He looks around fiercely, waiting for either of us to challenge him. 'One day, I'll move away from this shithole.'

'Where will you go?' I ask, after an awkward silence.

'America . . .' His eyes are dreamy.

'Nonsense,' interrupts Artur. 'A man's place is in his homeland, on his soil. The problems in this country have nothing to do with taxes and hard work, they're to do with greed and corruption, and people looking for shortcuts.' He gives his brother a nasty look. I have a sense that this isn't the first time they've had this argument.

In many ways, Abram is right. It would be churlish to argue that the Armenian economy has thrived since independence. For all that some might shout 'Boycott!', closure of the borders with Turkey and Azerbaijan has left the country heavily dependent on access through Georgia and on the Russian economy beyond. Iran's own international isolation means that it is unable to offer much in terms of diversification.

Remittances from Armenians abroad are a lifeline, accounting for roughly a quarter of GDP in some years, while membership in the Russian-led Eurasian Economic Union has tied Armenia even closer to Moscow. Add to that bureaucracy, corruption and the costs of war, and it's no surprise there's significant Soviet nostalgia here.

Throughout dinner, Ani does not take her seat. The men dine alone as she scampers around the table offering more wine, cleaning dishes and serving side-platters. She gives me a scandalised look when I offer to help.

'This is the Caucasus,' Artur laughs. 'Guests do not help.'

Flushed but looking satisfied, Ani finally joins us for dessert – fresh berries and strawberries from the garden.

'Where are you going next, Joe?' she asks.

'Well,' I squirm a little. 'The plan is to visit all fifteen Soviet countries, so I guess I need to see this conflict from the other side.'

'So, Azerbaijan?' Ani's voice is level, but the tension ratchets up a notch. Abram cracks his knuckles.

'I think it's good that you're going,' says Artur, warmly. 'You need to see both sides.'

I manage to temporarily sidetrack them from talk of their sworn enemy by discussing travel plans. You can see Azerbaijan from Kapan. The border lies a couple of miles from Artur's house. But getting there is not so easy. No traffic has crossed from Armenia to Azerbaijan for over thirty years. The once-seamless journey now involves travelling via Georgia or Iran. This means taking a midnight train to Georgia, and then a flight to Baku.

They are full of advice for the train journey. The post-Soviet rail network is one of the great iron legacies of Russian authoritarianism: the vast territories of the tsarist and Soviet empires were criss-crossed by over 90,000 miles of track by the late 1980s. Most of it is still intact, albeit some routes, such as Yerevan to Baku, have fallen into disuse.

There are three classes on these night trains. First class, sometimes called *luxe* and other times *spalny vagon*, is a two-bed compartment. Second class is *kupé*, and has the same set-up except with bunk beds, so it sleeps four. Then there is *platzkart*, a fifty-four-bunk open dormitory, with four bunk beds arranged round a table on one side of the aisle – as in *kupé* – and then another pair of bunk beds squashed in against the wall opposite, turned in the direction of travel.

'If you take *platzkart*, bring your own toilet roll,' advises Artur seriously.

'And some flip-flops and a pair of jogging bottoms,' adds Ani.

They assure me that I don't need to worry about safety. There's always likely to be at least one pair of curious eyes open, even in the dead of night. And while this might lead to an uncomfortable lack of privacy, it does a decent job of disincentivising potential pilferers.

'But the most important thing, whatever you do, make sure you purchase an odd-numbered seat,' says Abram. 'Those are the lower bunks, and everyone wants one. When they see you're young, some people will try to bully you out of the bottom bunk; don't let them do it.'

'Unless it's an old lady,' Ani reminds him.

Abram pauses, torn between justice and gallantry. 'Unless it's a *very* old lady,' he concedes.

But talk of Azerbaijan can only be put off for so long. 'I really don't see why you need to go there at all,' says Abram. 'Just go to Turkey. Azeris pretend to be different, but they're just Turks when it comes down to it. Mercedes-Benz is older than their country!'

'Have you heard the story about the time a Turkish delegation came to Armenia?' asks Ani. 'Tell him, Artur!'

Artur sighs and smiles indulgently. 'A Turkish delegate once came to Armenia and he saw all our banknotes, which have a picture of Mount Ararat on them – and says, "You do realise that's *our* mountain on your banknotes?" The Armenian diplomat nods respectfully and points to the delegate's lapel, on which there's a miniature Turkish flag, and he says – "You do realise that's our moon on your flag?"'

They all burst into hearty laughter at this. I manage a weak chuckle. I suppose every nation is a prisoner to its past; yet for Armenians, the chains seem especially heavy.

3
AZERBAIJAN
THE REPUBLIC OF OIL AND GAS

The cars may not have the same piercing, whining, jet engines of old, but there's still nothing quite like the noise of Formula One. The smells as well: the acrid fumes of fuel and the beautiful burnt rubber from braking on baking asphalt. The cars ripple through the heatwaves, popping like sparks as they speed by – blue and gold, red and black, deep matt-silver.

Baku is one of a select group of city-races on the Formula One calendar, and the three-and-three-quarter-mile circuit manages to take in four different eras of Azerbaijan's history. The start line is on Azadliq (Freedom) Square, with the cars facing the glass towers of modern Azerbaijan. Looming over proceedings is the baroque Government House, built to accommodate the Soviet parliament in the 1930s. The cars then speed off into the city, through classical architecture from the tsarist days, navigating past the twelfth-century Maiden's Tower and the walls of the medieval city, before slamming on the accelerator back along the famous Neftchilar Prospekt, and back to the start line.

The city is another level of opulence from the patchy roads of Yerevan, with their deep gutters and stray dogs. You can see why teams and fans love it here: the Hilton is a mere five-minute jaunt from the pit lane. This means easy access to Baku's nightlife: in the week since I've been here, the bars have steadily filled with fans sporting Mercedes, Red Bull and Ferrari clobber.

Locals that I talk to are less enamoured. It's hard to blame them: Covid lockdowns aside, I don't think I've seen disruption on such a scale before. The shops, restaurants and museums with the temerity to be standing in the path of Formula One's high-octane circus are shuttered ten days in advance of the race. The seafront promenade, where most Bakuvians come to walk in the evenings, has been made totally inaccessible to all but the select few who have a laminated pass dangling round their necks – the price of which, incidentally, is about as much as the average monthly salary.

Locals attending the Grand Prix all conform to a certain type that I've seen many times before when working with rich Russians. The grandstands are a sea of Botoxed lips pouting for endless selfies, the sun reflecting off a thousand pairs of designer sunglasses. I wonder what Artur back in Armenia would make of it all.

Azerbaijan pays a rumoured $55 million to host the race each year – in addition to the crippling costs on businesses from closing down the city centre for two weeks. You might be wondering where that money comes from and why people put up with it. To answer that we must go back to Neftchilar Prospekt, or, as it translates into English: Oil Man's Avenue.

Baku was the original oil city. Due south from the fertile foothills of the Caucasus, the land falls away into a dry, windswept plain that ends in a peninsula thrust into the Caspian. On this peninsula rose a medieval town enclosed by stone walls where Persian traders, Arab scholars and steppe nomads crossed paths with the Turkic-speaking locals in caravanserais, mosques and markets. But even then, travellers passing through here found the city's supply of thick black gloop worthy of mention. Marco Polo noted that 'this oil is not good to eat; but it is good for burning and as a salve for men and camels affected with itch or scab'.

In the late nineteenth century, oil's usefulness in powering the internal combustion engine began to be realised and Baku became a boom town. By 1901, the oilfields around the city provided a full *half* of the world's oil supplies. Fortune seekers flocked here from far afield and it became one of the Russian Empire's most cosmopolitan cities. Baku was the prize that the Nazis were attempting to secure before they got bogged down at Stalingrad.

The city's relative importance declined as production shifted to Siberia and the Arctic, but independence has brought enormous investment from Western petro-giants. In what has been dubbed the 'Deal of the Century', a consortium of foreign oil majors, led by BP, negotiated lucrative access to fields in the Caspian, as well as bringing the expertise to exploit them. Better still, the local authorities no longer have to share the proceeds with

Moscow. Money has poured into the public coffers and for much of the early twenty-first century the city has flourished. Flying into Baku by air, you can see the miles and miles of wells stretching into the Caspian. So much oil that you can almost set the water alight.

Foreign expats are out here in force. James Bond even paid a visit to the city in 1999's *The World Is Not Enough*. To accommodate them there are huge numbers of Irish bars, many of which have a seedy reputation: 'They're either expensive, full of hookers, or expensive and full of hookers,' one Scottish oil worker warns me.

All this foreign investment has left Azerbaijan in the odd position of being the most pro-Western country in the Caucasus, a role that is only set to grow as Europe seeks to wean itself off Russia's natural resources. Bolt and Uber compete for status as the most popular taxi service, with Russia's Yandex nowhere to be seen. Baku is also the only city in the region with Starbucks Coffee.

I say 'odd' not only because Azerbaijan is the sole Muslim country in the Caucasus, but it is also unabashedly authoritarian, having been under the control of one family (save for a brief interregnum) since 1969. This family doesn't much care if they disrupt people; if they want to host a Formula One race, nobody in Azerbaijan is going to stop them.

Entering the arrivals hall of any post-Soviet airport is like finding yourself on the set of *Finding Nemo*, surrounded by the seagulls shouting 'Mine! Mine! Mine!' as they scrap over a morsel of food. Unlicensed post-Soviet taxi drivers are, if anything, even more aggressive. Should you have the strength of character to fend them off, an easier option in Baku is the shuttle bus to the city centre. This sweeps out of Heydar Aliyev International Airport, along Heydar Aliyev Avenue, past the Heydar Aliyev Center to the bus station. Not far from here is Heydar Aliyev Park, in the centre of which is a statue of none other than Heydar Aliyev. I'm presuming you've spotted a pattern here.

Heydar Aliyev, a former KGB colonel, became the First Secretary of the Communist Party of Azerbaijan in 1969. A protégé of Soviet General

Secretary Leonid Brezhnev, Aliyev ruled the republic until 1982, after which he became the first Muslim to enter the Politburo in Moscow. In 1987 he was forced to resign as Gorbachev attempted to replace him with someone less ostensibly corrupt. For Aliyev, this turned out to be a blessing: shunned by the Communist Party, he reinvented himself as a nationalist, and was perfectly placed to return to power in a military coup once the Soviet Union had imploded and Azerbaijan descended simultaneously into civil war and conflict with Armenia.

His return stabilised the country and he spent the next ten years restoring much of the police state and the cult of personality that had existed in the Soviet days. But Aliyev was already an old man by 1993, and he must have seen enough geriatric Soviet leaders die in office to know that he too would have to find a way to secure his legacy. Fortunately, there was no pesky Party to appease any more, so the old man put his trust in an older, more reliable solution: blood. Power would pass to his son Ilham, and the Aliyevs would create a dynasty.

In the modern world, a few examples of this quaint idea exist, the Kims in North Korea and the recently deposed Assads in Syria being the most notable. In 2003, as his father's health waned, Ilham Aliyev was made prime minister in August, before winning the presidential elections in October with 76 per cent of the vote. These elections involved patterns that will become familiar throughout this book: the arbitrary arrest of opposition activists, state-media fawning over the government candidate, as well as your common-or-garden voter intimidation and fraud. Still, at least it provided some comfort to a dying old man. Heydar Aliyev passed away that December, safe in the knowledge that the transformation to a dynastic dictatorship was complete. His son has held on to power ever since.

To learn more about the ruling family, there is only one place to start. Of all the buildings named after the first president, the Heydar Aliyev Center is the crown jewel. Completed in 2012 and designed by Zaha Hadid architects, the structure ripples in white waves atop a lawn of perfectly mown grass. This grass is all the more striking as it's the only vegetation you'll see for miles around. The lawn is tended by an army of gardeners manning the sprinklers, lest it shrivel in the frazzling heat. The vast interior is oddly silent, with wood and white marble. I'm told the acoustics in the auditorium are the best in the Caucasus. All in all, it's a rather touching thing for a son to build for his father – my father will be lucky to get a rendition of 'Shine On You Crazy Diamond' at his funeral – only Part One, mind. Definitely not the whole ten-minute ensemble. Then again, he's never given me a country to rule.

And what would the Heydar Aliyev Center be without the Heydar Aliyev Museum? The permanent exhibition takes us through the official biography of the former president, starting with his birth in the remote province of Nakhchivan (actually, most scholars agree that he was born in Armenia, but that would be rather inconvenient) and his brilliant scholarly career. Little attention is given to his participation in the Second World War, nor his time in the security forces. Presumably a career locking up Azeri dissidents for the Soviet KGB is also not the vibe they're looking for.

We then move on to his rule – I would have thought that this would be an interesting sell. Many newly independent countries seek to create a national myth focused on a heroic overthrow of an oppressive tyrant. One might expect Aliyev, as leader of Soviet Azerbaijan for over twenty years, and a member of the KGB to boot, to be deemed guilty by association. But no. Instead there are pictures of the development of industry, of Aliyev in the fields sowing seeds and shovelling earth.

The museum's version of events has it that Aliyev was not booted out of the Politburo, but in fact resigned in protest, only to return gloriously half a decade later in a manner of which Coriolanus would have been proud:

> In May to June 1993, given the acute government crisis fraught with civil war and compromising Azerbaijan's very existence as an independent state, the mass movement demanding Heydar Aliyev's return became the dominant force in Azerbaijan. Faced with this ever-increasing popular movement, the authorities of the day had no other choice than calling Heydar Aliyev back to Baku.

No other choice indeed! I will use this as a template to place in the Joe Luc Barnes Museum if I ever conduct a successful military coup.

Then follow pictures of Aliyev the statesman, shaking hands with various dignitaries: the queen, Bill Clinton and CEOs of oil companies among them. There's a special section on Aliyev's main achievement while in office: the completion of the Baku–Tbilisi–Ceyhan pipeline, which means Azerbaijani oil can be pumped via Georgia to a Turkish port on the Mediterranean without having to pass through Russia.

Lastly, there is a fascinating room dedicated to the gifts that other countries' leaders gave to Heydar Aliyev. If you've ever wondered what to offer a man who owns a country, here is the place to come for inspiration.

Famously, Aliyev was gifted a framed original graduation certificate from the Leningrad KGB Academy from fellow alumnus Vladimir Putin when he came to visit in 2000. This is not something on display, but some of Putin's other gifts are, including a gold watch, a shotgun and a coffee set. There's also a sculpture of a bison from Belarus's Alexander Lukashenko and a crystal glass eagle from George W. Bush.

The museum has left me bursting with questions, and fortunately I've been pointed in the direction of a man who is brimming with answers. Altay Goyushov works at the Baku Research Institute, one of the few independent think tanks in the country, after being fired very publicly from his professorial position at Baku State University for speaking out against the regime.

We find a shady spot outside a tea house in Filarmoniya Park, next to the old city. Much as English men meet down the pub, Azeri blokes sit outside and drink tea. They do so slowly, deliberately, adding strawberry jam as a sweetener rather than sugar. Tea is often accompanied, as in Armenia, by a game of chess or backgammon.

Altay has kind eyes and a cigarette permanently on the go. I begin by relating to him what had preoccupied me at the museum: why did independent Azerbaijan not last two years before handing power straight back to the old Soviet elite that was ruling it before? Was there any point in overthrowing the communists at all?

'In 1993, when he came to power, we were in really bad shape,' Altay begins, flying out of the traps and speaking in strongly accented English. 'We'd lost the war [with Armenia] and were totally disillusioned with everything that was going on around us. That's why Aliyev is portrayed as the founder of the republic – as the man who actually made the Azerbaijani state viable. But this wasn't only in Azerbaijan, this sort of thing happened across the post-Soviet space: many of these newly emergent nationalists came to power for a short time, but then had to give it back to the old Soviet elite because they were not able to run the country.'

But in none of those countries, save for Turkmenistan, has a new ruling dynasty been established.

'We didn't know anything about Ilham Aliyev until the parliamentary elections of 2000. And his first public speech was really, really bad,' Altay chuckles. 'Ridiculous actually. He could not speak. He grew up speaking Russian, and he spoke very bad Azerbaijani. Plus his speech was synchronised badly with his hand movements. He would say, "We have to move forward" while throwing his hand backwards,' Altay laughs uproariously. 'Everyone said, "How can this kind of guy be a president? It's impossible! He's absolutely not a public politician, he cannot do anything!" But all these predictions were wrong. He became the president; he has been running the country for over twenty years. They say that now his achievements are even greater than his father's.'

'But you got on the wrong side of him?' I press him, referring to his sacking from the university. 'How did you become so outspoken against the regime?'

Altay pauses once more and takes a long drag on his cigarette.

'As a young boy, I was a hockey fan,' he begins slowly. 'I remember in the Olympics in 1980 when the Soviet Union Dream Team lost to the USA. I was in eighth grade at middle school. I remember crying at home because we had lost to the enemy. And it wasn't just me, people all around me were devastated by that match. But then just eight years later – when the USSR began to collapse around 1988/89, suddenly this surge of nationalism started. I saw those same people who had cried when the USSR lost to the USA were now screaming "Death to the Soviets. Death to the Russians". Before they had one religion – the socialist revolution or whatever – and overnight this was replaced by ethnic nationalism. They just replaced one Lenin with another Lenin. For me this was an awakening.

I saw that they had been brainwashed, and I realised that until now, I too had been brainwashed. Suddenly, just like that, I regained my freedom. And I realised that it would be something that I would never give up. I told myself: *never allow anybody to brainwash you again. Be independent. Maybe you will be wrong. But the most important thing is that you will never allow anybody to brainwash you.* I was twenty-three years old at that point.'

He would go on to study a PhD in History before becoming a Professor at Baku State University. By all accounts he was popular with his students, but his increasing use of mainstream and then social media to criticise the regime made his position untenable in the eyes of those in power.

In 2013, Goyushov was offered a comfortable severance package if he went quietly and signed a resignation letter that the university had drafted for him. His refusal to do this resulted in a stand-off as the students rallied to his side.[1] But this only delayed the inevitable; at the start of the next academic year he was informed that he would no longer be required to teach classes. Seeing the way the wind was blowing, he took up an offer of a fellowship in the USA.

I ask him if he feels safe and secure now that he has returned to Baku.

'You cannot feel secure in this country. Never,' he says. 'It's a dictatorship and you're criticising it. Who knows when they'll decide to do something about that? But, so far, they tolerate me. I've created autonomy for myself.'

'Why are there not more people standing up to the regime like this? Is it just fear?'

'Fear, yes. But not necessarily fear of arrest. It's actually more down to economics. We have what you might call an authoritarian middle class. It's mainly guys who were educated abroad but who have made their money through the government structures, or business structures also connected to the government. These guys, in order to earn money, must be loyal to the government, serving it either in the state sector or in the so-called private sector – which is not private as it's run by the family of the first lady.'

The family he refers to is the Pashayev family, who own everything from banking to oil through the ubiquitous Pasha Group. The marriage of the Pashayevs and the Aliyevs is almost medieval in its arranged convenience.

'They've made a few offers to me for "collaboration".' Altay gives a wan smile. 'That's just how things work here. Either you stay abroad to be independent, or you come here with no opportunities apart from being part of the government. And then there are dissidents like us who struggle to somehow find their way independently. For me it's easy, I don't care about my career or finding a job. But young people who work with me either have to find a professorship in the West, which is not easy to do – or if they stay here, they have to go to government-dominated structures. They don't have a choice.'

'What about Armenia?' I ask him, hoping to find some positive note on which to end our conversation. 'Now the war is over do you see any resolution to the conflict?'

He laughs again. 'There's a place you should go here in Baku – they recently opened this so-called trophy park with Armenian relics from the war. I had quite a public argument with the government about this. We said, you're talking about reconciliation, about living together, coexistence or whatever, and then you open this trophy park with mannequins of Armenian soldiers, and you allow people to abuse these mannequins. And you take *kids* there!' He's getting into his stride now. 'You're not just making a problem for your so-called reconciliation efforts, but you're also abusing your own kids! What kind of future are they going to provide with this kind of education?' He briefly pauses for breath, or maybe to smoke, he seems to do both in one motion. 'Eventually they agreed with us. They took away the helmets and mannequins, but the park is still there.'

'I guess Aliyev isn't that keen on letting the memory of this victory die . . . Does it make peace something that he doesn't really want?'

'This is a big question for me as well – because in the twenty years of his rule, winning this war is his only real achievement. And it's a big achievement, so I understand that he wants to build his legacy on it. But it's not a reliable foundation . . . There was a belief in Azerbaijan that after victory in the war things were going to be different: the people would demand more, they would have more say in the running of the country. And this assumption was completely wrong. Now people have begun to understand that things are even getting worse. The victory didn't make the public stronger, it made the ruler stronger.'

Next day I give the Military Trophy Park a go. It's on the edge of the city. The ground here is parched; the pitiless sun reflects off the gleaming glass towers overhead. It's so hot that the lashing wind makes it less bearable.

At the park's entrance are the words *Qarabag Azerbaycandir!* (Karabakh is Azerbaijan). This is a phrase that is daubed all over the city, appearing on big screens, projected onto towers and even written on bottles of water.

Each exhibit has been labelled systematically, with descriptions, in English and Azeri, detailing the dimensions, speed, range and production date of each individual weapon or vehicle, as well as the place where it was captured. Most of them were made in the Soviet Union period. Some items are quite tragically ancient, such as a 'towed howitzer' from 1946. There's even a captured ambulance on display – although a sign has been added below the description: *Note – this vehicle was used to supply weapons* – lest anyone let their sympathy run away with them.

At the far end of the museum is a mock-up of an Armenian military base, complete with obstacles such as razor wire, mines and trenches that the 'glorious army of Azerbaijan' (I'm quoting here) had to pass through to remove them from their positions. Beside each exhibit is a little bench, as though this were a park where one might want to sit and reflect on the view.

The triumphalism is understandable. In the Museum of Independence that I'd visited that morning, a young tour guide had held forth about the tragic events of the first Karabakh War in the early 1990s. Most keenly felt was the loss of Shusha – 'a cradle of Azerbaijani music and culture', which was wrenched out of Azerbaijani control by the rampaging Armenians. There was also a certain relish with which she detailed a massacre that took place in the town of Khojaly, where Armenian forces slaughtered over 600 civilians (this is the Azeri government figure).

'The Armenians skinned people, pulled out eyes, cut off ears,' she informed me, gesturing to some grisly photographs on the wall. Azeris often refer to this event as the Khojaly genocide – partly for international sympathy, but I suspect also in an attempt to belittle Armenia's own experience at the hands of the Ottomans.

In all, over half a million Azeris were driven from the Karabakh and its surrounding regions by Armenian forces. To have regained much of that land in 2020 brought a huge emotional release across the country.

This is not to diminish Armenian suffering in the same period – 200,000 Armenians living in Baku, Sumgait and other cities in Azerbaijan were forced out almost overnight during a wave of vicious pogroms. Indeed, the date of the Armenian assault on Khojaly, 25 February 1992, was likely timed to coincide with the fourth anniversary of the Sumgait pogrom.

Having seen both sides of the Nagorno-Karabakh conflict it's clear that, for the last thirty years, each side has used the suffering of its own people to lay claim to a nasty sense of moral superiority. Neither is willing to acknowledge the legitimacy of the other's grievances, nor the atrocities committed by their own forces. In Azerbaijan one man did attempt to do this, and his treatment is perhaps a good indicator of why more people do not step forward as peacemakers.

Akram Aylisli was an Azerbaijani prize-winning author; a national treasure in a country that, let's face it, is not hugely renowned on the international literary circuit. His books were part of the school curriculum, and he was twice elected as a member of parliament in 2005 and 2010. In 2013, his novel *Stone Dreams* was published in a Russian literary journal, *Druzhba Narodov*. The book sought to draw attention to the massacres of Armenians in Baku as the Soviet Union collapsed. 'If a single candle were lit for every Armenian killed violently,' he wrote, 'the radiance of those candles would be brighter than the moon.'

The ensuing scandal was predictable. Aylisli's name was dragged through the mud by the regime, who described 'his entirely slanderous work' as a 'deliberate distortion of the history of Azerbaijan', before issuing a decree stripping him of his prominent status as People's Writer. In February 2013, people gathered in the author's home town to symbolically burn his books. One politician even offered $10,000 to anyone who would cut off his ear.

You might argue that these are the inevitable consequences of a dictatorship that uses ethnic hatred and militarism to cling to power.

But in democratic Armenia the same attitudes hold sway. As we have seen, Armenians burn Azeri flags in public ceremonies; pillory their own prime minister for attempting to make peace, and sometimes refuse to distinguish between the Azeri people, alongside whom they lived peacefully in the USSR for seventy years, and the Ottoman Turks who perpetrated a genocide against them a century ago.

For an outsider, the intransigence of both sides can be a little maddening, and solutions are thin on the ground. As the Soviets were fond of saying: *Vostok – delo tonkoye*; the East is a delicate thing.

Ganja

I'm starting to feel claustrophobic in the glitzy, triumphalist atmosphere of Baku. I've also been told that the rest of the country is very different, with the wealth barely stretching beyond the city limits. To try out this theory I sweat my way towards the magnificent neoclassical building on 28th May Square, first opened in 1883 to serve as the terminus of the Tiflis to Baku railway.* 'Modernisation' has meant that the beautiful old station is no longer used: behind the palatial facade is a utilitarian structure with an underground ticket office. I'm a little miffed to have to show my passport in order to get a ticket for the four-hour train journey to Ganja, Azerbaijan's second city.

'Is this an international service?' I ask sarcastically as I hand it over for inspection. Not a flicker from the babushka.

I board a spanking-new train called The Stadler – named after the Swiss company that makes it. It's a double-decker and, mercifully, air-conditioned. It swaggers out of the shining station and we head into the dusty interior, leaving the coast far behind, and with it any vestiges of wealth and prosperity. The poverty here is as in-your-face as Baku's gaudy skyscrapers. The settlements we pass are sorry, shabby affairs, with gravel roads, shrubs and one-storey houses. The occasional lean cow can be seen hauling a plough through the bone-dry earth, a farmer plodding resignedly

---

* The Georgian capital, Tbilisi, while always referred to as such in Georgian, was known internationally as Tiflis until 1936.

in her wake. In the bigger settlements there are long-abandoned factories, relics of the days of socialist industry. Their stern concrete battlements look blandly across the landscape, pockmarked by smashed-in windows. Many of the railway lines are overgrown with grass.

The only sign that this land hasn't been abandoned by the state are the policemen who guard every level crossing. They stand to attention as the train passes. There are also brand-new signs at the entrance to passing towns, each showing young men's faces superimposed onto Azeri flags. These are the Shahids, or martyrs – the men from these villages who died fighting for their country in the recent war.

Ganja too has a woebegone look about it. The roads might be paved, but they're unlikely to be hosting the F1 anytime soon. Outside the hostel, an abandoned pink teddy lies face down on the crumbling pavement. It seems to portend ill. All the windows are shuttered.

Modernity is present in the street in the form of a poster of the Aliyevs: father and son surrounded by pictures of fresh armaments: helicopters, anti-aircraft missile launchers and suchlike. It bears the slogan: *Vezifemiz Azerbaycanin Erazi Bütövlüyünü Qorumaqdir* (Our duty is to protect the territorial integrity of Azerbaijan). Although it's hard not to defer to a word with five umlauts, I'd hoped to have left the nationalism behind in Baku.

On the plus side, people here are extremely hospitable, even if the level of spoken Russian has dropped precipitously. One woman refuses to let me pay when I enter her tea shop, she natters away to me in Azeri while I eat the extra-large portion of Napoleon cake that she brings forth. She eventually manages to scramble enough Russian together to ask where I'm from and squeals with delight upon finding out the answer. She then makes me pose for a picture next to my half-eaten cake. 'Handsome,' she says. I like to think I'll be up on the wall one day, next to the picture of Heydar Aliyev.

Bar service involves a similar amount of trial-and-error communication. I come across a cocktail place near Heydar Aliyev Square where I order a gin and tonic. The waiter takes me at my word and returns with a shot glass full of gin and a can of tonic water. I fight back a smile and ask for some ice and lemon. He shuffles over a couple of minutes later with a glass filled to the brim with ice, as well as a whole lemon, cut into eight pieces.

'If you need any help with translation, let me know,' comes a voice in English from the table across. A bearded man in his thirties, wearing an orange T-shirt and his hair in a ponytail, is also grinning at the DIY cocktail that I've just been handed. He beckons me over and we start chatting. His name is Shahrud, he works in Luxembourg but is back in Ganja for his father's funeral.

'He was only sixty-eight,' Shahrud sighs. 'A really healthy man as well, rode his bike everywhere; but then one day had a heart attack – they tried to give him a caffeine injection to save him, which was a crazy thing to do. He was dead within two minutes. If he'd lived in Europe, he'd still be alive.'

Shahrud is in the mood for a few bevvies and offers to show me Ganja's nightlife, which admittedly isn't one of its main draws. The city is prettier at night; it's now that perfect sultry temperature for walking on a summer's evening and the dark shadows allow the mind to imagine other surroundings than cracked pavement, stray dogs and abandoned teddies. We find a bar that stays open late and plonk ourselves on a table outside.

'*Qardash!*' shouts Shahrud, and the waiter comes over. We order two pints of Xirdalan, Azerbaijan's favourite lager (of all the civilisational 'gifts' that Moscow bestowed upon its Muslim subjects, alcohol was by far the easiest to swallow).

'Does *Qardash* mean waiter?' I ask.

He grins. 'It means "brother", or "bro"; something like that. In Russian they say *brat*.'

I nod in recognition; I'd been in enough Moscow taxis to know that every Caucasus taxi driver considered me his *brat*.

'Literally, *Qardash* means "snow stone", which is a little more poetic!'

Snow stone came over with our Xirdalans and some nibbles – salted chickpeas and *chechil*, smoked cheese, which he drizzles in lemon juice. For a nation of tea-drinkers, the Azeris don't half have some good beer snacks. I tell Shahrud so.

He frowns. 'There's honestly so little positive about this country. Coming back here after living in Luxembourg . . .'

We end up discussing our childhoods. Shahrud is stunned to find that I grew up in a village. Rural people are poor people in Soviet countries, pretty much without exception. The idea that an English village might be relatively prosperous comes as a bit of a shock to him, but not nearly as much of a shock as me telling him that many people in Britain are quite nostalgic for the 1990s.

'Nostalgic for the nineties?! Why?'

I try to explain about Britpop, Cool Britannia, retro football kits, nationalised rail, the milkman, a world without the cesspit of the internet and its crushing mass of constant information.

'We really grew up in two different worlds,' says Shahrud, shaking his head. 'The nineties here were fucking shit. People were so poor that at school we were prohibited from bringing bananas for lunch; they were so expensive that no one could afford them. The teachers were worried that kids would fight over them.'

The next day, Shahrud messages asking if I want to come to Park House Café by the river at 1 p.m. The river in question has that forlorn look of waterways in Spain or Italy in the summer: a struggling stream surrounded by a winter's worth of detritus.

Even before I've sat down, Shahrud offers me some of the strawberry-jam tea that I'd tried with Altay.

'Also, you need to try some *piti* – it's more of a Baku dish, but we eat it all across the country. Here,' he says, ladling some into my bowl, before finally introducing our dining companions.

'These are my nephews,' says Shahrud, pointing me in turn to Elton, a twenty-year-old sociology student with a look of mischief about him, and Nuriman, Elton's scowling brother who is a couple of years younger, but very well built.

'Nuriman used to do kick-boxing,' Shahrud explains. 'He was really good. He wanted to represent the country, but to do that he had to pay a bribe to the local sports minister – about fifteen hundred dollars.'

'Why?'

'Because the minister spent a lot of money getting to that position of power, and now he needs to earn that money back. That's the way this country works. It's the same in the schools as well. No one studies seriously here, they know that to pass the exams they just need to pay the professor at the right time.'

'Everyone does it,' says Elton. 'Half my class have already bribed the teacher and have begun their summer holidays early.'

'Joe, eat your *piti*!' says Shahrud. 'It'll get cold!'

Piti is a warm, meaty soup. It's genuinely delicious – little meatballs surrounded by a delicate thin dough that fizz in an oily broth. I rip some *tandir* bread and dip it in. It makes a nice change from kebab, which has been sustaining me for most of this leg of the trip.

'Will you go to university as well?' I ask Nuriman.

'Nope,' he shrugs.

'My sister only had enough money to send one child to university,' says Shahrud quietly. 'Nuriman is going to start working in a butcher's factory in Poland later this summer. The average salary in this city is around three hundred dollars per month, whereas in Poland he'll earn closer to a thousand dollars.'

One very noticeable difference between Azerbaijan and Armenia is the number of young people here. Since independence, Azerbaijan's population has grown by almost 50 per cent to over 10 million. In an economy that, as Shahrud puts it, runs on oil, the ruling family's business interests, and weddings, this leaves a booming population with limited options. War was one way of harnessing that, but with victory the country must now reckon with a harder question: what was the point of throwing off communism if it only meant replacing Moscow's grip with a home-grown dictatorship, one that leaves most of its people little better off?

I dwell on this as we spend an otherwise enjoyable afternoon drinking tea, smoking some shisha, before having a few more Xirdalans in the sun. But I have Georgia on my mind. Tomorrow I'm booked on the evening flight from Baku and I take my leave before we move on to the G&Ts once more. This time I insist on paying, partly to pay Shahrud back for all the beers he'd bought yesterday, but mainly because I couldn't pass up the chance to ask him to have *piti* on me.

4
GEORGIA
THE REPUBLIC OF THORNED ROSES

In 1948, at the outset of the Cold War, a number of prominent American socialists, among them John Steinbeck, were invited to the Soviet Union and led on a guided tour. Steinbeck wasn't particularly enamoured with Russia or Ukraine, but there was one place that he couldn't wait to get to.

'Everywhere we went in Russia, the name Georgia came up constantly,' he wrote. Eventually, he made it to Tbilisi and seemed to fall in love.

'The people [in Georgia] were better dressed, better looking and more full of spirit than any we saw in Russia,' he declared.[1] It's an image Georgia has retained. Tourists from the former Soviet Union flock here, and it is increasingly appearing on Western radars as an 'up-and-coming' tourism hotspot.

Georgia is around the same size as Scotland and, like Scotland, it has mountains and sea. Unlike Scotland, it also has good weather, meaning that its Black Sea beaches are thronged with visitors from May until September, and the mountains, stretching as high as seventeen thousand feet, are more spectacular than anything the British Isles have to offer.

I've wound my way past these peaks and across scorching plains in search of something else that draws in scores of tourists. All that elevated land and sunshine makes Georgia the perfect place for growing grapes. They've been doing so for 8,000 years, boasting the world's earliest recorded evidence of wine-making. Georgians are extremely proud of this fact.

The land stretches out like a pan under the enormous sky. To the west a cosy, pink hue is beginning to form; the early-evening light bathes everything in a warm glow, the neat rows of vines stand like troops on parade, casting dappled shadows onto the merry earth. To the north, in a far-off fuchsia haze, lie the Caucasus Mountains, the legendary natural wall between these lands and Russia – albeit a wall that has proved all too permeable over the centuries.

'Eat!' rumbles Nika in his guttural voice, shoving a plate towards me. Nika owns a vineyard just outside Telavi, the beating heart of Georgia's oenotourism scene. He's already topped up my wine glasses – glasses plural, as he'd like me to try everything at once. As usual in the Caucasus, conspicuous consumption is viewed as a sign of manliness, and Nika seems intent on giving my palate the alpha experience.

It's very, very easy to get fat in Georgia. Its culinary mainstays are *khachapuri* – hot, cheesy bread that comes in a variety of forms, the most famous of which is shaped like a rowing boat, the centre filled with butter and a raw egg. Then there are the *khinkali* – large, juicy dumplings – and *nigvziani badrijani*, thinly sliced aubergine rolls stuffed with a walnut paste garnished with pomegranates. Georgians also have their own variety of squiggly script for you to get acquainted with, so you'll be pleased to know that, even if you do remember all those new words, you won't be able to read the menu.

Fortunately, I have Nika, who encourages me to try *churchkhela* for dessert. These are strings of walnuts, briefly dipped into a mixture of grape syrup and flour, and then hung up to set for a few days, coming out looking like a foot-long knobbly truncheon.

And then there's the contents of those wine glasses. Nika himself is deeply attached to the land; his grandfather was sent to the Gulag for refusing to allow his family farm to be collectivised. He is also a huge promoter of traditional Georgian viniculture, eschewing the modern wine-making methods imposed by the Soviets in favour of distilling the grapes in a *qvevri* – a clay pot, like a Roman amphora, buried deep in the ground.

This little nation spent long stretches of its history under Arab and then Persian control, and clung on to its wine-making traditions throughout.

'When the Muslims came, first they cut our grapes, then they killed our people,' Nika tells me sombrely, before his face breaks into a satisfied smile. 'Georgian soldiers would fight with a bunch of grapes in our clothes so that, if they died in battle, the grape seeds would grow, even as our bodies lay on the ground.' The grapes of wrath, Mr Steinbeck might have called them.

Still, for Soviet citizens, coming from a land of long winters and monochrome tower blocks, you can see why Georgia was considered a slice of paradise. Their feasts, known as *supras*, were legendary, and would invariably become raucous as the guests moved from wine to *chacha*, a potent Georgian version of grappa. As Levan, a schoolteacher I meet in Tbilisi, puts it, 'Georgians were seen as Dionysian people for the entertainment of the Russians, like Italy or the South of France: funny, smiling, offering wine and sun.'

Tbilisi

The capital is the epitome of this open, friendly face that Georgia would like to present to the world. There's no visa trouble here – 365-day tourist visas are available to over ninety-five countries at the time of writing. That said, there's no airport shuttle, which means you'll have to negotiate with a taxi driver to take you up George W. Bush Avenue to the city centre.

By post-Soviet standards, Tbilisi has done a sterling job of maintaining its architectural heritage. Terracotta roofs bask in the sunshine, crowning the winding alleys of the old town, which lies splayed on the banks of the mighty Mtkvari River. Mornings start slowly here – in fact, barely anything is open until 10 a.m. Georgians seem to revel in their reputation for not working particularly hard. As in Yerevan, life is lived outdoors, but Georgians are better dressed than Armenians; both sexes are noticeably attractive, with a kind of olive-skinned Greek look. Georgia even has a place in Greek myth: in ancient times it used to be called Colchis, the land where Jason and his Argonauts sought the Golden Fleece.

In the tourist part of town, old cobbled streets play host to tiny pop-up restaurants, craft beer establishments, shisha bars and a surprising number of Thai massage parlours – which are a sure sign of a society reaching a certain level of civilisation.

There's a decidedly pro-Western focus to the city. Ukrainian flags are draped from every window. Political organisations proudly declare themselves in an alphabet soup of acronyms – NATO, EU, USAID; the graffiti too is written in English – 'Russians Go Home' and 'Never Back to USSR' are two of the more common refrains.

Much of the credit for this pro-Western, smiling Georgia is owed to one man: Mikheil Saakashvili, Georgia's president between 2004 and 2013. Misha, as everyone knows him, was a man in a hurry. A recent graduate when the Soviet Union fell apart, he took advantage of this new climate to attend law school in the US, briefly working on Wall Street and at the UN before taking up politics aged just twenty-five. By thirty-two he was justice minister, and by thirty-six he had led a bloodless revolution that toppled the ageing president, Eduard Shevardnadze, the former Soviet foreign minister.

The Rose Revolution of November 2003 was a first in the former USSR. Before Saakashvili, people wondered if these countries were simply unsuited to democracy after so many years under a totalitarian regime. One month before the revolution in Georgia, Ilham Aliyev in Azerbaijan had won his first election, succeeding his father as president after ruthlessly crushing opposition. The journey from communism to oligarchic dictatorship via a bout of nationalistic excess, as Altay suggested in Baku, was all too familiar.

But the success of the Rose Revolution changed that perception. It proved an inspiration for Ukraine's Orange Revolution a year later, as well as Kyrgyzstan's Tulip Revolution in 2005. This revolutionary tide greatly unnerved the Kremlin, which referred to them collectively as 'Colour Revolutions' supported by the USA.

As for Misha, he stood unopposed for president in January 2004 and won 96 per cent of the vote: a mandate to impose his revolutionary agenda. He slashed taxes and red tape, introduced a new national anthem and updated the country's flag to include no fewer than five St George's Crosses – a Little Englander's wet dream. To root out corruption, new university exams were introduced to stop rich kids bribing their way in; oligarchs were arrested and made to pay huge fines in exchange for their freedom – resulting in a trebling of the government's budget; he also sacked the entire police force in one day and made them all reapply for their jobs.

Georgia was the darling of the US foreign policy establishment.

George W. Bush visited Tbilisi in 2005 to a rapturous reception and spoke in glowing terms of the country's progress to a crowd on Freedom Square.

Saakashvili's reforms set the country on the path to join the EU, an objective that remains the stated ambition of both of Georgia's major political parties. On the face of it, the country would seem to have a lot going for it: freedom of speech, democracy, openness to foreigners and Western investment, as well as rocketing up the Ease of Doing Business index.[2] That said, even someone with Saakashvili's force of personality could not alter geography and age-old customs. Fifty-five per cent of the workforce remain employed in agriculture, and Georgia's northern neighbour, with its 145 million consumers, is a market that is hard to ignore. Russians continue to quaff Georgia's wines, and their tourists and émigré workers still flock to its beaches, despite there being no direct flights at my time of visiting.

Moreover, the EU has been reluctant to admit Georgia – ever since the start of Saakashvili's second term in 2008, there have been concerns that Georgian democracy is backsliding, that politics is becoming aggressively polarised, that its independent judiciary is fast disappearing and that cronyism is beginning to creep back in. For the past decade, Georgia has been ruled by the socially conservative Georgian Dream political party, controlled by Bidzina Ivanishvili, a billionaire oligarch who is rumoured to hold a 1 per cent stake in the Russian energy giant Gazprom.[3]

There are also some thornier issues to overcome. Georgia has been caught in a post-communist bind that will be familiar to followers of Eastern European politics. It wants to be seen as modern, cool and Westernised, while simultaneously attempting to restore the 'traditional values' that came under sustained attack by communism. With both parties accepting the market economy, the political battleground has shifted to the cultural sphere, the totemic issue being LGBTQ+ rights.

'Numerous polls have shown that Georgians would rather be next-door neighbours with a criminal, an alcoholic or a drug addict than a gay man,' Levan Kakhishvili, a social scientist, tells me.

This came to a nasty and very public head in July 2021, when armed thugs forced the cancellation of Tbilisi Pride and, for want of anyone else to attack, decided to assault the fifty or so journalists who had come to cover the event instead. They then ripped down the EU flag from the Georgian parliament building and set it ablaze. The government, for its part, couldn't quite bring itself to condemn this behaviour.

I get in touch with Giorgi Tabagari, an activist and organiser of Tbilisi Pride between 2018 and 2021. We meet in his office in a modern, red-brick building in the upmarket Vake region of the city, where I ask him about the events of that day. He tells me that the attacks on Tbilisi Pride were a quasi-military operation, with around 5,000 men recruited from across the country to disrupt the parade.

'Why was it so important for them to disrupt Pride?' I ask. 'What makes Georgia such a homophobic country?'

'It's not just Georgia,' he says. 'If you look at a map, all the surrounding countries have some of the lowest scores in terms of LGBT rights. Partly, it comes from this macho, southern culture: the gender stereotypes about what role men should have. Being gay is just unacceptable, it's a deviation from standard malehood. Culturally I would also say religion and lack of education – we missed out on a lot of progress that occurred elsewhere during the seventy years of Soviet occupation.'

Throughout the Caucasus, men have a distinct and defined role: they are the breadwinner, they ought to be rich, have a decent motor, flash clothes and be able to entertain guests at all times. It's at the root of why Artur, Shahrud and Nika have gone to such lengths to wine and dine me. But along with this obligation to be generous is a fierce and often destructive pride, a macho hot-headedness that even communism failed to tame. Against this intimidating backdrop, I ask Giorgi what exactly he's hoping to achieve through his activism.

'Social change,' he says simply. 'A mental revolution in a way. By 2019, the underground culture was thriving, there were bars and cafés which were safe spaces where we could hang out, and if you went to queer parties, you'd see maybe two thousand people filling up Bassiani.' He's referring here to a techno nightclub that is famous for its queer nights. There are certain people he believes he can't persuade, but he feels that young, employed middle-class people might be receptive to his ideas.

His own polling has shown a 25 per cent increase in tolerance for homosexuals over the span of three years. Other polls suggest that the shift has been even larger. In 2019, the Caucasus Research Resource Center found that just 10 per cent of Georgians would approve of doing business with a homosexual; by 2021 that had almost doubled to 19 per cent.[4]

'Obviously we're starting from a very low threshold,' Giorgi continues, 'but this proves that we were on the right track. As you can imagine, it's not easy – we've been targeted, threatened, and been in near-death situations several times. You need really resilient people to go through that.'

I ask him about the kind of forces arrayed against them. Giorgi is quick to point an accusatory finger at the Georgian Orthodox Church, which has grown considerably in strength since the Soviet times and is virulently opposed to the Pride marchers and what it refers to as their 'sodomic sins'.

The Georgian Church is a branch of the larger Russian Orthodox Church, and is often accused by liberal Georgian activists of being a front for continued Russian influence in the country.

'Russia is possibly the most important problem,' says Giorgi. 'They have agents funding institutions that influence and lobby the Church, and then you have right-wing groups that are also funded or driven by Russian foreign policy goals. It's not like there's suddenly people just coming onto the streets in a homophobic explosion – it's more organised, it's funded by Russia, possibly by US conservative groups as well. Russia instrumentalises homophobia for political gains, creating instability, undermining the idea of pro-EU integration.'

'Defending traditional values' has become an increasingly important theme in Russian domestic and foreign policy in the Putin era. It's embodied by the Russian president himself, his own version of machismo including such gems as riding a horse bare-chested; judo sparring; working out for the cameras; and flying fighter planes. Putin seeks to embody what Russians call a *muzhik*, which in Britain would probably be termed a 'proper bloke'.

Russian media and government officials have frequently portrayed the West as degenerate, aggressively exporting its alien values to the rest of the world. Battle lines were drawn as Russia passed a law banning the promotion of 'non-traditional' sexuality in the run-up to the Sochi Olympics in 2014. This caused a furore in the Western media and led to an attempted boycott of brands such as Coca-Cola who continued to sponsor the games. It has only grown in relevance since, with Putin likening those in Russia who believe in LGBTQ+ rights to a fifth column.*

The Georgian Church also used this line of attack when confronted by Western criticism over the Pride attacks. 'You want to force your profligate, obscene and depraved ideals on Georgia,' said a Georgian priest in a speech to the US and EU diplomatic missions. 'If anyone is violent, it is *you*, who force your warped views on the absolute majority.'

Right at the top of the list of targets is the trans community. What could be more emblematic of Western degeneracy, say the post-Soviet conservatives, than a society that cannot distinguish between man and woman? The trans issue is contentious even in countries where gay rights are well established, so I imagine it's particularly delicate in a culture like Georgia's where men and women have such clearly defined roles.

I put this to Giorgi relatively baldly: 'Does the trans issue make the gay cause more difficult in Georgia?'

He hesitates, but to his credit does not shirk the question: 'I dunno . . . Maybe . . . It would be horrible to say that. But it's really unethical to even talk about this. I usually prefer trans people to speak about their rights. I can speak as an activist on the general problems, but I would never be able to speak in the first person on trans matters because we are still a very diverse community, and we are put in this box of LGBTQI or whatever, but trans challenges are way different than the challenges that I have. They are the ones who are on the front line of not being accepted . . .'

I bite my lip. Giorgi talks with empathy and in good faith, and it's not like I have a better alternative. Still, it must be meat and drink for the Church and Russian propagandists to sow seeds of doubt.

---

* 'I do not judge those who can't go without their foie gras, oysters and so-called gender-freedoms, but the Russian people will be able to distinguish true patriots from scum and traitors, and simply spit them out like a fly that accidentally flew into their mouth,' Putin said in a state of the nation address, three weeks after his invasion of Ukraine.

'Are you hopeful that in the next ten or twenty years we'll see real progress?' I ask instead.

'I wouldn't be doing this otherwise,' says Giorgi. 'The validation is the progress that we're seeing. The other day I went to a drag ball and saw the post-pandemic generation just starting to go out, and I realised that it's inevitable that the authorities are going to lose this battle in the long run. Georgia is going to become as gay as Spain soon. They can't stop the progress because the TikTok generation don't just get education in the formal sense, there are plenty of other sources of information where they can educate themselves. As long as we manage to stay independent and away from the madness of Russian influence, then it will be possible.'

For Giorgi, everything hinges on the outcome of the Ukraine war: 'If Ukraine falls, we fall,' he says simply.

Georgians are far more invested in the Ukraine war than Armenians and Azerbaijanis. After all, they've had their own brushes with the Russian military since independence.

The roots of the conflicts here resemble those in the Karabakh. As noted in the Armenia chapter, the Soviet Union comprised over a hundred ethnicities, but only fifteen gained statehood in 1991. Georgia too was a melting pot, and tensions had long simmered, particularly over Abkhaz demands for greater autonomy. Georgian nationalists capitalised on these demands, using them to provoke confrontation with the Soviet authorities and rally support for their cause. On 9 April 1989, Soviet troops violently dispersed a peaceful pro-independence demonstration in Tbilisi, killing twenty-one people and wounding hundreds. The crackdown supercharged the independence movement and helped propel Zviad Gamsakhurdia, a prominent ultranationalist figure, to power, setting the stage for the violent conflict that would soon engulf the country.

By 1994, after three years of carnage, the ethnically distinct, formerly autonomous regions of South Ossetia and Abkhazia had broken away from Tbilisi's control. They were helped by a motley alliance that at various times included both the Russian military and Chechen fighters, who not long later would be at war with each other. Hundreds of thousands of Georgians were rendered homeless, particularly in Abkhazia. Peace talks stalled, and Russian troops were called in to keep the peace. The Kremlin claimed to be acting as a mediator, whereas Georgians viewed this as a Muscovite land grab.

It was hoped that the Rose Revolution might break the impasse – indeed, in 2004 Georgia successfully reintegrated another restive region, Adjara, which had come under the rule of a local strongman. But the other efforts made little progress; Putin goaded Saakashvili into a vain attempt to reinvade South Ossetia in August 2008 and he was met with a ferocious Russian response. In what became known as the five-day war, around 850 people lost their lives on all sides, more than 100,000 fled their homes, and the Georgian military was pushed back deep into Georgia. South Ossetia and Abkhazia have now become Russian provinces in all but name. Ever since, Georgians have used the quip that 'Russia occupies 20 per cent of our country'. This might be a neat line, but it's also rather depressing that, thirty years since the disaster of Gamsakhurdia's rule, Georgians continue to gloss over the existence of the Ossetians and Abkhaz. The onset of the war in Ukraine has only strengthened this sense of self-righteousness.

You might be getting the hint by now that Georgians have a little beef with the Russians. To get some background, I head to the Museum of Georgia on Rustaveli Avenue, the top floor of which is dedicated to the 'seventy years of Soviet occupation'.

The word 'occupation' is not accidental. I'm sure there were some Armenians and Azeris who read the previous two chapters and have been chomping at the bit for me to bring this up. To many it's an important distinction: these countries did not *become* independent in 1991, rather they *regained* independence.

In 1918, in the wake of the Russian revolutions of the previous year, the countries of the Caucasus, after a brief spell spent merging their resources as the Transcaucasian Republic, each declared their independence. Such independence was for the most part in name only – Azerbaijan was propped up by a British military force keen on securing Baku's oil supplies, and Armenia was on the point of being wiped out by the Turks until the Bolsheviks stepped in. The Democratic Republic of Georgia was originally a protectorate of the Germans, then the British, and its government struggled to assert control over the whole of the territory it had just claimed. It lasted little over two years until Lenin and Atatürk sliced it up between them in 1921. Still, the First Republic ushered in Georgia's first taste of democracy, and by 1920 it was recognised by most of the European powers. Besides, like the Armenians, Georgians have a tradition of statehood going back over a thousand years, which is why the Georgians use the term 'occupation' to describe the arrival of the Red Army in 1921.

In the Museum of Georgia the stark lighting produces long shadows, like graves stretching along the floor. The exhibits are arranged chronologically. The grim statistics frown down accusingly from the wall: 'Between 1921 and 1941, 72,000 people were shot and 200,000 deported from Georgia,' it reads. Significant numbers in a country of just 4 million. Beneath this are revolvers used by the original Soviet secret police, the Cheka. Their bullets are arranged artfully next to photos of victims. The exhibits move on to cover the anti-Soviet protests of 1956, 1978 and 1989, two of which led to massacres. The museum appears to be tailored to a Western audience; any Soviet achievement is notable only by its absence. Seemingly the lesson that the visitor is meant to draw from all this is that the twentieth century would have been a land of milk and honey had it not been for those pesky Russians.

This forgets one rather inconvenient element: not all Soviets were Russian. The Bolsheviks were a motley bunch whose high-ranking members also included large numbers of Jews such as Trotsky, Zinoviev and Kaganovich; Armenians like Anastas Mikoyan; and Poles such as the founder of the secret police, Felix Dzerzhinsky. Georgians were well represented too: Eduard Shevardnadze became foreign minister; Sergo Ordzhonikidze ran several economic ministries in the 1920s and 1930s; while Lavrentiy Beria became head of the NKVD security forces.

And finally, those killings the museum mentioned between 1921 and 1941 . . . the ones committed by the 'Russian occupiers' . . . The curators seem to be forgetting that Joseph Stalin, the Soviet leader for most of that period was, well . . . also kinda Georgian.

Joseph Dzhugashvili, as he was born, spent his teenage years in Tiflis, as Tbilisi was called in the tsarist period. Back then, it was a far less Georgian city than it is today – the population was majority-Armenian and there was a sizeable Russian contingent. Joseph was a fifteen-year-old country boy who arrived in the city in 1893. The son of a drunkard shoemaker, his mother saw his only way out of poverty was by sending him to a seminary, through which he could entertain hopes of joining the priesthood. Needless to say, he did not become a man of the cloth, but he did get an impeccable classical education and learned fluent Russian.

To his mother's horror, Stalin was eventually kicked out of the seminary for missing his exams, but by that time he had set about becoming a fully fledged revolutionary. He proved an important asset to Lenin in the Caucasus, running numerous criminal enterprises to help fund the Bolshevik revolutionary machine. In Baku he ran brothels and kidnapped and extorted the city's rich oil barons. Back in Tiflis he organised one of the biggest bank robberies in tsarist Russia, making off with around $5 million in today's money. The fact that the robbery led to forty deaths was a sign of things to come.

Vano Abramashvili, Director of Caucasus House, a think tank, smiles slightly when I ask him about Stalin's legacy today. 'We're a very small nation, and you need to understand the psychological complexes that come with that. Stalin is Georgian, and everybody knows him, and that's why many people are proud of him. I'm not personally, but these people close their eyes to many of the things that he did. He's purely a mythical thing.'

A historian, Davit Jishkariani, tells me that Stalin is loved by Georgians from the USSR generation. 'My father was born in 1961, not long after Stalin's death, he was named Joseph in his honour,' he says. 'Most Western historians only pay attention to his Georgianness. They say that this admiration of Stalin is nationalism and nothing else. But the generation who love Stalin will also mention that he was a cobbler's son, a guy from their social class. All this in combination makes him a bit of a folkloric hero here.'

I tell Davit that this isn't what I've heard from younger generations. In fashionable Tbilisi bars, where cocktails go for London prices, the locals show little pride in the legacy of Georgia's most famous son. In fact, Stalin is someone these young, Westernised Georgians would rather not discuss. There's a droll rolling of the eyes when I bring him up, the kind of look English people reserve for Americans who ask whether we've met the queen.

Davit nods comprehendingly. 'I teach at two universities, a private one, for the children of the elite, and a state one. In my classes, the private university students immediately start loudly criticising the USSR – this is how they control the national narrative. The rest of the students from the middle and lower classes don't dare say, "The USSR is represented differently in my family's memory" because they are afraid to be considered pro-Russian, or against the independence of Georgia. But working people see the elite enjoying their banquets and driving their Porsche Panameras around the centre of Tbilisi, while the rest of Georgia collapses with traffic, hunger, high taxes and so on. Those are the two different perspectives in this country. And that's also why Stalin's cult is still here – the cobbler's son.'

Gori

One place where I've heard the cobbler's son gets a better reception is his home town of Gori. It lies within striking distance from Tbilisi, so I arrange to go there on a day trip. I arrive at the station only to be told, once again, that I need a passport to buy a ticket. I'd left mine back at the hostel – Georgia is not Azerbaijan, after all; I thought Uncle Misha had got rid of this needless red tape.

'Why do I need a passport?' I ask.

'To buy a ticket . . .'

I breathe in deeply. 'Why do I need my passport to buy a ticket? I'm not leaving the country here; I'm only going about eighty kilometres!'

'Because I need to enter your passport number on the ticket booking system.'

'But why? For what purpose?'

She gives me a blank look. 'Young man, you can't book a ticket without a passport or national identity card. If you don't have your passport, you can take a *marshrutka* to Gori from Didube Bus Station.'

I'm seething, but there's a throng of people behind me, their passports and identity cards held obediently at the ready. Stalin would have been so proud.

I suppose this means it's time to introduce *marshrutkas*, which will be cropping up frequently over the coming chapters. A *marshrutka* is basically a minibus, usually with around fifteen seats, but performing the function of a fixed-route shared taxi. Some are operated by companies, but most are simply self-employed drivers, renting out seats in their bus for cash.

They existed in the communist period, but as state capacity collapsed and private citizens were permitted to use their initiative, *marshrutkas* quickly became *the* quintessential means of transportation across the former USSR. They serve as cheaper and faster alternatives to trains, sometimes even over long-distance routes. They are not, however, safer. The driver's income depends on getting as many passengers on board as possible, and then putting his foot down to squeeze in the maximum number of trips per day.

At Didube the scenes are rather chaotic. I'm assaulted by the smell of exhaust fumes, grilled meat and heavily perfumed women selling tat. There are dozens, perhaps hundreds of buses. Each *marshrutka*'s destination is written on a placard in the front window. Some are in Latin script, but they're mainly to the big tourist destinations like the Black Sea resort of Batumi; most are in Georgian. I can't make out a Gori anywhere.

'*Gamarjoba*,' I say uncertainly to a group of blokes who are sitting outside a kiosk, smoking, drinking beer. One is gently masticating on sunflower seeds, the remains of which lie scattered on the ground around him. They're all dressed in the classic Caucasus get-up of fake-snakeskin shoes, tight black T-shirts and jeans. They look up, their interest piqued.

'Which is the *marshrutka* to Gori?' I ask in English to blank looks. I try again in Russian. Use of the former coloniser's tongue usually induces a scowl in Georgia unless there is money to be made, in which case they quickly become your *brat*.

'Here! Here!' two of them bark excitedly, each attempting to chivvy me towards their respective vehicle, gold teeth flashing in the mid-morning sun. I opt for the man whose eyes are slightly less bloodshot and whose bottle of beer is only half-drunk.

I hop aboard and hand over the fee for the journey. That's all that's required; he doesn't even give me a ticket. Sure, this guy might be slightly tipsy, but at least he doesn't ask for my passport.

In Gori, I head out under a blazing sun. The town is reasonably poor and largely forgettable, similar to the provincial towns I visited in Armenia and Azerbaijan. The people are mainly old – as in many places, capitalism has sucked Georgia's best and brightest out of the villages and valleys and spat them out into the metropole. I wander down the road, past the old battlements of Gori fortress, coming across no one but the odd stray dog. Down a side street there's a group of kids playing football using some clapped-out Ladas for goalposts. Eventually, the houses rise higher; five-storey tenement blocks called *Khrushchevkas* come into view, arranged along the street that I've been looking for. Above me is a road sign that once appeared in every city east of Berlin. I'm standing on Stalin Avenue.

In 1956, Nikita Khrushchev gave what became known as his Secret Speech, in which he criticised the 'monstrous acts' that Stalin had unleashed on the people of the USSR. It ushered in a sea change in Soviet politics. Tens of thousands of political prisoners were released from labour camps; deported ethnicities who had been forcibly removed from their homeland were permitted to return home; Soviet citizens were briefly allowed to travel abroad, and the new-found freedom in the arts allowed books such as Alexander Solzhenitsyn's *One Day in the Life of Ivan Denisovich* to be published.

A de-Stalinisation campaign began. Cities were renamed: Stalingrad became Volgograd; Stalino became Donetsk. On Halloween 1961, Stalin's body was removed from the Mausoleum alongside Lenin and reburied in the Kremlin wall. They also came for the portraits and the plazas, the streets and the statues. All over the USSR, Stalin was scrubbed from his place of pre-eminence.

Uncle Joe didn't always go quietly: when Yerevan's enormous statue of Stalin was pulled down in 1962 it fell on several of the soldiers, crushing one to death. In Georgia resistance took a more human form. Two weeks after Khrushchev's speech, angry crowds gathered in Tbilisi to mark the third anniversary of Stalin's death and demonstrate against the new leader.

The authorities' panicked response, sending in soldiers and tanks, resulted in the deaths of an unknown number of protesters, possibly in the hundreds. The plaque that commemorates these events in Tbilisi is phrased with delicious delicacy: 'This monument commemorates the participants of a peaceful rally gunned down by the Soviet regime on 9 March 1956.' I guess it would rather spoil the sense of injustice if they'd mentioned that the 'peaceful rally' was in honour of one of history's greatest murderers.

Gori, however, did not change. Stalin Avenue remained, as did Stalin Park; the local football team is even called Morning Gori FC – named after the title of one of Stalin's poems. The only thing that has been removed is the Stalin statue in the centre of town, and that was in 2010.

'When they removed his statue, they did it at night,' Vano Abramashvili told me. 'People would not have let it happen otherwise. You can imagine all over Georgia, the importance of Stalin, but especially in Gori.'

There are more than just sentimental reasons for this. These days there is no shortage of people hoping to cash in on communist colossi. In Moscow's Red Square, for a small fee you can pose next to lookalikes of Lenin; in China the souvenir shops are stacked with Chairman Mao plates and posters; on a trip to Estonia ten years ago I even came across a store selling a mug portraying Stalin's face. It was captioned, 'Sorry, shit happens!'

Gori is no different. 'The Stalin Museum in Gori is easily the most expensive museum in all of Georgia,' Vano told me. People have come from far and wide to see Stalin's birthplace: some Russian fanboys are here examining the marble bust of Stalin at the head of a red-carpeted staircase; a group of Japanese tourists nose interestedly around his olive-green railway carriage; and a couple sporting the red, yellow and purple flags of the old Spanish Republic on their backpacks are gazing in morbid fascination at Stalin's death mask.

The museum itself is akin to the Heydar Aliyev Museum in Baku, more a collection of sentimental titbits seeking to soften the edges of the Man of Steel than a serious reckoning with history. There's a photo of Stalin from 1893, looking just like the young lads I saw playing football on the way here.

Another exhibit contains the police mugshot from his arrest in 1902. It's said that Stalin was a remarkably handsome young man. I'm afraid I can't agree. Even in the old photos, his pockmarks are obvious – he caught smallpox at a young age. This is not to mention his lame left arm, a result of being hit by a carriage at the age of twelve, which left him hospitalised for months – proof that wayward driving in the Caucasus is not a new phenomenon. I will grant that he had a cracking head of hair, something which my eyes have been drawn to increasingly since I turned thirty.

Just as the Museum of the Soviet Occupation had a mysterious case of amnesia when it came to Soviet achievements, when the Stalin Museum confronts historical events it does so in an oddly passive voice: 'In October 1917, a revolution occurred in Petrograd . . .' or 'The years 1937–8 saw numerous high-profile figures arrested . . .' – as though these things happened of their own accord and Stalin was simply an observer.

After lunch, I take a straw poll of Gori residents, asking people for their thoughts on Joseph Vissarionovich.

'Stalin made this town,' says Irakli, an old man who ends up nattering away to me on a bench in Stalin Park. He's swigging beer from a two-litre bottle, but seems quite lucid. 'There would be nothing here without him. If Stalin were alive today for just one year, everything here would be working again. Sometimes you need a strong hand.'

I ask Irakli if his children feel the same way. 'My children don't live here; they are in Tbilisi. There is nothing to do there, there is no work for anyone. This country is a great place if you are a tourist, or rich. If you have money, you can even kill someone and it's not a problem, you can just pay and you go free.'

'Didn't Saakashvili improve things?' I ask him.

'Misha?' he laughs. 'Oh, he improved things in Tbilisi, but not the rest of the country. He was just as corrupt as the others in the end. He ended up in jail. Not before he got us into a war with the Russians, mind.' He spits on the floor. 'I thought I'd never see my home again when they came here.'

'They were here?'

'Of course! The Russians bombed us. They occupied Gori . . .'

He's referring to the five-day war of 2008, when the Russian military infamously dropped cluster munitions on Stalin Square before launching an assault on the town, which they occupied for nine days.

'You know why we say that Stalin is the greatest of all Georgians?' Irakli asks, a sly grin emerging on his face. 'Because he killed more Russians than any other Georgian.'

I shake my head and take the beer he's offering me. After all, I've never had my home bombed, so I can understand how viewing his compatriot, the cobbler's son, as the nemesis of his enemies might provide comfort. As a Mongolian friend once told me, 'Sure, Genghis Khan was a bloodthirsty, murdering bastard; but he was *our* bloodthirsty, murdering bastard.'

In 1988, the Nobel Prize-winning scientist Andrei Sakharov voiced his fear that the collapse of the Soviet Union would not lead to freedom for all peoples, but instead the creation of 'mini empires', which would seek to wipe out minorities in a fit of nationalist excess. Alas this has proved all too prescient. The excesses unleashed by independence in all three states of the Caucasus led to the deaths of tens of thousands in total, as well as the displacement of 1.5 million, almost 10 per cent of the total population.[5] Road and rail links, once seamless, have withered, making everyone poorer. Formerly grand train stations are now empty husks. On the face of it, this doesn't make the best case for independence.

There's a danger, of course, that this narrative nicely parrots that of the Russian imperialist. Perhaps it's best to view Moscow's role as a kind of geopolitical shark: if you swim in waters with a shark, it's unlikely to bother you until it smells blood. Unfortunately, the power vacuum left in an empire's wake can often lead to just that. Independence for some often means a new form of oppression for others, and the Kremlin has been ruthless in exploiting the tensions that have stemmed from this.

Irakli was keen to share another of his favourite Georgian aphorisms before I left: 'You know who Georgia's favourite neighbour is? – The Black Sea.'

CENTRAL ASIA

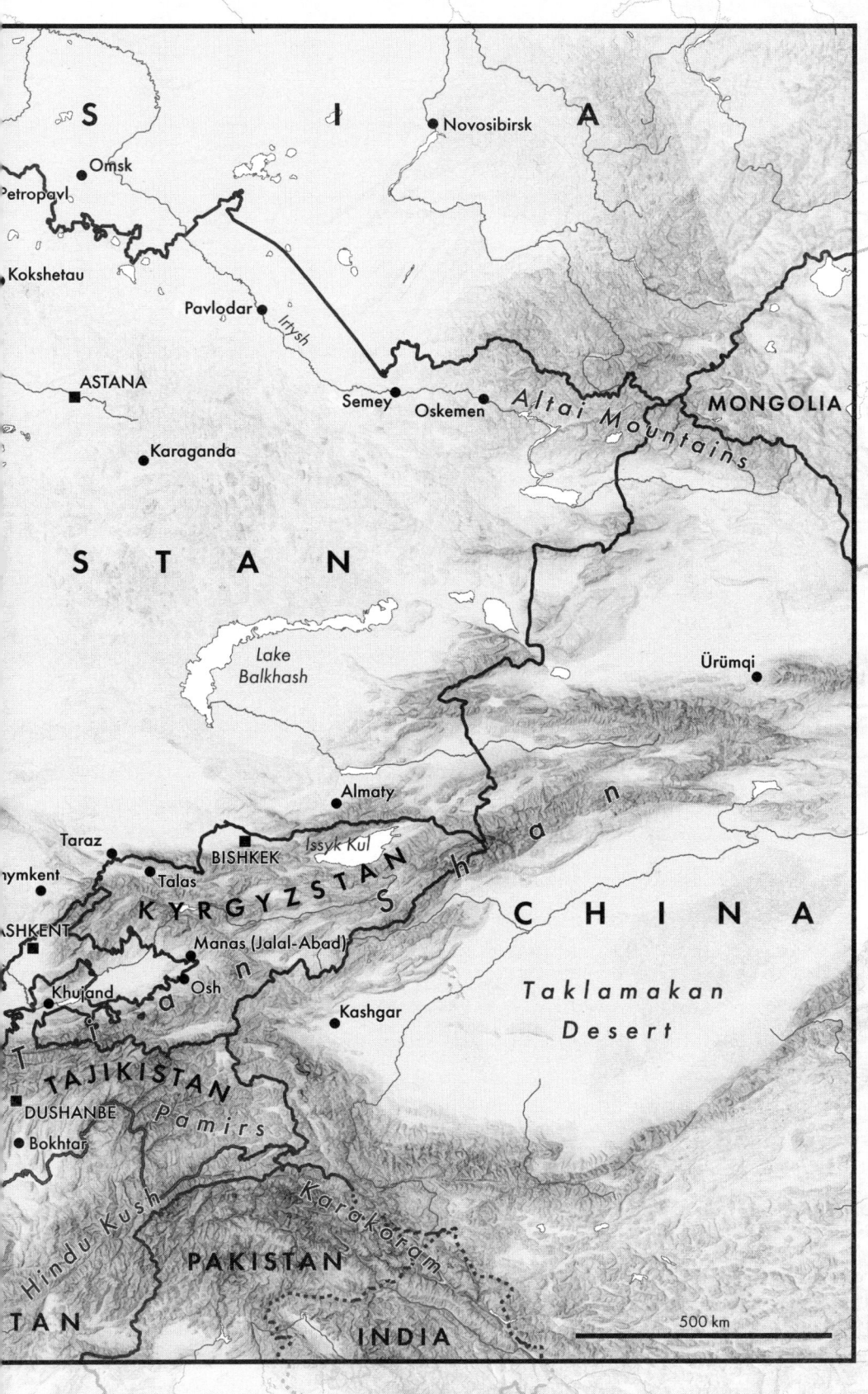

5
KAZAKHSTAN
THE REPUBLIC OF COMPROMISE

I took some time off after my Caucasian adventures. Following Irakli's advice about Georgia's favourite neighbour, I headed to the shores of the Black Sea for some well-earned R&R.

There I met a Kazakh woman called Klara, an IT worker who lived in Kazakhstan's capital, Astana. As soon as she found out about my post-Soviet odyssey, she made it her mission to make her country my next destination.

'The last I heard about Kazakhstan,' I said, 'there were huge street protests where you burned down your own parliament.'

'Oh, that was the old parliament building!' said Klara, as though this made it OK. 'Besides, that was back in January, everything is much calmer now.'

But Klara couldn't help slipping increasingly wild anecdotes into her tales. She informed me that the word *Kazakh* – like 'Cossack', to which it is related – means 'wanderer'. The Kazakhs were once a nomad people, like the Mongols, who have lived on the vast Eurasian steppe for thousands of years. Over time they split into three great tribal unions called *zhuzs* (which in English probably translates as hordes): the Junior *Zhuz* in the west; the Middle in the central and eastern steppes; and the Senior in the south. Kazakh folklore ascribes each of these a character: hot-headed fighters in the west, poets and intellectuals in the middle, and elders in the south.

'Historically it was important not to marry into other *zhuzs*,' said Klara. 'Every Kazakh is supposed to know the names of their last seven ancestors on their male side.'

The hordes weren't the half of it; on another occasion, I was asking her how she'd ended up moving to the capital city. 'Oh, it's a fun story. So my mother was kidnapped by my father, and then—'

'Sorry, what?'

'My mother was kidnapped by my father,' she repeated simply. 'Anyway . . .'

I put it to her that a land of hordes who jealously guard their bloodlines and where kidnap is apparently a legitimate means of wooing a prospective spouse might not sell the country to readers.

'Oh but there's so much more than that!' she protested. 'In Semey, we have the remains of the USSR's first nuclear testing site; and we've got the cosmodrome where Yuri Gagarin took off into space; oh and the Gulag: Solzhenitsyn was imprisoned here – Dostoevsky too! Plus the world's newest and most beautiful capital city, I'll show you it all!'

I have to admit, she had me at Gulag.

Karaganda

The steppe stretches in all directions under the massive sky. There are no trees, no hills, no natural points of interest of any sort, save for a herd of horses grazing by the roadside. The openness of Central Asia makes itself felt immediately. Kazakhstan alone spans an area larger than Western Europe. It's a welcome contrast to the disputed, mountainous landscapes of the Caucasus. Four of Central Asia's five countries – Kazakhstan, Kyrgyzstan, Uzbekistan and Turkmenistan – descend largely from nomadic hordes who have roamed these plains for millennia and speak closely related Turkic languages; Tajikistan, in contrast, is Persian-speaking. The region's population also shares a common thread of Islamic faith, though the practice and influence of religion vary widely. Centuries of transient empires and migration along the historic trade routes of the Silk Road have left a mark on these societies, which lie strategically between Russia, China and Iran. The shared experience of Russian conquest in the nineteenth century, followed by Soviet rule in the twentieth, has left Russian as the lingua franca, along with a legacy of centralised political control. When the Soviet Union collapsed, independence was largely seized by the existing elites rather than emerging through popular choice, ensuring that top-down governance continues to reign over the region's young, restless population – from the deserts in the west to mountains in the south and vast steppes in the north.

But these northern plains are not featureless. Factories dot the landscape, their chimneys raised like middle fingers in defiance of the mighty heavens. Thin trails of smoke seep from them and a vast network of pylons and railway tracks sprawl from their feet. Karaganda and its environs are home to some of the largest-scale coal-mining on the planet. One of the biggest employers in the region is steel giant ArcelorMittal. Such abundance of raw material and lax regulations are a big draw for any steelmaker.

'We don't like them here. They don't care about employees; they pay us nothing, and don't give a shit about our safety,' my taxi driver tells me.

'Do you work down the mines?'

'Used to. I'm an invalid now; was forced to retire. My lungs can't take it any more.'

'Would you like to be back down there?'

'Of course!' he says, displaying that gritty courage you often get in mining communities, where a hard day's graft is the highest form of honour. As it happens, this former miner is taking me to one of the predecessors of ArcelorMittal; another institution that has a rather patchy record when it comes to worker rights.

Around a century ago, Karaganda didn't really exist. Coal had been discovered here in the late nineteenth century, but the nascent mines were soon abandoned – for some reason it proved difficult to persuade people to leave their families behind and toil down the pit in the middle of the frigid steppe. Besides, there were too few houses and nowhere near enough food to supply a large-scale mining settlement. But all that changed in February 1927, when Article 58 of the Russian penal code was brought into force.

Article 58 justified the arrest of those suspected of counter-revolutionary activity. The law cast a wide net as the precise meaning of 'counter-revolutionary activity' was left deliberately vague, leaving Alexander Solzhenitsyn to ask: 'Who among us has not experienced its all-encompassing embrace? In all truth, there is no step, thought, action, or lack of action under the heavens which could not be punished by the heavy hand of Article 58.'[1]

People may not have fancied moving to the steppe, but fortunately for economic planners the Soviet justice system had suddenly created a large pool of labourers who had little choice in the matter.

Interestingly, Russian and German share the same word for camp: *lager*. And whereas in Nazi Germany people came to dread the *Konzentrazionslager*, in the USSR it was the *Glavnoye Upravleniye Lagerey* you had to worry about.* This translates as Main Directorate of Camps, although in English we also use the Russian acronym: Gulag. Surrounded by barbed wire and watchtowers, these camps represented a series of islands in the remotest parts of the Soviet empire. It was not for nothing that Solzhenitsyn called his seminal work *The Gulag Archipelago*.

However, there was a key difference between the Soviet Gulag and the Nazi death camps: the majority – actually, the *vast* majority – of Gulag inmates survived the experience. From 1921 to 1953, the total number of people passing through Soviet forced labour camps is estimated to be around 18 million.[2] The number of those who died is disputed, but is thought to be around 1.5 to 1.6 million.[3] These numbers suggest that while the Gulag experience was unimaginably brutal, it was not necessarily the death sentence it is often portrayed as.

The Karaganda Camp (or Karlag) was created in 1930 to solve the problem of supplying the coal mines. It grew so rapidly that, by 1940, the area of the camp covered 6,500 square miles – slightly smaller than Wales – and was home to 65,000 prisoners. The Kazakh SSR became a repository for all manner of 'undesirables', from the political dissidents convicted under Article 58 to the so-called rich peasants, or *kulaks*, who were seen to be standing in the way of the equal distribution of land. They were joined by whole groups of 'disloyal' ethnicities such as Poles and Chechens, Koreans and Crimean Tatars. In the early 1940s, half a million ethnic Germans, who had been living along the banks of Russia's Volga River for almost two centuries, were also forced to relocate here.

Between them they played a large part in the building of Karaganda, which went from a small settlement in the late 1920s to a city of over 200,000 twenty years later. The camp headquarters, and now the site of the Karlag Museum, was in a small town called Dolinka, about 30 miles

---

* Technically the Main Directorate of Correctional Labour Camps (*Glavnoye Upravleniye Ispravitelno-Trudovykh Lagerey*).

from Karaganda proper. There are few other visitors, so the young lady at the ticket office, whose name is Nazgul, is happy to give me a free tour. I try not to do a double take at the sound of her name.*

She takes me to the dormitories first. It's draughty even at the height of summer. Rough woollen sheets filled with straw are draped over bunk beds whose supporting planks are so thin I doubt they would have supported any but the scrawniest of inmates – though I suppose the diets here were unlikely to have left anyone particularly rotund.

'Local people used to ride here on horseback and throw *kurt* over the walls of the camp for the prisoners to eat,' Nazgul tells me.

Kurt is a hard, extremely salty ball of dried cheese. It's not particularly appetising but lasts a long time and has been used for centuries as a protein-rich snack for those spending days in the saddle. The traditional Kazakh diet is heavy on these milky staples. Another is *kumis* – fermented horse's milk – which I was made to sample on my first evening here. It wasn't the tastiest of concoctions, but I imagine that both *kurt* and *kumis* would hit the spot if you've been forced to build a coal mine on Oliver Twist's rations. I also imagine that this story isn't true – the idea of noble, empathetic Kazakh horsemen coming to the aid of the desperate, oppressed prisoner is, well, a stretch. However, there is well-documented evidence of large-scale black-market trade in food and rations in the Karlag, whose walls were more porous than other camps due to its size and proximity to Karaganda.

There's a nursery here – women were also on the camp, and while older children were generally separated from their parents by the authorities after their arrest, special dispensation was made for those who were pregnant, or with infants. A touch of humanity in the system? Think again.

'The children were blindfolded while they breastfed from their mother,' says Nazgul, her tone perfectly level.† 'Once old enough, they were taken to orphanages to be raised.'

---

* She later informs me that Nazgul means 'Charming Flower' in Kazakh.
† It must be said that I later found nothing to substantiate these 'blindfolding' claims, but thought I'd note them for posterity.

We come to the commandant's study, set up as it would have been in the early 1950s: portrait of Stalin on the wall behind the desk and some heavy bookshelves, well stocked with the works of Lenin, Marx and Engels. The only touch of personality is betrayed by an old gramophone.

'Concerts were organised on Sundays and Mondays,' she tells me. 'Those were the days when the prisoners were tortured; the music drowned out the screams.'

The other rooms are dedicated to the fate of the Kazakhs – that is, the people who had lived here for centuries before these lands became an integral part of the Gulag.

In 1897, under the tsars, the land we now call Kazakhstan was 82 per cent Kazakh. The early years of the twentieth century saw the authorities encourage Slavic people to settle in the areas that had traditionally been inhabited by Kazakh nomads.

'Kazakhs lived at one with the steppe,' Klara told me. 'They travelled to where food and water was before moving on. This way, the land was allowed to recover in the meantime. The European arrivals began to change that, and the Soviets put it on fast-forward. They were obsessed with collectivising people. The idea of being a nomad didn't fit into their concept of a worker-led revolution. Maybe Marx skipped our role in his grand theory of history,' she said, giving me a wan smile.

The result of this crash-collectivisation was famine. The room has exhibits on the famines of 1919–22 and 1932–3. Kazakhs suffered disproportionately as they lived on fertile land that could produce a lot of wheat. They were forced to abandon their nomadic lifestyle and produce food firstly for the Red Army, and then for Stalin's five-year plans. Those who resisted were shot. Many fled to China or Mongolia. Many more starved. In the Soviet census of 1926 the Kazakh population was 3.6 million; by 1939 this had dropped by a third to 2.3 million. By 1959 Kazakhs numbered a mere 30 per cent of the population of the Kazakh SSR.

Along with the demographic assault came the attempts to destroy Kazakh identity. The room next door has a small exhibition dedicated to the entire class of Kazakh intellectuals who were exterminated in the purges of the late 1930s. This was a process that happened throughout the USSR:

intellectuals, artists, dissidents were rounded up and shot as Stalin sought to eliminate any competing sources of authority – political, military or cultural. Just as their way of life was destroyed and their people forced onto farms, their thinkers, authors and anyone who might be able to articulate the uniqueness of the Kazakh identity were wiped out by NKVD bullets.

Klara had told me about the legend of the Mankurt.

'When a warrior was captured in battle, his head would be shaved by his captors and a piece of damp camel skin would be wrapped tightly around it. He would then be left, tied up in the desert sun, which would dry the camel skin and cause it to contract. His hair would also have no room to grow, so it would grow inwards, into his skull. The resulting pressure on the head would break the prisoner's mind, causing him to lose all memory, all sense of self, all knowledge of his past and his family. Once broken, he became the perfect slave: the Mankurt, loyal only to his master.'

This myth does not come from the distant past but from a 1979 novel set on the Kazakh steppe, *The Day Lasts More Than a Hundred Years*, by Kyrgyz author Chingiz Aitmatov. The idea was then developed into a film, produced by Turkmen director Khodzhakuli Narliev in 1990. In the film's final scene, the broken Mankurt, unable to recognise his own mother, shoots her with an arrow on the orders of his new master.

'This is what the Soviets did to the Kazakh people, to all the people of Central Asia. They tried to destroy us so completely that we would not even recognise who we were,' said Klara.

Astana

In 1996, Kazakhstan's first president, Nursultan Nazarbayev, announced that he was going to up sticks from Almaty and move the government and state bureaucracy to a brand-new city, 600 miles further north. The plan came as a shock to the Kazakh elite. Temperatures across this region regularly tumble below minus forty in the depths of winter, and the steppe offers little protection from the vicious winds. It had taken an army of slave labour to bring Karaganda into being. Why go to such efforts to build another city where none had a right to exist?

Nazarbayev's cheerleaders claim that he was being strategic. Kazakhstan was the most Soviet of the former Soviet republics. For reasons that we have just explored, Kazakhs did not represent a majority in their new country. The 1989 census had ethnic Kazakhs and Russians around equal, with 38 per cent and 37 per cent of the population respectively; there were also large numbers of Ukrainians, Germans, Belarusians and Poles, taking the number of 'European' peoples in Kazakhstan to around 53 per cent. Creating a coherent country out of this Soviet soup, while also contending with the demands of nationalists to emphasise the Kazakh nature of this new state, seemed a nigh-impossible task.

Nor did it help that the Russian population was generally concentrated in the north of the country. Louder Russian nationalists, including Solzhenitsyn, questioned whether Kazakhstan would be better off partitioned, with the predominantly Russian areas joining the new Russian Federation.[4]

The old capital, Almaty, was in the south of the country and out of the way: it was hemmed in by mountains and had little room to expand. Besides, rumour had it that Nazarbayev found it stuffy and pretentious. A new capital in the north, the theory went, would bring the Kazakh civil service with it, thus unifying the country by balancing out the demographic superiority of the ethnic Russians. Others opine that he wanted to start afresh, to build a city untainted by the Soviets, a decidedly Kazakh capital for his people. But the more I walk around this city, the more I think that Nazarbayev built it for himself.

Klara's apartment building is an ordinary post-Soviet affair: a new-build stretching twenty floors up. If you thought communist architecture was depressing, the dismal designs served up by capitalism offer little improvement, although admittedly more glass. One irritating feature, which was also evident in Georgia, is that you have to pay every time you use the lift. Klara is on the twelfth floor. She lends me the equivalent of an elevator Oyster Card, which charges me twenty tenge (around five cents) for every upward journey. Although exasperating, part of me has developed a grudging respect for the idea. At least people are being made to pay for not bothering to use their limbs.

The street too would hardly be noteworthy were it not for thick concrete pillars that dominate its centre, rising every fifty feet or so in a neat line that stretches into the distance.

'We call it the monument to corruption,' grins Klara. 'It's meant to be a light-rail project going all the way to the airport, but it's been suspended because, well, no one knows where the money has gone. It's been abandoned for years now. They keep talking about completing it, but, as we say in Kazakh, *köp söz, boq söz.*'

'*Köp söz, boq söz?*'

'It means "lots of words; lots of shit". It's a useful expression when dealing with our politicians,' she smiles. 'The light rail is probably the least corrupt thing about this city. You'll see what I mean as you walk around,' she laughs. 'Right, I'm calling a taxi, are you going to be all right on your own?'

I assure her I'll be fine. 'Do you take a taxi to work every day?'

'Of course, it's so cheap. And besides, it's not like there's much public transport,' she adds, gesturing to the abandoned pillars.

Why are the taxis here so cheap? Well, funnily enough, the answer to that question is the same as the answer to 'How come Kazakhstan could afford to build a brand-new city in the middle of nowhere?'

The answer is oil. Lots of oil.

The Soviets knew that, like Azerbaijan, Kazakhstan had copious oil reserves. The Tengiz oilfield, one of the world's largest, was discovered in the west of the republic in 1979, but remained undeveloped due to Soviet disinterest and lack of know-how. When Chevron et al. were allowed to develop the site after Kazakhstan became independent, production began to ramp up. The field was producing a modest 65,000 barrels of oil per day in 1993.[5] Today the daily total is over 600,000.[6] The project brought billions into the national coffers and meant that Nazarbayev, like Peter the Great before him, was in a position to build the city of his dreams.

The streets have a showroom quality to them – traffic flowing steadily but with empty pavements running alongside. I see no sign of schools. Coffee shops, libraries and bus stops also seem few and far between.

But Astana is not short of one thing: monuments. In the middle of the city is the Nurzhol Boulevard, which translates as the 'Way of Light'. At its centre is a 300-foot-high tower in the shape of an upturned shuttlecock, with a giant golden disco ball nestled in the centre. This is the Baiterek, and the design was sketched by Nazarbayev himself. From the viewing platform inside the orb, I can see Astana spread out beneath me in all its mad glory.

Heading east along the Way of Light is the presidential palace. Nazarbayev didn't sketch this one. He didn't need to. The building is a straight up rip-off of the White House, only eight times larger and with a naff azure dome. It's flanked by two golden towers of whose purpose I'm not quite sure.

For other projects, Nazarbayev did take some architectural counsel. Certain people salivate at the prospect of a brand-new capital; chief among them are Western architects who sniff out their chance to try out projects that democracies have blanched at. Norman Foster was first in line.

Across the Ishim River from the fake White House lies Foster + Partners' Palace of Peace and Reconciliation, an enormous glass pyramid designed to be a meeting place for the leaders of all the world's religions. Turn 180 degrees and another of Foster's gifts to the Kazakh people dominates the landscape: the Khan Shatyr, or Khan's Tent.

Shaped like a yurt, but 500 feet high, the Khan's Tent houses a shopping mall and entertainment complex. My guidebook tells me that the roof is made of ETFE, an acronym able to absorb heat, even in minus 30°C, which helps give the mall a constant year-round temperature. Apparently, there's also a monorail train at the top of the tent, as well as a swimming pool, replete with beach, whose sand has been shipped in from the Maldives.

To my surprise, the mall is packed. Not only with the nouveau riche who frequent the Gucci and Louis Vuitton stores, but with ordinary folk who have just come for a bite to eat, or to mill around people-watching. I'm left wondering where they've all come from. From what I know of the city's past, Astana is, like London, a city of migrants. Only Astana's case is far more extreme. Whereas around 30 per cent of London's population were born in the city, I'm pretty sure the figure for Astana is around 2 per cent.[7] But after a morning here, I'm struggling to see the appeal. Who would want to move to such a hostile city with no public transport and nothing but mad monuments to recommend it?

It turns out that plenty would. According to Kazakhstan's Bureau of National Statistics, in 1997 the population of Astana was 287,000. In just twenty-five years, it has grown to a city of 1.4 million. The website also has some before-and-after photographs of the city's surroundings, with miles of apartment blocks sprouting where once fields had lain.

I'm keen to hear more stories of those that have moved here, so after lunch I head for a haircut and some guaranteed conversation. My barber is Alinur, who, as expected, is anything but Astana-born-and-bred.

'My family are in Ekibastuz,' he tells me. 'It's not far, maybe three hours by car.'

'Why did you choose to come here?' I ask. 'I've heard the winters are pretty bad . . .'

'This is Kazakhstan – the winters everywhere are pretty bad! And Astana is an awesome place. The money here is good. It's modern. It's safe.'

'Don't you think it's a bit empty?' I ask, thinking of the miles of deserted pavement I've had all to myself.

'During the day, of course it's empty. People are working! If you work hard, this city is good to you. Why? What have you been doing here?'

'Oh, just walking around, seeing the monuments . . .' I suddenly feel quite self-conscious, drifting around at leisure while he furiously snips my hair into shape.

'Walking?' Alinur laughs, giving me a pitying look in the mirror. 'No wonder you think it's empty! Why walk when you can take a taxi?'

'I prefer walking,' I say, rather snappily. It's not often I feel European, but I do take a certain pride in coming from the only continent in the world where it's considered civilised to navigate a city on foot. I turn the question back on him. 'Why does everyone here want to drive everywhere?'

'Do you realise how cold it gets here in winter?' he laughs. 'No one wants to walk in that. Also, we're Kazakhs! We're used to riding horses. It is not in our genes to walk!'

These are fair points. Perhaps I've chosen the wrong country to make a stand for bipedalism.

'Can you ride a horse?' I ask.

'Of course! I learned in my family's village. There, horses are everything.'

Alinur is delighted when I tell him that I've already tried *kumis*, the fermented mare's milk. I even noticed that one of the pizza places in the mall had horsemeat as one of their toppings, though I think they missed a trick by not calling it pepper-pony pizza.

'Horses are useful for us at all times,' says Alinur happily. 'We ride them, we milk them, and then, when they are too old, we eat them,' he laughs, a little too heartily for a man holding a pair of scissors close to my face.

That evening, Klara takes me to meet some friends. This includes Sasha, an ethnic Russian and the only person I have yet met in Astana to have been born here.

'The city has had four names in my lifetime,' he tells me. 'On my passport it says I was born in Tselinograd – which means Virgin Lands City; after the collapse of the USSR it became Akmola, which was its original name. But when the first president decided that this would be the new capital, he used all his powers of imagination and renamed it Astana, which means "capital". Oh, and there was also a short period when it was named Nur-Sultan, after the president himself, before people began to realise that this was ridiculous, so now it's Astana again,' he laughs. 'Anyway, I hear you went to the Karlag – you survived, I take it?'

I tell him of my surprise that there had been so few visitors.

'I guess it's not exactly on the way to anywhere,' Sasha says drily.

This is a good point. Whereas tragedy tourists can visit Auschwitz on a half-day trip from Kraków and be back on the Tyskies by mid-afternoon, southern Siberia is anything but convenient.

Sasha leans in. 'You see, Joe, in your country the Gulag is a part of history; with us, it's still the present for many people. Going there means confronting more than an abstract event. This is what happened to our families, our grandparents. Who wants to go and see the conditions their grandparents lived in? And it's not like the Nazi death camps either, where you have Germans who did this to other races. In Kazakhstan, we did this to ourselves.'

I take a quick look up the table; Klara and her friend Zhansaya are busy in conversation. 'Do most Kazakh people see it like that?' I ask him. 'Do they look at you as a Russian who grew up here and say, "We were all in it together?", or do they blame you as a Russian for what happened to them?'

'Good question,' he smiles. 'It's certainly convenient for some Kazakhs to disassociate themselves from the communist past, especially the leadership – Nazarbayev and our new president Tokayev were both high up in the Communist Party and they'd rather people forgot that. I think generally it's difficult to sort people into victims and oppressors. Some people have both in their family – one grandparent who was imprisoned by the system, another who helped run it. Where do you think the guards from the camp went? A lot of them stayed around here. None of us can be truly "guilt-free" when it comes to our Soviet past.'

'I can!' says Zhansaya, who had overheard the last part. 'My family grew up in Mongolia. We only moved here when I was a year old.'

'She's an *oralman*,' says Klara, answering my quizzical look.

During the 1920s and 1930s, hundreds of thousands, perhaps millions, of Kazakhs left the Soviet Union for neighbouring Mongolia or China, fleeing the brutal collectivisation policies of the Bolsheviks. Many lived there for generations, keeping traditional Kazakh culture alive outside the USSR. When Kazakhstan became independent, another of Nazarbayev's nation-building ploys was to invite all ethnic Kazakhs to 'return' to their homeland from abroad. The returnees (*oralmans* in Kazakh) were offered money to resettle, as well as housing benefits.

'But not everyone welcomed us,' says Zhansaya. 'We were often discriminated against because we only spoke Kazakh – can you imagine?! Lots of people in the cities can't speak Kazakh at all, only Russian, so they looked down on us. My parents' generation had it really hard. In fact, *oralman* has become quite a loaded, derogatory term now. These days the politically correct term is meant to be *kandas*, which means "person of the same blood". Apparently, it's more inclusive.'

In demographic terms, however, *oralman* policy has been a huge success. Since 1991, almost 1.1 million ethnic Kazakhs have 'returned' to their native land; today the country is about 70 per cent Kazakh. The grand Soviet idea of the mixture of nations, which reached its height here, is drawing to a close. Many ethnically European peoples have made similar choices, returning to their own 'home' countries. Around a million ethnic Germans from across the USSR moved to Germany in the early 1990s. Russians and Ukrainians have also left in large numbers. It's an interesting contrast – the man who was born in the city being made to feel like he doesn't belong, while the government welcomes those born outside the country with open arms.

'We used to have a word, *Kazakhstani*,' says Sasha. 'It described people who were from Kazakhstan, but not ethnically Kazakh. You hear it less and less these days. Kazakhstan is becoming as nationalist as all the other republics. Some call it historical justice,' he says, with the trace of a smile.

'What do you call it?'

'Nobody cares what I call it.'

I came to Astana with an air of snobby scepticism. The idea that a city can be conjured from the frigid Central Asian wasteland might offend anyone who believes in sustainable, organic evolution. But the capital has continued to grow regardless – an unstoppable, swarming force swallowing up the steppe. I have to admit it's started to grow on me as well. Of all places, it reminds me most of Beijing: a sprawling city in a harsh climate, but whose young, ambitious citizens have an overwhelmingly positive attitude to life and the prospects it offers. People here are used to life getting better; there's a palpable sense that if you work hard enough, you will get rewarded. And yes, the winters are horrendously cold, but the place is inhabited by people who take that for granted.

The suffocating narcissism is harder to get used to. Many of Astana's features will be familiar from the Azerbaijan chapter: you land at the Nursultan Nazarbayev International Airport; you can visit the Nazarbayev Center, where there is another room of 'Gifts That Were Given To The Great Leader'; and if you want an education, then the best minds in the country gather at the Nazarbayev University. These naming traditions have unfortunately become standard practice in much of post-Soviet Central Asia, but Klara is keen to remind me that there are less despotic precedents.

'Maybe Nazarbayev thinks of himself as our George Washington,' she muses. 'He probably thinks that if the first American president gets a city named after him, why not him?'

Nazarbayev shares something else in common with Washington. In 2019, after almost three decades in power, Nazarbayev voluntarily stepped down, handing over the reins to his nominated successor, Kassym-Jomart Tokayev. He moved into an elder statesman role, using the title *Elbasy*, or Father of the Nation, which had been bestowed on him in 2010.

You might be wondering why I'm praising him for this. As I'm presuming you've guessed by now, Nazarbayev's regime was a dictatorship, with a nasty, bullying side to it just like any other. If he was really serious about transferring power, he might have, I dunno, held the occasional fair election or something. But once you've started on the road to dictatorship, elections are a risky option – you never know if the next guy will have you locked up, or shot. If the dictator can avoid a revolution or palace coup, power is more often than not prised from his cold, dead grasp.*

So, without wanting to shill for dictatorships, I think we can at a very minimum conclude that it could have been a lot worse. After thirty years of independence, Kazakhstan is still here; it remains in one piece (a rather large piece at that); there have been no wars on its territory; it has seen a reasonably smooth transfer of power; and GDP per capita has risen by about seven times since 1990. Considering the conflicts we've covered so far, these achievements are not inconsiderable.

---

* Nazarbayev's continued influence was one target of the violent protests known as Qandy Qantar ('Bloody January') in early 2022. While rising fuel prices served as the trigger, protesters in Almaty soon began chanting 'Shal, ket!' ('Old man, go!') in reference to the former president. Later that year, the decision to rename Astana 'Nur-Sultan' was reversed, and in 2023 he was stripped of his title Elbasy. However, much of his wealth has survived, and his daughter Dariga and her husband Timur Kulibaev remain among the country's most powerful oligarchs. For his part, Nazarbayev claims just to be a pensioner enjoying a 'well-deserved retirement', albeit a very wealthy one.

Almaty

'Almaty is fine. It's a nice city, but the people there are lazy. Nobody does anything. In Astana people work, and they work hard; in Almaty people sit around drinking coffee.'

This was Klara's warning about the former capital.

Whereas Astana represents a fresh beginning and is a self-consciously Kazakh city, a place defined by the steppe, whose flat landscape poses no challenge to its self-importance, Almaty, lying prostrate at the foot of the Tian Shan mountains, is mellow, more urbane. Its leafy avenues, despite being set out in a remorseless Soviet grid, are rather pleasant. Even at the height of summer the city is very green, and water flows peacefully down from the mountains into concrete channels dug by the roadside. Although Almaty has grown since independence, the centre of town hasn't undergone too much redevelopment. You could argue that losing its status as the capital was the best thing that ever happened to the city: it's given it some space to breathe.

Almaty is decidedly Soviet. In the centre is the Park of Panfilov's 28 Guardsmen, named after a Russian general who led a unit of mainly Kazakh and Kyrgyz soldiers during the Battle of Moscow in 1941. Legend has it that twenty-eight of these soldiers held up a group of German tanks as they advanced on Moscow, buying the defenders precious time to prepare their defence.* The fight on the Eastern Front is often depicted as a solely Russian triumph, but the other Soviet republics also suffered huge losses. Up to 600,000 Kazakhs are estimated to have died in the Second World War – comparable to the losses of Britain or France. The monument to the Panfilov 28 depicts soldiers from each of the fifteen republics, reinforcing the idea that it was a brotherhood of nations fighting the Nazis.

Indeed, Almaty is more of a melting pot than anywhere I've been thus far. In the month I end up spending here, I find that it is home not only to

---

* Like many wartime stories promoted in the Soviet Union, the tale of the 'Panfilov 28' is almost certainly a myth, maintained for propaganda purposes despite evidence to the contrary.

Kazakhs, but to Russians, Kyrgyz and Uzbeks; I even meet a young Uighur woman whose family recently found a way to get out of neighbouring China. The city remains the financial capital of Kazakhstan, and many of the major banks are headquartered here. There are bars, tea houses, the fabled Green Bazaar and a wider range of restaurants than anything I've seen since Moscow.

This Soviet multiculturalism is reflected most profoundly in language. Almaty is still a predominantly Russian-speaking city. This has saved me a fair bit of time as, not being a fluent speaker of all fifteen official languages of the new republics, I have thus far been getting around by learning basic greetings in each country and then switching to either English or Russian depending on my audience.

Navigating which second language to opt for has been a bit of a minefield. Armenia wasn't too bad – most people speak good Russian unless they're from the diaspora, in which case the chances are their English will be decent. Azerbaijan was more interesting. Baku was for most of its history a multicultural, Russian-speaking city. As we have seen, ethnic cleansing put a stop to the multiculturalism, but Russian has lingered on. It remains the language of the elite, and many parents prefer to send their children to Russian-language schools over Azeri ones. Outside the centre of Baku, though, it was a struggle to make myself understood.

Georgia was something else entirely. Speaking Russian in Tbilisi gets you, at best, some very nasty looks. I heard a few stories of people being refused service or confronted in the street for using it in a private conversation. You might think this is understandable, given Georgia's recent history, but others have assured me that the problem goes back far beyond that. There were riots in Tbilisi in 1978 when the authorities sought to enshrine Russian as a state language alongside Georgian.[8]

But in Kazakhstan, Russian is not simply the language of inter-ethnic communication. In some cities, and especially in Almaty, many Kazakhs are native Russian-speakers. To find out more about the language issues in the country, I arrange to speak with Dosym Satpayev, a Kazakh political scientist. He invites me to meet him near his home at Coffee Varka, one of hundreds of examples of Almaty's vibrant café culture.

I came across Satpayev's film *Nomads of the Dead Steppe* while I researched the famines at the start of the twentieth century, and he traces Kazakhstan's Russian-language roots back to this time.[9]

'In the film we tried to get across one very important idea,' he tells me. 'That Kazakh society is a post-traumatic society, especially compared with other Central Asian countries. If you look at Kazakh history, we had, let's say, the *base-level* trauma – the October Revolution; civil war; collectivisation; extreme repression of the intelligentsia etc. But on top of that, Kazakh society lost millions and millions of people through famine. And we didn't only lose people. Soviet power also destroyed traditions, the connections between generations.'

Due to the inbound migration from other parts of the union, in Satpayev's youth 70 per cent of the city's population were Russian.

'There was only one Kazakh-language school in the city. Just one!' he says.

But it's not just demographics and the education system that have helped maintain Russian's incumbency in the post-Soviet era, both in Kazakhstan and elsewhere. Box-office blockbusters and bestselling books are not always translated into Kazakh or Georgian, given the resources it takes to dub a film or translate a novel into a new language. Therefore Russian often becomes a way of accessing world culture. The old economic links remain as well – huge numbers of migrants from Central Asia and the Caucasus continue to work in Moscow and Saint Petersburg, and small things like road signs, satnav systems and apps are often single-language Russian imports.

But Kazakhstan is changing. When I first arrived at Klara's apartment, she greeted me with the words BORN QAZAQ emblazoned on her hoodie. I had noticed this spelling variant at the airport and on my passport stamp.

'Why is it Qazaqstan now?' I asked her.

'Kazakhstan is the Russian spelling; in our language, we write it as Qazaqstan.'

'And there was me thinking that you were just hoping to be worth more points than Kyrgyzstan in Scrabble.'

I got a slap for that.

In Almaty, the Kazakh language has begun to revive. Over the past two decades there has been an influx of *oralmans* and migrants from rural areas who never grew up learning Russian.

Anar, a Russian-speaking banker, tells me that she recently attended a music festival where many of the songs were in Kazakh. 'It's amazing to hear songs in our own language, I'm so proud!' she smiles.

The Ukraine war has also had a galvanising effect on the Kazakh language. In a 2023 press conference with Vladimir Putin, President Tokayev chose to answer his questions in Kazakh. Images of the Russian delegation, who had been expecting him to speak their mutual language, simultaneously reaching for their translation headsets as Tokayev began his response caused hoots of delight here when they did the rounds on social media.

But while the Kazakh cultural revival is gaining momentum, the Russian language, and indeed pro-Russian attitudes, still hold a strong presence in the country. Nowhere is this more evident than on the short stretch leading south-east towards the Kyrgyz border.

We're hitching again. The Altyn Orda bazaar on Almaty's outskirts is sweaty, heaving with the sights and smells of grubby commerce. A pasty white chap in an oversized shirt with his thumb stuck out gets some odd looks, but eventually an old couple pull in, dodging a rogue *marshrutka*, and consent to give me a ride as far as the junction to Bishkek.

'You Russian?' asks the man, whose name is Rasul, smiling encouragingly as I slide into the back seat.

'No; English.'

'Oh.' He looks disappointed.

'We like Russia,' says his wife. 'We love Putin; we respect him.'

I'm wondering what I've said or done that has challenged this notion, before she continues. 'Why is England interfering in Russia's affairs?'

'Careful, Asel,' Rasul mutters. 'This man is our guest . . .' He makes a sardonic nod in my direction.

'Five years, you served!' she hisses, before continuing to hector him in Kazakh. I have a feeling I know what's coming.

'Wars are between governments, not people,' Rasul pronounces solemnly. 'And this war won't last long either; all the negroes and foreigners in the Ukrainian army won't want to fight in minus ten degrees. Look at Napoleon, look at the fascists – when winter came, they froze and ran away. You British are just doing what the Americans want; Johnson can't stop licking Biden's ass.'

I'm sceptical as to how many ethnic minorities are in the Ukrainian armed forces, and have no desire to contemplate the presidential posterior, so I allow these comments to pass. I knew these opinions existed across the former USSR, but I haven't yet heard them expressed so boldly. On the contrary, the Russian invasion seems to have alarmed most Kazakhs. Anar had told me that she'd made a pact with her father that they would both volunteer to join the Kazakhstani army in the event of a Russian invasion. Dosym Satpayev was scandalised when the war began and has since written articles excoriating Russia's behaviour in Kazakhstan's version of *Forbes* magazine. Klara was similarly disgusted.

However, huge numbers of people in Kazakhstan continue to tune in to Russian state television. It was available in every hotel room I visited; I've seen it in bars, restaurants, even the barber's in Astana. There are still plenty of people ready to believe that the invasion of Ukraine is in fact a war between NATO and Russia, that Russia is acting in self-defence, and that it's only a matter of time before NATO becomes reasonable and withdraws its support for the fascist regime in Kyiv.

I wonder if my travelling companions miss the Soviet times.

'Of course – we were young! Everything is better when you are young . . .' Rasul pauses for a moment, thinking. 'Sport used to be better. I was a sports social worker. There used to be a stadium for everyone to use; now you need to pay a thousand tenge just for renting ice skates. Back then, everyone used to play sport . . .' He pauses again. 'But we've had improvements too . . .'

It's this sense of compromise that I rather like about Kazakhstan. The Soviet Union isn't labelled as either 'good' or 'evil', it's simply a legacy to deal with. The same goes for language – if you ever watch a game of football on television here, you'll notice that the commentators will switch between Kazakh and Russian, the assumption being that the audience is largely bilingual. Many Kazakhs think nothing of speaking one language at home and another at work, doing their shopping at the Kazakh-speaking market before drinking in a Russian-speaking café.

Yes, it's been lucky with oil; yes, it has gaping inequality and is a corrupt dictatorship, but for all that, I rather like the place. Besides, as we've seen in the Caucasus and will soon discover in the rest of Central Asia, it could be a lot worse.

6
KYRGYZSTAN
THE REPUBLIC OF UPRISINGS

There's a colony of seagulls waiting for me after customs, their Ladas parked pell-mell in the dirt beside the road. I pick one at random and negotiate a $5 fee for the fifteen-minute drive to the capital. A lot of pushing and shoving ensues between my driver and his rivals, all of whom want one last chance to make their case.

'Look at his shitty car!' one shouts. 'I offer you four dollars! Four dollars!!'

I stay loyal to my man and he repays my faith once we are under way, pulling out a bottle of knock-off Jägermeister and pouring it down his gullet.

'Thirsty?' I ask.

He grins into the rear-view mirror. 'For my health.'

I'm sure it is.

Kyrgyzstan, roughly the size of the island of Great Britain, is bordered by Kazakhstan to the north, Uzbekistan to the west, Tajikistan across the Pamirs to the south and China beyond the Tian Shan range to the east. While the free-spirited Kazakhs are people of the plains, mountains define their southern neighbours. Among these are some leviathans, including Lenin Peak (23,406 feet) and the highest, Victory Peak, at 24,406 feet. Such terrain led the Kyrgyz tribes to lead a semi-nomadic lifestyle, spending their summers in high-altitude pastures called *jailoos* and their winters in the valleys.

As we've seen with separatist movements across the Caucasus, high mountains generally contribute to a strong regional identity at the expense of the central authorities. While the other Central Asian countries quickly succumbed to authoritarianism following the Soviet collapse, Kyrgyzstan has traditionally been the most democratic of the five. And when Kyrgyz leaders *do* show signs of accumulating too much power, the people are not afraid to remove them. There have been three revolutions here since independence – in 2005, 2010 and the most recent in 2020. Such a weak state is a breath of fresh air after a month in Kazakhstan. I didn't need a visa, I've seen no evidence of any army, and the lack of traffic police means that my driver is free to drink his 'health tonic' with impunity. As I do my evening's admin, the pleasant surprises keep on coming: no one asks me for my passport when checking into the hotel, nor when I change dollars into Kyrgyz som; jaywalking is normal, and even if it's illegal, I don't see a single CCTV camera.

Bishkek

As students of Marxist dialectics, communists love a contradiction. Perhaps it's unsurprising, then, that the only former Soviet capital to shed its Soviet name at independence is the one that has changed the least. Until then, the Kyrgyz capital was called Frunze, in honour of the Red Army general who did so much to conquer this territory for the Bolsheviks; but in 1991 the new Kyrgyz government restored its historic name: Bishkek.

Cranes are beginning to dot the city centre, but the echoes of the old civilisation lie largely undisturbed. The massive, polished-white parliament building glowers down on the main square, solid, angular and uncompromising. The square itself is Soviet to a tee – more a parade ground than a place for public gatherings, the streets branching off it in rigid ranks. A clock tower stands like a sentinel to the east of the square, built by Armenian artisans. It's said that the clock stopped chiming soon after the USSR collapsed.

As in Almaty, there are channels for water beside the road, empty in the sizzling late-August heat; unlike Almaty, they are riddled with cracks, which extend all the way up to the pavement. The splendid marble facades are also long overdue a wash. The mercilessly stuffy summer has slowed the pace of life to a crawl.

Women sit at intersections under red umbrellas, selling drinks from the barrels stored next to them. Men wearing Kyrgyzstan's traditional tall, felt hat, the *kalpak*, stand smoking in the shade.

With the exception of KFC, the vanguard of globalisation has yet to arrive, giving the city centre an authentic feel. For a second, I think I catch a glimpse of a BP garage, but on closer inspection the petrol station is painted in the signature green and yellow livery of another BP: Bishkek Petroleum.

There are no shuttlecock towers or pyramids here, nor silly circus tents or museums to the Great Leader. Instead, a quiet, green city sits in the shadow of the Ala-Too Mountains, whose snowcapped peaks wink invitingly down at us.

Writers, Stalin believed, are the engineers of the soul. So if we're looking to understand Kyrgyzstan, there are few better places to start with than the home of the country's most famous author. Chinghiz Aitmatov, the man who gave us the Mankurt, is by quite a distance the largest literary figure to come out of the country. Born in 1928, he witnessed most of the Soviet period, as well as the early years of independence, before his death in 2008.

As I was being driven into town on the first day, I asked my Jäger-slugging chauffer, Marat, if he'd be interested in taking me to see Aitmatov's house in the suburbs of the city, which has now been turned into a museum. Once we're under way, he's quick to regale me with his life story.

'I have three degrees,' he begins. 'One in economics, and two in law. But there is no work for me back home. There I can earn fifty dollars a month, maximum. Driving in Bishkek, I can earn ten times that.'

Home for Marat is the southern city of Jalal-Abad.* I wonder how bad things must be there if Bishkek is the city of his dreams. The ordered disintegration of the centre is quickly replaced by the dust and gravel of the suburbs. After a couple of miles, the roads have disappeared altogether, leaving us to wind through a parched field. The satnav constantly reroutes us; perhaps it too is alarmed at how quickly the metropolis has surrendered to rural destitution. We bump onwards before arriving at a makeshift

---

* Jalal-Abad was renamed Manas in September 2025, after the legendary hero of the Kyrgyz national epic.

roadblock – a couple of tyres with some sandbags stacked against them. A man in military garb rises from a wooden chair beside the fortifications. Marat looks at me. I shrug. Is this a bandit? They have a conversation in Kyrgyz. The soldier asks him to translate.

'Where are you going?'

'To the museum.'

'No museum here.' The soldier gestures behind him at the dusty yellow field.

'He has a point,' mutters Marat.

'This zone is forbidden,' the young soldier adds, eyeing us suspiciously.

There's nothing for it but to loop back to the main road, this time approaching our quarry from the leafier and more robustly built Mir Avenue. The satnav appears more comfortable now, pointing purposefully dead ahead. But its confidence is misplaced: we drive on, only to find another roadblock.

'Seems your museum is well defended,' grins Marat.

This time we're faced with some proper barricades, bristling with the rifles of half a dozen soldiers. In a fit of gallantry, Marat decides to stop the car fifty feet away and suggests I walk towards the guns alone. The soldiers laugh among themselves as I approach. The commander nudges one of the young recruits, angling his head towards me in a go-and-see-what-the-foreigner-wants kind of way. The private is only a kid, his hair has been shaved mercilessly short under his oversized beret. He starts demanding things of me in Kyrgyz, trying his best to adopt a low voice.

'I'm here to see the museum,' I tell him in Russian. 'The Chinghiz Aitmatov Museum.'

There's indecision in his boyish eyes. I get the impression he hasn't understood a word I've said. He looks back at his superior officer for help. The captain strolls over nonchalantly.

'Passport,' he growls, holding out his hand without looking at me. He peruses it absently, presumably to buy himself some thinking time.

'Where are you going?' he asks eventually.

'To the Chinghiz Aitmatov Museum.'

'Which museum?'

I point it out on the map. 'The House of Chinghiz Aitmatov . . .'

'Who?'

'Chinghiz Aitmatov . . . you know, the author!'

'I don't know him.'

'But he's like your Shakespeare!'

'Who?'

I close my eyes.

'This is the president's residence,' says the captain, with a tone of finality. 'No museum here.'

I traipse back towards Marat, who has got the Jäger out once more. I take him up on it this time.

'The soldiers didn't even know who Aitmatov was!'

'Well, they are soldiers; most of them drop out of school at fourteen,' he shrugs. 'So they didn't let you in?'

'No; it's the president's house apparently.'

'Oh, so that's where he lives,' Marat whistles when I let him know whose castle we've spent the morning besieging.

The Kyrgyz leader is a rather different character to those we've encountered thus far. Two years ago, in one of the more remarkable political turnarounds of recent times, Sadyr Japarov broke out of prison, had himself installed as acting prime minister and then was democratically elected president within the space of a few months.[1] This isn't to say that the path from jail cell to statesman isn't a well-trodden one, but Japarov is more Nelson Muntz than Nelson Mandela. His eventual arrest for kidnap and hostage-taking in 2013 was only the latest in a string of criminal allegations, ranging from a raid on a bank, the storming of parliament, and the armed seizure of a crucial electrical substation.[2] But none of this stopped a large portion of the country voting for him when the time came.

'What do you think about the president?' I ask Marat as we set off back to town.

He snorts. 'We Muslims say that politics is dirtier than the toilet: you can clean a toilet, but whatever you try in politics, the dirt is always there.' He shakes his head. 'All of them – they deceive and deceive. Why do they make these promises and then pretend they didn't? This is the twenty-first century! I can show you a video of a politician making the promise he says that he never made! So, why not choose someone like Japarov? At least he is a bit different . . .'

This attitude is widespread. For three decades, Kyrgyzstan was consistently dubbed an 'island of democracy' in Central Asia. It earned praise from NGOs and international organisations for its free media, its separation of powers, the occasional free and fair election, and being the first Central Asian country to have had a female head of state. Levels of English here are the best in the region and civil society is bright and engaged in public affairs. As one activist put it to me, 'In Bishkek, everyone is a philosopher!'

And while none of these are bad things, in that time the country did not grow richer. The minimum wage in Kyrgyzstan stands at 2,460 Kyrgyz som ($28) a month. Yeah. A month. Small wonder that hundreds of thousands of its citizens are working abroad, the vast majority in Russia. Remittances from these workers constitutes 20 to 30 per cent of Kyrgyzstan's GDP.[3]

While a minuscule middle class were content to live on international aid money, the lack of jobs and meagre wages for the majority has led to a lack of the very things that glue a society together: the traffic jams on the crumbling roads make even basic journeys a chore, smog chokes the city in winter, and schools burst at the seams. And Bishkek isn't so bad compared to the rest of Kyrgyzstan: shanty towns have sprouted around the city as people migrate from the countryside, where the dearth of opportunities is even more acute.

Presiding over all this has been the political class, for whom 'democracy' has really meant repetitive cycles of corrupt, unpopular presidents losing an election, falsifying the results to claim they won, only to be kicked out by a protesting public taking to the streets. When this happened for a third time in 2020, Japarov was sprung from prison in the ensuing revolutionary chaos. More than one member of parliament has spoken out about how his thuggish cronies broke into parliament and coerced its members into accepting him as acting prime minister.

Chief among these cronies was Kamchybek Tashiev, a long-time ally of Japarov. Some cheekier local activists refer to him as 'Mr Stone' – the Kyrgyz word *tash* means 'stone'. But that's a rather kindly moniker compared to his first name, which translates as 'lord of the whip'. Perhaps he was destined for a life of hard power, a role he now fulfils as head of Kyrgyzstan's formidable security services. So close is the bond between Tashiev and Japarov that they are collectively known as *Eki Dos* (Two Friends), a phrase that has become shorthand for the pair's joint domination of the country's politics.

Since then, Japarov has consolidated power through a new constitution, expanded the authority of the security services, curtailed media freedoms and suppressed dissent, entrenching an increasingly authoritarian regime in Kyrgyzstan. He has promised that his rule will bring stability and create the conditions for growth. Indeed, the initial economic indicators are good. He has been helped over the past year by Russian money pouring into the country as companies seek to avoid Western sanctions, but it is a mark both of the disillusionment with democracy and the desperation for change that, even in this land of uprisings, people seem willing to give strongman rule a chance.

Later in the week I arrange to meet Cholpon Chotaeva, a history professor at the American University of Central Asia. She invites me to meet her in an upmarket coffee shop called Vanilla Sky. She has an air of hauteur and grace as she strides over to our table and orders herself a latte. She does so in Russian, the lingua franca of Central Asian coffee shops. It's sobering to realise that the cost – $2.50 – is around 10 per cent of the average monthly salary.

As it happens, the news cycle dictates the first question I ask her. Yesterday the world learned of the death of Mikhail Gorbachev, the man who did more than any other to bring about the country's independence.

'Do you think independence has been good for Kyrgyzstan?' I ask her.

'Let's say I don't think we were ready for complete independence. Of course, in August 1991, when independence was declared, it was a time of euphoria. People got excited, especially intellectuals like my parents. They hoped or expected a lot after the collapse of the Soviet Union. But how it turned out was completely different.'

I tell her about my conversation with Dosym Satpayev, the political scientist in Almaty. He spoke about a generational split in attitudes. Whereas he described the period as a 'beautiful time', his parents saw it very differently. 'The whole thing was a very big psychological shock for them,' he said, telling me how his father had spent the late 1980s carefully saving for a car only to see his life savings wiped out by the economic whiplash of the Soviet collapse. 'This money just disappeared. Millions of people were in the same situation. That's why if you talk to the young generation and the older generation, there's a different position towards independence.'

I find it interesting that Chotaeva's parents, despite being the same age as Satpayev's, were in favour of change.

She nods. 'Perhaps my parents were different from that Soviet generation. They got a lot from Soviet Kyrgyzstan, my mother was a professor with a very good salary, but there were huge problems during that time. I remember there were empty shelves in the department stores, and to get just a small, simple item of clothing you had to use your connections. My father actually had a lower salary than my mother – he was the director of an automobile service station – but his customers were the Party elite, so he had very good contacts and relationships with people in department stores. I remember we had special shops to get things like Indian tea or Moscow sausage, for example, which were not sold in ordinary shops for ordinary people. So it wasn't a nationalist thing per se, it was more them seeing the opportunities.'

Our talk turns to identity, and the Aitmatov museum I'd tried to visit earlier. Chotaeva gives me a brief history lesson, explaining there was no 'Kyrgyzstan' until relatively recently. For centuries, Kyrgyz life consisted of seasonal nomadic migrations between the steppe and the mountains. Politically, however, they were usually part of a larger empire. By the early 1800s this was the Uzbek-dominated Kokand khanate, while tribes in the east paid tribute to Qing China. By the mid-nineteenth century, the Russians came on the scene. However, it was left to the Soviets to draw the borders of the first 'Kyrgyz Republic' – albeit a Soviet Socialist one – ladling it out of the regional pilaf of peoples and territories.*

'This has left my parents' generation, for example, with an identity split between Soviet and Kyrgyz. They saw positive sides in both of them,' she says. 'After all, it's hard to say that the Soviets were wholly oppressive. Things here weren't as bad as some other republics. During collectivisation, the Kyrgyz avoided the worst of the famine because the leader here, Abdrakhmanov, refused to take grain from locals and give it to Moscow. For this he was killed, of course, in 1937. But unlike in Kazakhstan, there was no famine here. On top of that, the Soviets introduced the Kyrgyz alphabet, brought in the first Kyrgyz professional literature. I mean, they rescued the intelligentsia, right? The way intellectuals were raised before in the religious Islamic schools was completely different from the Soviet time.'

'You could say they destroyed the original intelligentsia though . . .' I point out. As in Kazakhstan and many other republics, intellectuals in Kyrgyzstan were caught up in the purges of 1937–8.

'To some extent, yes,' she says thoughtfully. 'They were very destructive in a way. They killed a lot. I'll tell you a story from my family history: my grandmother was the daughter of a tribal chieftain. In the 1930s, these local elites, along with the rich peasants, were repressed, killed, or sometimes sent far away to Siberia. All her family was sent over there and never came back. But she survived. She was young and beautiful and a local Red Commissar fell in love with her and ensured she wasn't deported. They ended up marrying. So it's hard to say what is positive or negative about the Soviet time, but it was bold, right? I suppose they're sort of part villain, part heroes.'

---

* Technically, the first 'Kyrgyz Republic' was actually what we now call Kazakhstan. In 1920 the Soviets created the Kirghiz ASSR, which in fact encompassed the Kazakhs, then commonly called 'Kirghiz' in Russian usage. What became Kyrgyzstan started out in 1924 as the Kara-Kirghiz Autonomous Oblast. I won't get lost in the weeds here – the key point is that Kyrgyzstan's borders, like Kazakhstan's, were drawn for the first time by the Soviets.

I'm unsure what to make of this Red romance. As in the Gulag, I wonder whether the selective mercy makes the system of oppression even worse. I tell her that, to me, the city still has a Soviet feel to it, even if some of the street names have changed.

'Well, they have been changed in official papers, but not in everyday speech,' she corrects me, pointing to the city's main thoroughfare – Sovietskaya Street – as an example. 'I don't think we should completely destroy or remove parts of our past like in Ukraine or somewhere else, but, of course, it's another issue over there . . .' She tails off.

Perhaps it's surprising to hear a reasonably well-off professor equivocate on the idea of her country's independence, but it's hard to exaggerate the economic disaster that the collapse of the Soviet Union caused here. Although the Kyrgyz SSR was one of the poorer republics, it did have a reasonably strong industrial base and played an important role in the USSR's military industrial complex. The Lenin Arms Factory in Bishkek churned out ammunition; important elements of the Mir satellite programme were centred here at the Space Research Institute, which employed over 1,000 people, and many of the USSR's torpedoes were produced and tested in the waters of Issyk Kul, the country's largest lake.[4] With the Soviet collapse, these specialised industries diminished in importance – they were a small part in a hugely complex supply chain that only made economic sense in the service of a superpower. After all, what use does a landlocked country with no intergalactic ambitions have for torpedoes and satellites?

The removal of subsidies was equally painful. Unlike other European empires, which exploited their colonies for raw materials, Russian nationalists saw that *they* were the ones with the resources and began to see the other republics, particularly Central Asia, as deadweight. For the team around Boris Yeltsin, economic shock therapy was the only solution to Russia's economic woes. This meant an end to subsidies, both within Russia and towards the republics that relied on it.

The cuts came in two forms. Firstly, the new Russian Federation stopped supplying the other republics with cut-price oil and gas, causing fuel and energy costs to spike. Then there was the central budget, which had been used to redistribute wealth around the USSR. In 1991 these budget transfers made up 35.2 per cent of the Kyrgyz SSR's budget (and 12.2 per cent of its entire GDP).[5] By 1993, much of that had disappeared. Russia's trade with the five Central Asian republics fell to 10 per cent of what it had been in 1991.[6] Kyrgyzstan found that 50 per cent of its industrial production had been wiped out, there was a huge hole in its government budget, and many of its non-Kyrgyz population (a disproportionate number of whom were skilled workers) had left the country, mainly for Russia and Ukraine.

Geography also contributed to the economy's torrid ordeal. There are two major populated areas in Kyrgyzstan: in the north of the country is Bishkek, the capital; in the south is the Ferghana Valley, with its principal cities of Osh and Jalal-Abad. In between are mountains.

Under the Soviets, the Kyrgyz economy functioned because its borders didn't much matter – things necessary for the south's industries could come in by rail from the Uzbek SSR, and goods to and from the north could pass through the Kazakh SSR. There was little need to travel between the two. But no sane person would give an independent country Kyrgyzstan's borders and hope that it would prosper. Since independence, it has often felt like there are two Kyrgyzstans – North and South. Getting from one to the other means taking a ten-hour trip through the winding mountains, on roads that are often blocked in winter.

To discuss how the country deals with this, I get in touch with political scientist Alibek Mukambayev. I read one of his pieces criticising the government's failure to invest in infrastructure, particularly the railway. He invites me for lunch, ordering for both of us – naturally.

'I've got us some *beshbarmak*,' he says. 'This is the traditional food of north Kyrgyzstan, and of Kazakhstan as well. In the south, they barely eat this; they're more likely to eat Uzbek dishes.'

The *beshbarmak*, when it arrives, turns out to be boiled horse meat with noodles and onions, and is tastier than it sounds. But Alibek is at pains to point out that the mountains don't merely divide the country gastronomically. He talks about the soft accent that defines southern Kyrgyz compared to the more guttural northerners, and economically he says the divide is most acute. 'You know, it's currently cheaper to transport one tonne of gasoline from Russia to Kyrgyzstan than it is to move it from Bishkek to Osh!' he says.

Alibek's grand idea is that a railway should be built through the mountains to connect the major cities of Bishkek, Jalal-Abad and Osh.

'It might be expensive to build, but the project would easily pay back loans through revenue raised from tickets and cargo,' he enthuses.

The government, however, has opted to upgrade the road between the north and south. 'They want something they can open right now; they want a quick success,' Alibek explains. 'And obviously building a railway is difficult and requires expertise. Right now, there's neither the will nor the money to commit to long-term projects like this.'

This is a problem that has beset many of the country's infrastructure projects. Bishkek's terrible air quality is partly due to its reliance on a large coal-fired power station that gets turned on in winter. Those not connected to the gas network resort to burning their own supply of low-quality coal to remain warm. Exasperatingly, the country could be a hydroelectric superpower given the number of rivers that begin here – but five of its seven hydroelectric power stations were built in the Soviet era, when planners could rely on powerful central government backing and engineering capacity. The lack of a tax base or investor confidence makes it extremely difficult to get these projects off the ground these days.

'If only you had some large communist superpower nearby who could help you out,' I muse.

He laughs. 'Right, it's only the Chinese that could build it easily, but they have to get something in return for that.'

Indeed, in 2024 Beijing did agree to finance over half the cost of a railway in Kyrgyzstan, but it will not pass through Bishkek or Osh. The new line will be laid across Kyrgyz territory but will mainly serve to connect China and Uzbekistan.

Whenever there is a new infrastructure project in Central Asia, it is very often the Export-Import Bank of China that funds it and the China Road and Bridge Corporation that builds it. It is no coincidence that Xi Jinping chose the Kazakh capital Astana to launch his Belt and Road

Initiative in 2013. All five Central Asian states have been happy to accept Beijing's help for everything from road-building to oil refineries, tunnels to 5G, railways to schools, with lending running to tens of billions of dollars.

But what the Chinese might be getting in return for their investments in Central Asia is a strained topic. On the one hand, governments here love the low-interest loans that come with few strings attached; but there is a wariness of running up too much debt to their giant neighbour, as well as unease about the labour camps and destruction of mosques in neighbouring Xinjiang province. Leaving Soviet Russia only to fall into the grip of communist China is not exactly a fairy-tale story of independence.

One sector that doesn't require Chinese investment to prosper is tourism. As much as Kyrgyzstan's mountains are a pain to get around, they are staggeringly beautiful.

I take a tour to Song Kul, a lake right in the heart of the country at an altitude of over 10,000 feet. The tour group is an odd mix: there are some foreigners, but most are locals in their early twenties who have made their money in Russia. It's the last week of the summer pasturing period; the lake lazily laps the grassy bank from where cows crane their necks to take a leisurely sip. The water stretches out in front of them like a small sea, the land around it untouched by humanity save for a small colony of yurts on the northern shore. The only nods to modernity are the miniature solar panels standing outside each. The air is the most pristine I've tasted since the Gulag, but it's undeniably chilly up here. Some shepherds are already dismantling their yurts, ready to take them down into the valleys for winter.

To warm ourselves up, we mount horses to go for a lakeside trek. It's remarkable how horses can transform a person. Our small, bumbling minibus driver suddenly becomes a bareback gaucho, the picture of competence and manliness. He gallops, whooping across the plateau, turning his steed on a sixpence. His shouts echo for miles through the thin air and the endless silence on top of the world. My steed, in contrast, has taken one look at me and decided I'm a soft touch.

'Give her a kick!' shouts the instructor once I've struggled into the saddle. I dig my heels into the horse's belly; she responds by tossing her head sardonically.

'I said *kick her*, not tap her!'

'I don't want to hurt her,' I shout back.

'Ugh, city dwellers!' he sighs, before calling the dogs. Their snarls quickly get the dozy mare breaking into a trot.

My urban skillset is unlikely to get me far here, but it does give me some sense of how alien Soviet demands for the emancipation of the urban proletariat must have seemed to the rural Kyrgyz a century ago. Indeed, for some people here, it must be as if the Soviet Union never existed. We're simply too remote. They live as they always have: after the ride, a stooped old matriarch offers me *kumis*; that evening we dine on mutton broth from a freshly slaughtered ewe; the only thing not sourced locally is the bread that has been brought up from the valley.

While tourism alone can't save a country, it seems a good place to start. If I were advising the Kyrgyz tourist board, I'd say that a lot of the ingredients are here – a rich cultural heritage, a gem of a Soviet relic for a capital city, and undisturbed, wild mountains begging to be explored. It strikes me as a means of bringing some dignity and income to a way of life that has survived Muhammad, Marx and the post-Soviet malaise.

7
UZBEKISTAN
THE REPUBLIC OF ISLAM

'Imagine you become president of independent Uzbekistan in 1991,' Alibek said to me. 'Next door, you have problems in Afghanistan; you have a civil war in Tajikistan; you have rising Islamism in the population . . . You can see why the Uzbek state is built like a castle to withstand a siege!'

Fortress Uzbekistan is apparent from the outset. The border is more heavily protected than any I've crossed thus far. Mounds of razor wire are piled high and sentry towers are silhouetted against the rising sun. The train comes to a halt in a goods yard, surrounded by Chinese shipping containers. Beyond these, I can just about make out Tashkent 8 miles away. From this distance, only its most Soviet elements can be seen: the white factory chimneys with their distinctive red hoops, as well as the ubiquitous TV tower.

After ten minutes of waiting, the air conditioning turns off. I glance at my watch, grateful that it's only 7.30 a.m. An hour later, we still haven't moved. The compartment is becoming stifling. The carriage attendant wanders by and is surprised to find someone still aboard; most of the passengers got off at Shymkent, on the Kazakh side of the border.

He is rather affable, but is followed not long after by some Uzbek customs officials, who are decidedly not. Predictably, they have brought a German Shepherd with them.

'Which republic are you from?' snaps one, examining my passport.

'Great Britain.' I feel this isn't the right time to point out that it's a kingdom, not a republic. He nods and disappears with the passport; his colleagues examine my luggage.

'You have any dollars?'

'About two hundred.'

'Any books? Camera equipment? Recording equipment?' They continue asking the standard repertoire of twentieth-century questions.

'Just a phone.'

Unconvinced, he begins shining his torch under the seats. His colleague is rifling through my rucksack; he opens my washbag and pulls out the Durex.

'What are these for?'

The dog growls, enough to deter me from cracking a joke.

Tashkent

I'm expecting a lot from Tashkent, the city that has been the heart of Central Asia ever since General Mikhail Chernyaev decided to take it without the tsar's permission in 1865. By 1989 it had grown to become the USSR's fourth largest city, and the biggest east of the Urals. Today it serves as the capital of Uzbekistan, one of just two double-landlocked countries in the world.* It makes up for this isolation by acting as the region's fulcrum, the only Central Asian state to touch all the others: to the north, at twelve o'clock, is Kazakh steppe; the peaks of Kyrgyzstan and Tajikistan bask together in the eastern afternoon around three and four; Afghanistan settles down for supper at six; from seven onwards, the sky begins to darken over the Turkmen deserts to the west.

Like the Kazakhs and the Kyrgyz, the Uzbeks are a Turkic people. Originally nomads from the plains north of the Aral Sea, they swept into the region in around 1500, conquering the cities that criss-cross the ancient Silk Road. Unlike the Kazakhs and the Kyrgyz, they decided to settle down. Establishing several small kingdoms called khanates, they sought to prosper in a region that for centuries had dominated the trade between China, the Middle East and Europe. Unfortunately, their timing wasn't the best – they arrived here just as Vasco da Gama discovered a sea route to India, and the Silk Road began a slow slide into irrelevance. This hasn't stopped the

---

* Pub quizzers among you will doubtless know that the other, of course, is Liechtenstein.

route's romantic image lingering on. Even as I pass through the ticket hall I spot a poster of a camel-caravan approaching an oasis under a burning sun; another depicts ancient mosques and smiling old men drinking tea under plane trees.

The burning sun part is accurate, but, walking from the station to the hostel, there are no ancient mosques, no greybeards supping tea nor a grain of sand in sight. Here too the cranes are everywhere, overshadowing the broad, tree-lined avenues with neat Soviet buildings.

But something is amiss. I soon begin to count, stopping when I get to a hundred. Apart from four Hyundais, a Kia and eight Chinese electric vehicles, the other eighty-seven cars are all Chevrolets. It's as if the whole city is one vast showroom. There's every Chevy model imaginable, from the cheap and cheerful Spark to the workhorse Lacetti. High rollers cruise along at the wheel of Malibu sedans. There are even a couple of Tahoe SUVs, the Bactrian camels of the twenty-first century. To add to the sense of spooky uniformity, about 80 per cent of these Chevrolets are white.

Upon independence, the Uzbek authorities continued to treat the car industry as part of the planned economy. Punitively high tariffs – 100 per cent of the value of the car – were slapped on any foreign car imports, forcing people to buy domestically.[1] That only left the problem of creating a car industry. Fortunately, there was one company willing to move into the Uzbek market, South Korean conglomerate Daewoo. In the 1990s the company was the largest investor in the country, providing not only cars but telecommunications equipment, as well as buying a portion of Uzbekistan's lucrative cotton crop.

Daewoo signed its first agreement with Uzbekistan in 1992, and by 1995 had already set up a manufacturing plant in the country. In 2001 Daewoo was acquired by General Motors, who saw little wrong with the cosy deal they had inherited and continued to produce around 200,000 cars a year for the Uzbek market under their Chevrolet branding.

I rendezvous with Madina at Oybek metro station. Madina was formerly a doctor, but a few years back she spent a semester in Saint Petersburg while retraining to become a psychologist. This is where she met Leo, who has put us in touch. She bounces over in a short black dress and gives me a warm hug.

We head for a cosy place called Coffee Nation, which Madina informs me is run by a pair of recently arrived Belarusian immigrants. I'm reluctant to have a second morning coffee, I didn't sleep much on the train so was lured in by Uzbekistan's biggest coffee chain, Bon!, upon arrival. It turned out to be more *comme ci, comme ça*, but shook me out of my slumber nonetheless. Besides, I've been looking forward to trying some Tashkent tea, which is famous across the former Soviet space. The recipe is generally black tea with lemon, mint and honey. The pretty Belarusian waitress at Coffee Nation serves it enthusiastically. Madina purses her lips.

'Generally, you won't find Tashkent tea on the menu in Uzbekistan. Here we just call it tea, or *choi*, and it's only sugary in the touristy places . . . and in other former Soviet countries,' she adds, eyeing the waitress irritably. 'If you have it in a real *chaikhana*, or tea house, you'll just have it black, with perhaps a little lemon on the side.'

'You brought us to Coffee Nation,' I point out, feeling a curious desire to come to the defence of the sultry waitress, who has since drifted to beguile another table of customers. 'Why not show me a *chaikhana* if you want it done properly?'

'Women don't usually go to tea houses,' Madina says shortly. 'They tend to be male-only places.'

This shuts me up. Blokey *chaikhanas* had been a characteristic of Azerbaijan too.

'It's different in the home,' Madina continues. 'There it's usually the woman's job to serve the tea. When you pour it into the guest's cup, you should only pour a small amount. This is to make sure the tea stays warm, but also to show that the host is attentive, as it's a pain to be constantly topping up someone's tea. This way it shows our respect for the guest.'

We go for a walk, cutting through the busy traffic on crossings. Construction is going on all around us, but we soon emerge into a quieter area.

'This is Yakub Kolas Street,' says Madina, lowering her voice slightly. 'The houses here are old but they're very prestigious. Lots of artists and writers lived here in the Soviet period. You can see the trees, and how peaceful it is – even in the centre of the city. These days the nouveau riche want to move here, so now there's this odd mix of very wealthy people as well as poor old babushkas who want to hold on to their houses. You see that school over there . . .' She points to a building behind high walls, the words *110-Maktab* are written on the sign over the ornate gates. 'It means School-110. It's a state school, but somehow only people with the richest parents seem to be able to get their children a place there. In the mornings, I sometimes run around here, and you can see all the expensive cars parked outside. Funnily enough, none of them are Chevrolets . . .'

We pass some upscale restaurants and a bakery. I'm beginning to get confused by the written language. The school sign had been in Latin script, but the bakery's is in Cyrillic.

'In the past everyone studied at school using the Cyrillic script, but we switched to Latin in the mid-nineties,' Madina explains. 'The idea was to make Uzbekistan feel more accessible to the rest of the world, but adapting to the change has been very difficult for the older generation. They keep pushing back the deadline for the official switch to Latin because of the amount of trouble it's caused.'

'We have a similar thing in Britain,' I tell her. 'Half the population still uses pounds and ounces; the other uses grams and kilograms.'

'What are pounds and ounces?'

I spend the length of Yakub Kolas Street attempting to explain, but have given it up as a bad job by the time we reach Amir Timur Square.

'What about Russian?' I ask instead. 'People seem to speak it quite well here . . .'

'It's very common in the centre of Tashkent, yes. It's still the main interethnic language and we have many nationalities here; for example, the Korean population here will speak Russian. And it's also the language among big businesses.'

Tashkent reminds me a lot of Almaty: the Soviet centre slowly being invaded by high-rise glass towers, the Russified but patriotic middle class, the native-speaking recent arrivals from the provinces and the epic TV tower watching over it all. These parallels felt even more striking because, back in Almaty, I had befriended Zuliya, an Uzbek who had grown up in Kazakhstan. She had shuddered at the conservatism and backwardness of their ancestral homeland.

'The word for an Uzbek daughter-in-law is *kelin*. It's the expectation that when an Uzbek woman marries, she does so into her husband's family. Before long, she comes under the thumb of her mother-in-law,' Zuliya told me, saying that she could never see herself with an Uzbek man for this reason. 'Whenever I go to visit my own family it's bad enough. They basically expect me to become a domestic servant – cleaning windows, cooking, looking after my younger siblings. What sort of life is that?'

I tell Madina about Zuliya's impression of Uzbek culture, and my confusion as Tashkent, superficially at least, doesn't seem that conservative. Here I was being shown around the city by a multilingual doctor whose dress ended high above the knee.

'It's only the centre of Tashkent that looks like this,' says Madina darkly. 'If you go further out, the attitudes change completely. I'm originally from Samarkand, which is much more traditional. Women are expected to dress differently there. It's even worse in the villages. So your friend is right, Uzbekistan isn't quite as "progressive", let's say, as Almaty. It's quite unusual to meet someone like me – thirty years old, unmarried, educated and with her own small business. Having said that, twenty years ago this situation would have been almost impossible, and now there are several of my friends who are in the same position. So perhaps things are changing.'

'Do you think women in Uzbekistan were better off under the Soviets?'

'Well, Soviet rule had its own problems. There was no economic freedom – for anyone. Without that, how was a woman meant to pursue her independence? But I guess if you wanted to find something even more totalitarian than communism, it would probably be Islam,' she laughs.

Until this point, I've avoided saying the 'I' word, hiding behind euphemisms like 'tradition' and 'culture', but we can't reasonably go much further without discussing it. Islam permeates life in Uzbekistan to a greater extent than anywhere we have been thus far. I'm also visiting at a time when Afghanistan, which lies on its southern border, has just been taken over by the Taleban.

'Does Islam worry you?'

'I think the type of Islam that the Taleban follow would worry any free-thinking person. It has quite a strong influence in the city as well, even in the supposedly "Russified" areas. When I was teaching medicine at the university here, religion would often become a problem. There was one student, with one of those religious beards – you know the one with no moustache, just a straggly mess hanging off the bottom of his face? I told him to shave it, not because of Islamophobia or for aesthetic reasons, but because of hygiene! We have strict standards in the medical profession about facial hair, and hair in general. This isn't about religion; I wouldn't have let him come in with a ponytail either!'

'How did he react?'

'You could tell he wasn't used to being told what to do by a woman, so he stared at me insolently for a second or two, but when he came in the next day he hadn't shaved it *all* off, but it was neater at least. I thought perhaps I'd been harsh on him, but it turned out that he'd only shaved because he wanted something from me. After the lesson he came up to me and said that he had Friday prayers later that week, so would I give him permission to miss the class? Obviously, I said no. He immediately got angry and started threatening me – "I will report this! This is a Muslim country; I have a right to pray!" It was true, he did have that right, but I explained to him that this was not a matter of constitutional rights, he can go and pray any time he wants, but the university also has its own rules, and these include turning up to class! This was a medical university after all – would he leave midway through an operation to go and do his prayers?'

'What did he say?'

'Again, he didn't like being told this by a woman, so I had to send him to another member of the faculty who said exactly the same thing. It's a shame, but I suppose that's the way the country is going.'

On what now roughly corresponds to the territory of Uzbekistan were once the khanates of Khiva and Kokand and the Emirate of Bukhara. When these states were independent they adhered to a strict form of Sharia law. Even as tsarist protectorates these lands stuck closely to the tenets of Islam, and it was only after the October Revolution in 1917, followed by a brutal course in modernisation under Stalin, that things began to change. Women were unveiled and sent into the fields to work; the Arabic script that had been employed for centuries was abolished; mosques were shut down, madrasas closed, and religious leaders and intellectuals persecuted, arrested or shot.

But even after seventy years of socialism, Islam did not entirely disappear. Back in Bishkek, Professor Chotaeva told me how her elderly Uzbek neighbours had continued to stick to the old ways. 'When I was a child, we had some Uzbek family friends. When we came as school kids to their house, we would always see their grandfather praying in his room. We would try to be silent, just so as not to disturb him. Islam was still there, it just had to be hidden from the authorities.' The Bolsheviks may have dreamed of remoulding the various peoples of the USSR into a single, uniform *Homo Sovieticus*, but we ought to be wary of overestimating their success.

I want to see more of the Islamic Tashkent that Madina spoke about. Fortunately, I have a man for the job. Saif was in my hostel room during the Baku Grand Prix. He did his prayers five times a day in the dormitory as the other travellers looked on, a little baffled by his unselfconscious piety. Still, he was a lovely chap and keen to help in my project, telling me to get in touch if ever I made it this far.

I'm instructed to meet him at the entrance to Hazrati Imam Mosque, a short metro ride north-west of the city centre. Tashkent's metro stations are as magnificent as anything I've seen since Moscow, and I get off every couple of stops just to have a look around. Particularly impressive are Kosmonavtlar (Cosmonauts) and Ming Orik (Thousand Apricots) stations. The first is appropriately themed like a space station, whereas the latter has an imposing array of frosted-marble walls and chandeliered ceilings that belie its rather charming name.*

My stop is just a couple of miles from the centre, but beyond the barriers of the metro is a very different Uzbekistan. The tree-lined boulevards are no more; the roads are dusty and the people enigmatic. Women wear bright, shapeless dresses; many are veiled, shifting wraith-like through the gathering dusk. Men are bearded, wearing flowing robes and a traditional Uzbek skullcap, the *doppi*. I make out a minaret in the distance and follow the mass of narrow, twisting lanes towards it as the sky begins to pale.

I quickly lose my bearings in the lean alleys and am only spared the embarrassment of calling Saif when I hear the call to prayer, whose magnetism corrects my wayward course. Five minutes later, the alley widens to reveal an open square. On the far side, the mosque's turquoise domes are set spectacularly against a western sunset. Worshippers stream through the great yellow-brick archway, beneath abstract art in labyrinthine shapes on glazed cobalt tiles. All around the beguiling drone of the *muezzin* continues.

'*As-salamu alaykum*, brother,' smiles Saif, spotting me. 'Is this your first time at Hazrati Imam? We have the world's oldest Quran inside!'

I read this scrap of information while travelling here on the metro; unfortunately, it's not true.† Still, the Uthman Quran has an interesting backstory. It lay in Samarkand for centuries until it was filched by the Russian army and put on display in the Imperial Library in Saint Petersburg. Later, in an example of some of the marvellous contradictions of Soviet rule, it was returned as a gift by the atheist Lenin to the Muslims of the Russian Empire in 1924 – an attempt to curry some favour before the assault on the opiate of the masses began in earnest. He initially chose to bestow his gift upon the city of Ufa in the Russian SFSR, but eventually bowed to repeated appeals to have it moved to Tashkent.

---

* Time travellers will also appreciate the metro carriages. The teal-blue 81-714 model, built in the Leningrad Wagon-making Factory in 1989, can still be seen all across the former Soviet Union, from Baku to Kyiv.
† The Uthman Quran, as it's called, is indeed very venerable, but the oldest Quran currently resides in Birmingham, of all places.

We stand in silence for a while, listening to the haunting drone of the call to prayer.

'You know it was banned under the previous government?' says Saif quietly.

'Why?'

He chooses his words carefully. 'There are some people who think we should not show our religion too openly.'

'It seems to be pretty open here.' I gesture towards the long-bearded laggards rushing to join the evening congregation.

'Here, it can be controlled; it is not a threat on the edge of the city. We will not go inside, if you don't mind?' he adds. 'You might attract attention.'

Across Russia and Central Asia, and especially in Uzbekistan, the 'threat' of Islamism is often used as an excuse for wider crackdowns. A series of car bombings took place in Tashkent in 1999, for which the Islamic Movement of Uzbekistan, a terrorist group, was blamed. The government's reprisals saw the arrest of over 5,000 people, many of whom were innocent worshippers.[2]

In another case in the eastern city of Andijan in 2005, the charge of 'Islamic extremism' was used to justify the arrest of twenty-three local businessmen. Many suspected that the town's officials were using the charges as a pretext to seize their businesses, leading to widespread protests. When these turned violent, the government responded by showering the demonstrators with bullets. The massacre has never been fully investigated; the government has the official death toll at 187, but some estimates are an order of magnitude higher.[3]

'Do you think the government is right to try to shackle Islam?' I ask Saif.

'Brother, you have to remember that the modern state is a game; it is uninterested in equality and justice. Politicians learn how to abuse the word that they call "law"; they steer it to the left and right for their own benefit. Islam seeks to return to a system where the word "law" itself is a constant and immutable. The law should be the shield of the people. The law should not be invented for the benefit of individuals. That's why

Islam should stand above the state so that everyone obeys the law equally, regardless of social status. In an Islamic society, laws exist on the basis of Islam and not laws invented by man. Politicians should not oppose it with their invented system.'

He's speaking almost robotically. I decide not to push any further. Saif's mood has become rather dour, so I'm pleased that he has invited Eldon, a friend of his, to dinner with us at Besh Qozon, a favourite haunt of locals.

'*Besh qozon* means "five cauldrons",' Saif informs me. 'This restaurant is famous for *plov*, our country's most famous dish.'

I admit that *plov* might not sound particularly appetising. Something about the word has a nasty, onomatopoeic quality. But to dismiss it on those grounds would see you miss out. *Plov* is just another way of spelling pilaf or pilau – i.e. rice cooked in stock and spices. The three staple ingredients are rice, lamb and carrots; all these are simmered together in oil and sheep's fat inside a massive iron cauldron called a *qozon*. Think of it as an Uzbek paella. There are five of these *qozons* on the go, each presided over by a cook holding a spatula as large as a spade.

'Each region has its own traditional *plov*,' Saif tells me as we watch one of the cooks tipping gallons of oil into the bubbling *qozon*. 'Samarkand *plov* is a favourite for a lot of people, it's a little healthier. But tonight, because you are a guest, brother, we will have wedding *plov*, which we reserve for special occasions.'

Eldon arrives just after the bread is served. He's more genial than the serious Saif. He owns a chain of mobile phone repair shops and has an entrepreneur's glint in his eye. As the food is delivered, both Saif and Eldon close their eyes and hold their hands out in front of them as though in prayer; they mutter something before wiping their hands over their face. They laugh as they open their eyes to find me staring at them.

'You don't do this in England?'

I tell them how at primary school we used to chant 'For what we are about to receive, may the lord make us truly grateful, amen'. 'But I haven't done that since I was about eleven,' I add, sheepishly.

'Food should be respected,' says Eldon. 'Bread above all else, it must always face the right way up. It's immensely rude to turn it upside down.'

I hadn't been told of either of these traditions by Madina.

'What about the straws?' I ask.

'Straws?'

'Come on, you must have noticed!'

It's a phenomenon I've seen all over Central Asia. Every time a woman orders a beer, it arrives, without fail, with a straw. When I once made the mistake of pulling one of these straw-toting pints towards me the waiter rushed to stop me, as though one sip would see me overdose on oestrogen.

'Why do women get given a straw in their beer?' I ask them.

Saif shifts uncomfortably.

'Sorry, I guess you don't drink.'

'No.'

'What about you Eldon?'

'I drink, sure.' He pauses, avoiding my eyes.

'Well?!' I ask, growing impatient.

He shrugs. 'Isn't it obvious? No one wants to see a woman tipping beer down her throat. It's disgusting.'

Samarkand

There is more to Uzbek transport than Chevrolets and Soviet metros, and the journey to Samarkand represents the best of it. This is the first and only time on the trip where I'll be able to travel by high-speed train, the Afrosiyob, which covers the 200 miles or so from Tashkent to Samarkand in just two hours. Considering my last train took four hours to cross the Kazakhstan-Uzbekistan border, this is light speed.

As we begin to motor, first through Tashkent's suburbs, then open countryside, I'm reminded strongly of the wealth inequality I saw in Azerbaijan. We VIPs, settled in our comfy, reclining chairs, gaze upon passing cotton fields, where rows of workers load their harvest onto carts pulled by donkeys. At level crossings there are tailbacks that stretch for half a mile. The old Soviet belief that the countryside only exists to service the urban workers still seems to hold true. The farmers can wait while the metropolitans whizz by.

All too soon, we arrive in Samarkand. It's a name, like Babylon or Timbuktu, that has a hold on our collective imagination, promising some vague oriental splendour. Every Central Asian despot worth his salt has had a crack at this ancient jewel, from Alexander the Great to Genghis Khan. Russian influence arrived comparatively recently: General von Kaufmann took the city in the name of Tsar Alexander II in 1868, almost 2,200 years after it had been conquered by his master's Macedonian namesake. But the city owes much of its splendour to another warlord, who made Samarkand his capital in the fourteenth century: it was from here that Timur set out to bend the earth to his will.

You might not have heard of Timur, a name that means 'iron' in Uzbek. He took an arrow to the leg when he was a young man, which led him to walk with a limp for the rest of his life. Those far enough away from Samarkand to escape his wrath dubbed him Timur the Lame, which became Tamerlane in the West. For those in his path, the Iron Cripple wasn't so funny. He had a habit of making towers of his enemies' skulls each time he conquered a city. When he sacked Delhi in 1398, massacring up to 100,000 people in the process, these skullscrapers reached quite a height. His expeditions even went as far as Georgia and Armenia, 1,000 miles to the west, where he dragged tens of thousands into slavery. According to higher-end estimates, Timur's campaigns may have wiped out 5 per cent of the world's population. His empire stretched from India to Syria and the wealth from these conquests was lavished on his capital, Samarkand, which became one of the wonders of the Middle Ages.

The city's main draw is the Registan, a central square that is home to three medieval madrasas, squaring off like peacocks. The oldest was built almost six centuries ago and has undergone some heavy restoration starting in the Soviet period. But even in the Victorian age it was deemed a marvel. British statesman George Curzon came here in 1888 and described it as the 'noblest public square in the world'.[4] As a result of this fame and beauty, for the first time in Central Asia, I'm not the only foreigner in the city. In fact, it's thronged with visitors. Coachloads of middle-aged Europeans potter around in the wake of guides, each of whom is equipped with a loudspeaker. The audio assault makes taking in the peaceful majesty of the first madrasa rather difficult. There is a quaint quad, with trees that have been carefully positioned to throw dappled light on the enchanting mosaicked walls.

'This was the Madrasa of Mirzo Ulugh Beg,' one Uzbek guide is saying in passable Spanish. 'Built between 1417 and 1421, he was the grandson of Timur and a great philosopher and astronomer. Here everyone was permitted to learn, for free, provided they were between the ages of fifteen and forty-five – and male, of course.' The group of blonde Spanish women whom he is showing around do not seem particularly offended by such an exclusionary policy. Instead they've begun to try on the selection of naff hats and shawls for sale in one of the alcoves, giggling raucously. The guide begins speaking more loudly. 'The academic year in the madrasa ran from Libra to Aries, and the subjects taught were philosophy, logic, maths, astronomy, literature . . .' But he's wasting his time, the *españolas* have spotted the handbags. The guide takes his microphone off in disgust and starts to harangue the stallholder, whose eyes have lit up.

Seeking a bit of peace, I wander towards Gur-e-Amir (the Tomb of the King), Tamerlane's final resting place. There's an air of hushed excitement among those who have splashed out for a ticket.

At the heart of the stone mausoleum sits Timur's ornate marble sarcophagus, its sides alive with swirling calligraphy. It has a legendary story: on 19 June 1941 Soviet archaeologists opened the grave in order to analyse the remains. Local lore has it that there was a curse placed upon the tomb, punishing those who might disturb the rest of the Iron King. Three days later the largest offensive in human history began, as Nazi Germany invaded the Soviet Union. Uzbeks will tell you that it was only when the bones were returned to their rightful resting place and given a full Islamic burial in November 1942 that the Soviets began to turn the tide of the war.

Despite the mythology, the Soviets were never particularly enamoured with Timur – perhaps because he came close to conquering Moscow in 1395, or perhaps Stalin didn't like the competition – steel is, after all, a mere alloy of iron. Whatever the reason, the Soviets preferred to promote the achievements of Timur's intellectual grandson, Ulugh Beg, as well as the fifteenth-century poet Alisher Navoi. But in independent Uzbekistan that has all changed. Where Soviet monuments once stood, shrines to Timur have taken their place. Tashkent's Revolution Square became Amir Timur Square, and at its centre Karl Marx was shunted aside to make way for a resplendent horseback statue of the old warlord. Meanwhile, in Uzbek schools he is a staple of the curriculum.

'Everything is about Timur,' Madina told me. 'We learn about all his battles, about all the laws he made, who he defeated, some of his quotes.'

'Do you not learn about any of the bad stuff?'

Timur's name is mud in places like Iran and India – neither Delhi nor Isfahan recovered from the ravages of the Timurids for decades.

'I guess it's a bit like any leader,' shrugged Madina. 'A bit like Putin . . . people respect him because he is strong.'

I can understand this: we've already looked at the pride that Stalin inspires in half of Georgia. Viewed from six centuries' distance, I suppose even 100-foot-high skull towers can be viewed with a little sangfroid. After all, there are Rues Bonaparte across France, busts of Caesar in Rome, and outside the British Houses of Parliament a statue of Richard I, probably the worst king in English history, who bankrupted the country to go on a campaign of slaughter in Palestine. My favourite Mongol adage comes back to me once more: a bloodthirsty murdering bastard, but *our* bloodthirsty murdering bastard.

Still, it's nice to finally be in a country with a sense of history, you might be thinking. *At least the Uzbeks aren't building craven monuments to last week's tinpot dictator*. Unfortunately, you'd be wrong. On a lofty mound away from the touristy bustle of the Registan, another marble mausoleum overlooks the city. The burning sun illuminates the golden letters on the tomb, inscribed upon it in Uzbek and in English:

> This is a sacred and eternal place where the first president of the Republic of Uzbekistan, the Great Statesman and Politician, The Respectable and Honorable son of Uzbek people, Islam Karimov, rests.

I begin taking pictures, but a guard quickly emerges, ordering me to desist. Petulantly I point to a woman who, not five feet away, is also holding her phone up to the Great Leader's resting place. 'How come she's allowed to?'

'I'm doing a video call!' she snaps at me, before turning and continuing to whisper in reverential tones in front of the tomb. It was no problem to be happy-snappy in Timur's mausoleum thirty minutes ago. But it seems that this mausoleum is different. Islam Karimov's shadow still lies over the country he ruled for twenty-five years from independence until his death in 2016.

Karimov is another Samarkand local. His childhood is shrouded in mystery; some rumours say that his mother is Tajik, while others claim he spent much of his youth in and out of orphanages. In fact, two out of the fifteen original leaders of the former Soviet republics grew up in orphanages, the other being Saparmurat Niyazov of Turkmenistan, who we will come to later. You might think that this is a glowing reflection of Soviet social mobility – Stalin the cobbler's son, Khrushchev the farmhand, and two Central Asian orphans making it to the highest ranks. It's hard to see this happening in Western Europe or the USA. However, there are a couple of caveats. Firstly, *a lot* of Soviet kids grew up in orphanages – an inevitable consequence of years of civil war, purges, collectivisation, famine and forced resettlement, followed by a Nazi invasion that in itself claimed 20 million lives. Second, these orphanages were in many ways ideal for the authorities: they allowed for the creation of perfect Soviet citizens. Unfettered by parental sentimentality, religious, cultural or linguistic traditions, orphans would grow up living and breathing the state ideology, Marxist-Leninism, and the state language, Russian. Karimov learned the system and what was needed to survive and thrive. His engineering and economics background saw him rise up the ranks of the State Planning Committee (GOSPLAN), before a series of purges got him fast-tracked into the republic's top job.

Karimov's schooling in the planned economy is important in the development of independent Uzbekistan. It's in this context that the homogenous car industry begins to make sense. He was determined that his new state would not be reliant on anyone.

'Karimov was a very cruel authoritarian, but he was the only leader in the post-Soviet area who could say "Fuck you" to Mister Putin,' Dosym Satpayev had told me. He sought to maintain Uzbekistan's ability to produce its own goods. He also wanted something that he could sell to the rest of the world to keep money flowing into the state coffers. This is the reason behind another of the more unique aspects of Uzbek society, the reason, in fact, that I first heard of the country.

Back in 2011 I visited the International Slavery Museum in Liverpool. After a reasonably harrowing exhibition on nineteenth-century cotton-farming in the USA, the museum had a small display on modern slavery. Here the unlikely name of Uzbekistan came up, due to the millions of people who were being pressed into service every autumn to harvest the same white gold that caused so much misery in the American South. This wasn't just the poor and those in rural areas: schoolchildren and teachers alike were taken out of the classroom, doctors left hospitals, all to ensure that the cotton quotas were hit.

This wasn't so much Karimov's policy as a hangover from the Soviet period, when vast swathes of land were designated as cotton-picking zones, displacing other types of agriculture. Cotton is a thirsty crop, so rivers were diverted to provide sufficient moisture. Cotton became part of the identity of Uzbekistan to such an extent that the country's most successful football team, Pakhtakor, literally translates as Cotton Picker FC. In harvest season, all that can be seen along either bank of the Amu River are flat fields, speckled with fluffy white balls being rolled into huge bails. The export of cotton, whether in the form of the raw material or finished goods like T-shirts, has historically accounted for around 10 per cent of Uzbekistan's total exports, a vital source of revenue for an otherwise impoverished country.[5]

I asked Madina back in Tashkent if she had ever been forced to pick cotton.

'Obviously,' she said. 'Everyone did. Well, maybe not in Tashkent, they didn't want to upset the people in the capital, but the rest of the country would all do it. Every September, for six weeks, we were taken out of university.'

'Even from medical school?'

'Even from medical school, to go and work in the fields. It wasn't so bad actually. At first it was hard, I remember the first day I was told that I needed to harvest sixty kilos – can you imagine? That's more than my bodyweight! After about an hour I was in tears as I'd only harvested two kilos and the farm manager was shouting at me and my friends to hurry up. By the end of the day, I only managed to collect twenty-five kilos, and that was literally going as fast as I could. I was tired, aching everywhere, sunburned . . . Most of us got shouted at and threatened with bad marks at the university if we didn't improve.'

'But you said it wasn't so bad in the end?'

'Ah well,' she grinned, 'once you discovered how it really works, it was OK. The local villagers were so good at picking it that they easily exceeded their quota every day. Some of them would think nothing of picking a hundred and twenty, maybe even a hundred and fifty kilos. So once they had picked their quota, we would pay them to pick ours as well.'

'But you still had to be there, you couldn't go back home?'

'No,' her smile widens. 'And most of us didn't want to either. Of course, some people got homesick, but most of us . . . you have to understand that our university experience is not like yours where you all move somewhere else to study. We continue to live at home when we're at university, with generally quite conservative Muslim parents. This period that we got to spend away from our parents, with all our course mates . . . Let's just say there was quite a lot of romance during cotton season. Quite a few friends' marriages began there!'

Madina's story is far from unique. I ask most people about their cotton-picking experience – of course, many hated it, seeing it as demeaning and pointless, but nostalgic grins drifted across the faces of others. One old gentleman told me that it was his favourite time of year as a child. 'We got to be in the fields, the weather wasn't too warm, we skipped classes, and our friends were there. Plus the teachers had to pick along with us!' he laughed.

Still, I suppose a few positive anecdotes are a flimsy defence of modern slavery. The International Labour Organization took a similar view, and along with the Cotton Campaign, a human rights and advocacy group, worked with major brands from around the world to force the government to change its labour practices. Their big concern was child labour, and advocacy on this issue led to over 300 brands joining a global boycott of Uzbek cotton.

'Slowly, we noticed a change in how the government was treating the issue,' Cotton Campaign spokesperson Raluca Dumitrescu told me in a telephone interview. 'When Nike, Burberry, Adidas stop buying your product, the government takes notice, right?'

Initially, the government stopped sending children into the fields, replacing them with adult labour instead. But in September 2016 a heart attack brought Islam Karimov's twenty-five-year rule to an end. Under his successor, Shavkat Mirziyoyev, Uzbekistan has slowly begun to open up: visa-free travel was introduced for many tourists; the state-controlled cotton sector was privatised, and the government began to ensure that everyone was paid for their work. In 2021 the International Labour Organization officially announced that there was no longer any state-imposed forced labour in the Uzbek cotton harvest. This allowed the Cotton Campaign to drop their boycott of Uzbek cotton, giving the green light for brands to invest here again.

The disappearance of forced labour in Uzbekistan was meant to herald a break from the coercive practices of the past. But it takes more than a stroke of a pen to end a way of life that had remained unaltered for decades. Dumitrescu tells me that the way some private companies treat their workers is just as exploitative. Switching to new crops is expensive, and for many farmers the only option is to keep toiling in the same cotton fields.

Meanwhile, the strain of feeding these vast fields has taken its toll on the region's ecology. Central Asia's two great waterways, the Amu Darya and the Syr Darya, see their levels diminish every year. Rising in the mountains and flowing west across desert and steppe, these rivers once fed the Aral Sea, the world's fourth-largest lake, whose fertile shores supported thriving fishing towns that sent their catch across the USSR. But as their waters were siphoned off to irrigate endless cotton fields, the lake was choked, shrivelling to a fraction of its former size by 1991. Rusting ships now lie stranded hundreds of miles from its ever-shrinking remnants. Today, relentless overuse of these rivers, compounded by rising temperatures induced by climate change, threatens the water security of the entire region.

But does this tell us more about independent Uzbekistan or about the disasters of Soviet policy? You might ask the same question about the rise of Islam. Nature abhors a vacuum, and as in Georgia, where we saw the revival of Christianity, perhaps the strictures of Soviet power have ushered in an Islamic reaction here and across Central Asia.

This is a young country, with more than half its people under thirty, and its future could tip in several directions. Karimov's shadow still lingers; in many ways the USSR's collapse was simply suspended here, its authoritarian habits and state planning carried on under a new flag. Mirziyoyev is working to change that narrative, having opened the economy, eased censorship and courted foreign investors. Tashkent and the tourist towns of the Silk Road have boomed.

But there are risks. The new post-Soviet generation of restless, optimistic Uzbeks has high expectations. Political sclerosis or economic disappointment might trigger disillusion, pushing people into the arms of Islamist movements, especially in the more conservative Ferghana Valley.

And looming above it all is the question of water, for which the Aral Sea has become a parable in sand. By the shores of that vanished sea, in this land of white Chevrolets, you can indeed drive a Chevy to the levy – and there is no doubt that the levy will be dry.

8

TAJIKISTAN
THE REPUBLIC OF EMIGRATION

The train is very old. The sagging seats and the rugs on the floor are the same shade of faded burgundy. A tired, stained curtain clings on to the rail above. The bathroom at the end of the carriage reeks of cigarettes. I decide to do my ablutions now – it will smell worse tomorrow morning.

In the four-bed compartment, I have a group of Uzbeks for company; they're on their way back from Tashkent to a town called Qarshi. I will be travelling further, staying on board until we pull into Tajikistan's capital, Dushanbe, tomorrow morning. They're a merry bunch, but after explaining for the umpteenth time that no, I do not have children; yes, their daughters look very pretty in the pictures they show me; and no, I do not wish to marry them, I stick my headphones on and lie back, figuring this might be a good night to get some kip. My companions spoil this plan by ordering some tea and plonking the pot on the table about six inches from my head. It slides ominously towards me as we brake.

Unable to shake the thought of waking up with a scalding face, I decide to go and investigate the restaurant car. I get hold of two litres of beer in a plastic bottle, sit in the otherwise deserted carriage and stick on the recording of an interview I'd done back in Almaty with Marius Fossum, the head of the Central Asian branch of the Norwegian Helsinki Committee, a human rights organisation. Marius had warned me that Tajikistan was much more repressive than the three Central Asian countries I'd visited so far.

'Kazakhstan differs from somewhere like Tajikistan,' says his tinny voice in my ears. 'The state is much, much stronger in Kazakhstan and the authorities have more self-confidence. When the authorities imprison dissidents in Kazakhstan, they lock them up on charges that, at least in the eyes of the state, are related to what they've done wrong – so things like "sowing discord", which might get you put away for five years. Their Tajik counterparts, on the other hand, will just strike you with "extremism" charges and lock you up for twenty years or so.'

'Is there any chance of things improving in Tajikistan? Isn't there meant to be a succession at some point?' comes my voice. The ageing President Emomali Rahmon was born in October 1952, just two days before Vladimir Putin.

'There will have to be a succession because you can only live for so long,' Marius agrees. 'Everything points to Rahmon grooming his son to take over.' But unfortunately, he continues, there is little reason to believe that anything will improve. As in Azerbaijan, a weaker son taking over will have to be even more ruthless to consolidate power, and the regime is already extremely paranoid, arresting people just for studying in other Muslim countries, for speaking Arabic, or being doctors.

Tajikistan is a weak state still recovering from a debilitating civil war in the 1990s. Its economy is even more heavily dependent than Kyrgyzstan's on remittances from migrant labourers in Russia. Until recently, a large portion of its GDP was also derived from trafficking drugs from neighbouring Afghanistan.

'I'm not sure how the Taleban takeover has altered that,' Marius adds. 'But there are almost no prospects, and no safe way for people to vent their frustrations. They've been going after people for blog posts, or imprisoning people for liking posts on social media. It's really dangerous. And if you express dissent, they crack down brutally. Torture has become routine . . . anything from an iron on your body or just basic beatings, to a lot worse. They get creative pretty quickly. We were told about something euphemistically called *Petrovich*, which was basically a car battery.'

'Car battery?'

'And cables.'

'Jeez.'

When I return to the compartment, the Uzbeks have left. We must have passed Qarshi already. It's a shame, as I wouldn't have minded their company. Instead, I drift off to sleep, my worries about scalding tea replaced by dreams of high-voltage cables.

The next morning, after a breezy Uzbek customs check, which fortunately does not involve Poirot searching inside my washbag, the train enters Tajikistan. I immediately see what Marius means about the economy. People in the fields look desperately poor; there are mounds of garbage piled up in the village roads; the buildings are baked dry by the sun. You can tell a country doesn't get much attention when kids start chasing the train.

The waiting hall at Dushanbe station has been turned into a makeshift customs office. When a state is this visibly weak and disorganised, it makes you consider what a country is from first principles. There is nothing giving this ramshackle customs-hut any authority apart from people's tacit acceptance. It resembles little more than a village checkpoint. We tend to see states as natural, tangible places with defined histories and iron-clad boundaries, inviolable except with the express permission of the authorities. Tajikistan has a couple of fences strung around it that any mug could hop over. Indeed, given that a sizeable chunk of its economy comes from smuggling Afghan heroin, it seems many do.

A chap in military garb pulls me out of the queue and ushers me into a small cubicle; he asks if I need help filling out the forms, which are written in Tajik and English. He points to the place where it says SURNAME and explains in broken English that I need to write my surname. He points to the place where it says PASSPORT NUMBER and tells me that this is where I need to write my passport number. I quickly get the gist, but the guard seems to think that his help has been indispensable and demands $50. I laugh in his face. Not today sunshine. I'm calculating that this kid is unlikely to whip out the car battery over my refusal to pay his bogus tithe.

'Maybe five dollars?' he asks, pleadingly.

I keep my hand in my pocket, but am generous enough to point him in the direction of a couple of American accents I'd made out through the din.

Dushanbe

The Tajik capital is so remote that it wasn't until 1960 that it lost its former name of Stalinabad, a full seven years after the demise of the General Secretary, and once again became Dushanbe. Back in 1921, Dushanbe was a village of only around 3,000 inhabitants. Its name means Monday, which is presumed to be related to a weekly market that took place here on that day. There were few indications that this spot had the makings of a national capital. But, Stalin being Stalin, when he decreed that a city would be built here, a city it became. Until the railway arrived in 1929, entire streets' worth of materials and libraries' worth of books were hauled here from Uzbekistan on the back of camels. But once the sleepers were in place, it began to grow rapidly.

I walk across the bustling square facing the station and through the rather grandly named Sadbarg Trade Center, which consists of a couple of second-hand electronics stores, a pharmacy and a clothes emporium. Indeed, the first striking thing about Dushanbe is people's clothing: while women are garbed in the same brightly coloured, amorphous dresses as in Samarkand, almost all men are uniformed in slim-fitting suits and skinny ties, giving them a strong resemblance to the Tokyo salaryman. From Sadbarg I make my way to Rudaki Avenue, the city's main thoroughfare and the easiest way of orientating oneself in Dushanbe. It's a kind of Tajik Las Ramblas, with a pedestrianised avenue between the lanes of traffic where one can walk under the dappled shadows of the chinar trees. The bottom end of Rudaki takes us through the older part of town, with low, colonial-style buildings painted in a pinkish hue.

Fixed to the front of many of these buildings is the portrait of President Emomali Rahmon. No two portraits of Rahmon are quite the same: some have him swanning through cornfields, others have him interposed over the national flag, his hand raised in an Alan Shearer celebration. Ever present, however, are his massive, bushy eyebrows, which make him look like another Gallagher brother.

Unfortunately, this is far from the only gaudy element to the city. After passing the opera house and the country's only KFC, the buildings along

Rudaki start to take on an air of self-importance. Each ministry is increasingly grand and pompous; the covering foliage thins, and we enter New Dushanbe, full of the kind of dystopian monuments that I saw enough of in Kazakhstan. These include Central Asia's largest library, a marble edifice in the shape of a book; an enormous triumphal arch, also of white marble; and the world's tallest flagpole: a 541-foot-high mast that was completed in 2011 and was specifically designed to be ten feet taller than the one erected in Baku the previous year. Sadly, Dushanbe didn't hold this prestigious record for long – the Saudis built an even bigger one in Jeddah in 2014.

Eeriest of all is Maydoni Istiklol, or Independence Square. I'm sure some of you have played that game where you see how many steps you can walk with your eyes closed. I think the maximum I'd manage in London would be about ten, and even then I'd get nervous – you never know when some wally on an e-scooter is going to whizz out of nowhere. But alone on this colossal maidan I manage to make it to fifty. If Tajikistan is looking to set any more world records, this is the place to do it.

More of these grandiose monuments are evidently in the pipeline. The northern stretches of Rudaki are a building site, with cut-and-paste neo-Stalinist blocks sprouting up. Chinese companies loudly proclaim their handiwork: large characters bearing a series of insipid abstract nouns beam down on the uncomprehending populace: UNITY; STRUGGLE; PRAGMATISM; INNOVATION.

That evening, I go to a restaurant called Toqi Teahouse to meet Farangis, an old university friend, along with her husband Komron. We order some barbecued lamb ribs as well as a dish called *kurutob*.

'It's our national dish,' Farangis tells me. 'It's kind of like a bread salad.' I feel this description doesn't do it justice; I can't see many dinner guests getting lured in by the prospect of 'bread salad'.*

'What are the ingredients?' I ask. 'Apart from bread . . .'

'Well, the word comes from *kurut*, which are like these hard balls of cheese which . . .'

'I know all about *kurut*,' I stop her. 'It's all I ate in Kazakhstan.'

---

* Although tell them you're doing *panzanella* and watch how they change their attitude.

She waves a dismissive hand. 'The Kazakhs don't know what they're doing; they usually eat them whole! No – you need to dilute the *kurut* in water and then mix it with tomatoes, cucumber, fried onions, whatever . . . It's a traditional highlander's dish – the idea is that you make it with whatever ingredients you have available. And then you add the bread.'

It all adds up to something rather marvellous – mushy and salty and cheesy but with the fresh tang of veg. I wouldn't mind being a highlander if this is what they eat. We get stuck into the food, which is traditionally meant to be shared, and chat about how they've been since the university days.

'I need your help,' I say. 'I have to give a talk to some students in the north next week, about studying abroad in England. How did you two get there? Were there scholarship options?'

'There are a few,' says Farangis doubtfully. 'I got mine through the British Foreign Office, called the Chevening Scholarship. There are only around five or six spots available for Tajikistan each year; it's quite competitive.'

In Tajikistan, a career-orientated woman is swimming against a deeply conservative current. Like in Samarkand, women in Dushanbe are dressed very modestly, but here the authorities are far more prescriptive. In 2018, the Ministry of Culture printed a 367-page book on what a 'good woman' should wear.[1] Tajik ladies must tread a narrow line: on the one hand, the regime's paranoia about Islamism has seen the hijab banned, while black, tight-fitting or transparent clothing is also discouraged. On top of this, there's the unspoken rule that her real place is in the home – raising children, tending to in-laws, keeping the family fed – and a woman who puts her career first risks being seen as selfish or unnatural.[2]

The conservatism also seems to stretch to drinking habits – my search for a bar earlier that evening had not been particularly fruitful. Even at the promisingly named Beer House people arrived and left in groups; no one sat at the bar for a natter. I had to remind myself once again that I was in the capital of a police state, where casual chats with strangers can often get you into trouble.

*

Over the next few days, I plod the streets of the capital in search of what makes Tajikistan tick. The first question you might ask is who exactly are the Tajiks? They will tell you that they are the original inhabitants of Central Asia, heirs to the Silk Road kingdoms of Sogdiana and Bactria, here long before the Turkic tribes swept out of the north. Conquered by the Arabs, they became Sunni Muslims, but continued to speak Persian. Indeed, across a swathe of land stretching from Iran (where it's called Farsi), through northern Afghanistan (Dari), to Tajikistan (Tajik), the peoples all speak a mutually intelligible language. The Tajik flag is basically an inverted Iranian flag, and Rudaki Avenue, which we walked down earlier, is named after one of Persian literature's most prominent poets.

I take a trip to the National Museum. I've been to several of these so far on the trip, but this one typifies the post-Soviet authoritarian way of presenting the past: a textbook study in dictatorship curation.

I pay two surcharges at the entrance – one for being a foreigner, and the other for the right to take photos. On each floor I'm greeted by a young female guide who is followed around by a couple of older colleagues. These minders keep a distance of around ten feet and pretend to be looking away whenever I glance at them. But they watch her beadily, lest she be tempted to do anything risqué like voicing an unscripted thought.

The information they do offer is of the safest, most nondescript kind, covering banalities such as the exact number of square kilometres in Tajikistan, or the layers of bauxite deposits from the Precambrian period. They do so in the same blank tone I always reserved for the Lord's Prayer at school. I'm chaperoned through an endless series of exhibits on the country's flora and fauna – my guide insists that this includes tigers, though none have been sighted since the 1970s. After forty-five minutes or so, we finally get to the humans. The authorities appear to have deemed events that happened over a millennium ago to be safe enough for study. Much is made of the various dynasties of ancient Persia, especially the Samanids, under whose rule the world was introduced to Rudaki's poetry and Avicenna's medicine. There are innumerable pots, pans and coins from across these dynasties, the guide keeping up a constant patter of trinket trivia, such as the dimensions of the pans or the differing ratios of silver and tin in the coins.

Unfortunately, as in museums across Central Asia, many of the prize artefacts are replicas, the originals now filling Western galleries. Most famous of these are the Oxus Treasures, a collection of 180 gold and silver bracelets made over 2,000 years ago in the Achaemenid Empire, which were discovered in Tajikistan around 1870. They have been residing safely in the British Museum for the past century or so, readily accessible to any Tajik who has the good fortune to be granted a British tourist visa, can afford the air fare, and has the iron will required to elbow their way past the hordes of Chinese tourists in Bloomsbury. The British Foreign Office, in what they clearly believed was a diplomatic master stroke, gifted replicas of these treasures to the Tajik government in 2013, proudly boasting: 'Visitors to the new Tajik National Museum will be able to admire these high-quality golden replicas just as many thousands of visitors from all over the world admire the originals in the British Museum.'[3]

I'll let you decide if that does anything other than rub salt in the wounds, but the fruits of this diplomacy were clearly limited. At the time of writing, citizens of Australia, Canada, the USA, France, Germany, Japan, Argentina and fifty-five other countries can visit Tajikistan without a visa. Britain is not among them.

Given the dearth of original Persian artefacts, you might imagine that the museum would have put more effort into its twentieth-century collection, but the past hundred years are summed up in rather laconic fashion. The 300,000 Tajiks who were sent to fight on Eastern European battlefields in the Second World War are given an exhibit or two, then there's a jump through time and we end up in the obligatory 'Gifts That Were Given to Our Great President' room. You could reach the end and be forgiven for thinking that Soviet rule and the civil war never happened.

The minders allow my guide to accompany me alone to the exit. 'What did you think of our museum?' she asks, her attitude suddenly far brighter.

'Very . . . illuminating,' I remark. I've seen too many Soviet museums to be surprised at the historical amnesia, but this marks a new low.

'This is the biggest museum in Central Asia,' she enthuses.

I glance out of the window, but the view is blocked by scaffolding and construction workers beavering away. 'Is it about to get even bigger?'

'No, but over there we are about to construct the largest theatre in Central Asia,' she says with pride. 'Across the road we are also constructing a new palace for the president. You know, when the Russian president came here, he said, "This city is like Moscow: everywhere is construction and everywhere Tajiks!"'

'Have you been to Moscow?' I ask her.

'I visited once. It was interesting, every time I took a taxi and saw the driver's name on the licence, I could see he was Tajik; it was the same in restaurants.'

'Did you speak to each other in Persian?'

'No, only in Russian. I think when we are in Russia, maybe we are ashamed of who we are.'

Back in Kyrgyzstan, Professor Chotaeva had wondered aloud whether her country was ready for independence. Kyrgyzstan is landlocked, divided in two by insanely high mountains with no real way of travelling between them, and what little industry it had was decimated by the Soviet collapse. All of those things also apply to Tajikistan – only here, the situation is even worse. By many measures it was already the poorest Soviet republic, and its geography ensured that it had deep divisions on both ethnic and regional lines.* The northern communist elite who had long dominated politics were resented in the more agricultural south. Aspiring powerbrokers were quick to capitalise on the economic chaos of the Soviet collapse by recruiting masses of recently unemployed men to local militias.

This was a combustible pyre, and the alcoholic, often absent President Nabiyev had not inherited much of an army to do any firefighting. The capital quickly found itself besieged by rebel forces in late 1992 as full-scale

---

* According to the 1989 Soviet census, Tajikistan was 23 per cent Uzbek and 7.6 per cent Russian. The majority Tajik population was not uniform – peoples such as the Garmis had strong regional loyalties, and the Pamiris, while classified by the Soviets as 'Tajik', were in fact ethnically and linguistically distinct.

civil war broke out. It lasted until 1997, although the majority of the casualties occurred in the early years, including around 50,000 deaths between May and September 1992.[4]

Despite this smorgasbord of causes, in official discourse today it is more common for the Tajik government to blame the civil war on a single culprit: Islamism. They point to the fact that the primary democratic opposition in the early 1990s was presented by the Islamic Renaissance Party; there was also the fact that neighbouring Afghanistan, which had its own brutal war against the Soviets in the 1980s, was a ready supplier of both weapons and radical Islamist ideas across the porous Amu River. This simplified narrative also resonated with the kingmakers in Moscow and Tashkent. Uzbekistan, which not only controlled access to the country but also feared unrest spilling over into its own population, had a strong interest in the welfare of the large Uzbek minority. Russia, whose troops remained stationed in Tajikistan, wanted a reliable, secular partner in Dushanbe. And so out of the flames of a burning nation came Emomali Rahmonov, an electrician by trade and the head of a collective farm in the Kulob region. Rahmonov was seen as a compromise candidate: Kulob is in the south of Tajikistan, but he was accepted by the northern warlords as a reasonably malleable figure with solid communist credentials. Russia and Uzbekistan also approved, especially as the rooting-out of the Islamists became an even greater priority after the Taleban capture of Kabul in 1996.

Still, Rahmonov was little more than a figurehead in a country that had fallen apart at the seams. A shaky peace deal was agreed in 1997 that guaranteed 30 per cent of cabinet posts would go to the opposition. But the government lacked the resources to rule with much authority. The president's perceived pliability was such that, in the 1990s, people joked that he was simply the mayor of Dushanbe, with the warlords carving the rest of the country up among themselves.

Then came 11 September 2001, and suddenly everything changed in Central Asia. As in a game of musical chairs, if you were in power when the music stopped on 9/11, you won big. Dictators from around the world rallied around the wounded hyperpower as it was gripped by righteous fury: Putin's carpet-bombing of Chechnya was suddenly seen as virtuous; in Uzbekistan, the Friendship Bridge in Termez became a key logistics hub for the NATO invasion of Afghanistan; meanwhile, Tajikistan was also happy to turn its airbases over to the Americans. Suddenly, Rahmonov had a far stronger hand. This US military presence, as well as funding, did a lot to stabilise the country at the start of the 2000s, and he set about systematically eliminating his rivals. It has led to a remorseless, ratcheting increase of his power, and with it a cult of personality. Rahmonov dropped the Russian suffix -ov from his name in 2007, simply becoming President Rahmon. His gilded status was cemented in 2015, when the Tajik parliament bestowed on him a new official title: Founder of Peace and National Unity, Leader of the Nation.

As for Islam, it still exists, but only in highly circumscribed form. The opposition Islamic Renaissance Party was banned in 2015. Meanwhile, overt demonstrations of faith are frowned upon and are prosecuted in a way that has become legendary among Tajikistan's neighbours.

'Tell me, brother – is it really true about the beard thing over there? I mean, are they banned?' Saif messages me from Tashkent on my third day here.

I snort into my afternoon cuppa. I'm about to send a derisive, stop-reading-all-that-fake-news response when it strikes me that Tajik males are indeed a rather clean-shaven bunch. I sit watching people ambling along Rudaki in their skinny suits, and I wonder if Saif is on to something. I do a bit of digging and uncover a speech from Rahmon in 2017, in which the president encouraged his people not to try and show their righteousness externally, and instead to 'love God with their hearts'.[5] I can't tell if this amounts to a ban, but maybe the threat was enough. Happily, my waiter is sporting a fair bit of stubble, so I ask him what he makes of this injunction.

'There is no ban,' he assures me. 'In Tajikistan, we are free to dress as we want.'

Nevertheless, he spends the rest of his shift glancing at himself in the mirror, stroking his stubble, seemingly deep in thought.

*

The next stop is a reunion with my friend Mahliyo. She and I met a few years ago in Beijing, where she was working as an English teacher. To her students, she called herself Meghan. I believe that name will be easier for the reader as well. A previous attempt to see her was stymied by armed skirmishes that had broken out between Kyrgyzstan and Tajikistan in the disputed Ferghana Valley – an ethnically mixed region around the size of Wales, yet home to some 15 million people, roughly the population of the Netherlands. Conflict over borders here has rumbled on since independence, with each side often producing its own Soviet-era maps to stake their claim to individual villages and farmsteads.[6] The most recent conflict resulted in over 100 casualties and caused 136,000 Kyrgyz to temporarily flee their homes.[7]

Fortunately, a ceasefire was announced after three days of fighting, which has held for a couple of weeks now, leaving the way clear for me to visit Meghan in the impeccably named Proletarsk, a small town in the north of the country near the city of Khujand.

Well, the way isn't exactly clear. Like Kyrgyzstan, Tajikistan is sliced in two by a mountain range. The countries are almost mirror images of each other, with the densely populated Ferghana Valley at one extreme and their capitals at the other, separated from them by peaks reaching silly heights, the tallest being Ismoil Somoni Peak at 24,590 feet. Until 1962 it was called Stalin Peak; then it was called Peak Communism, but then, well, you know the drill by now . . .

A disused piece of land opposite Dushanbe's cement factory has been turned into a makeshift bus station. But there are no buses or even *marshrutkas* here, only a series of gnarly off-road SUVs. This is slightly disconcerting – is the road so bad that it can only be traversed with a 4×4?

I'm quickly surrounded by seagulls, vigorously offering their services. Too lazy to negotiate, I allow myself to be bundled into the nearest car, a silver Toyota Land Cruiser. First, a fat old lady clambers in. Then a family of three. I politely offer them the middle row, intending to sit in the front, but the driver's mate bars my way, jabbering something in Persian. The meaning is pretty clear: 'I'm riding shotgun. You're going in the boot, sunshine.'

So it's from the back of the car, among the mounds of luggage and shopping bags, that I contemplate the road ahead. There is one part of it in particular that concerns me: to get through the mountains between Dushanbe and Khujand means passing through the 'Tunnel of Death'.

A little melodramatic? Well, the tunnel has fought hard to earn its reputation. Until recently, there was just one road between northern and southern Tajikistan, but at 11,000 feet, it was so high that it was only useable in summer. In the 1980s the Soviets began a project to build a tunnel at around 9,000 feet, which would be open all year round and save drivers four hours of travel time. Unfortunately the USSR collapsed before it could be completed, and work was further delayed by the civil war. Eventually the Tajiks secured funding from their Iranian cousins to finish the job. The work took longer than expected, and the government grew impatient, opening the tunnel in 2006 despite it being unfinished. What had originally been planned as two tunnels, each with a dual carriageway, became a single tunnel with one lane in each direction.

'There's no lighting in there, no pavement either,' one spooked-out girl at the hostel told me. 'But the worst thing is that there's no ventilation – so if someone has an accident and you're stuck in the middle of the tunnel . . . good luck making it two miles to the exit when you're choking on carbon monoxide fumes.'

Those are the sort of merry thoughts I'm having, cramped into my little corner of the boot, as we leave Dushanbe behind. On the plus side, the brand-new toll road out of the city has been priced in a way that ensures the riff-raff (i.e. the entire country) can't afford it. Our only real company is lorries. The landscape is stony, arid. The remnants of a few landslides sprawl by the side of the road. As we get higher, we begin to overtake trucks who are driving with their bonnets open, presumably to aid their overworked radiators in the struggle to cool the engines.

Traffic starts to build as we near a summit – and then, there it is – the 'Tunnel of Death' looms ahead of us like Shelob's Lair. The driver asks all of us to close our windows. We plough into it and darkness engulfs us. Spectral dust hangs in the air, drifting in the beams of our headlights. The road bumps and bucks the Land Cruiser, and splashes of water leap onto the windscreen from the innumerable puddles. A Lada is bumbling cautiously along in front of us – too cautiously for our driver. We can all tell what he's thinking; the lights of an oncoming car are in the distance, but its speed is difficult to judge. He's going to go for it. I put my head in my hands. The Land Cruiser surges forward, passing the Lada and re-entering our lane with around twenty feet to spare.

'How long is this tunnel?' I ask the guy sharing the boot with me.
'About five kilometres.'
I groan.

But we make it. There isn't the proverbial light at the end, the gloom merely seems to relinquish its hold on the vehicle and we emerge gently into the sunlight, covered in dust. I'm not the only one feeling relieved. There's a large gravel car park at the tunnel exit. One driver has his prayer mat out and is sending his thanks to the heavens.

The landscape improves as we descend; we enter a picturesque valley where the road passes through the town of Ayni. Shortly afterwards we burrow into another interminable tunnel, this one built by the Chinese Road and Bridge Corporation and opened in 2012. It's of distinctly higher quality than the Tajik-Iranian effort, a lesson, perhaps, in the merits of Unity, Pragmatism, Struggle and Innovation. Between them, these two tunnels have taken around seven hours off the journey between the two biggest cities in Tajikistan. What used to take eleven hours now takes four. This, in the quite literal sense, is nation-building.

An hour or so later, at Meghan's request, relayed down my phone to the unwilling driver, I am dropped off at a junction. The mountains are long gone, having given way to a landscape of rolling fields and a warm Mediterranean palette. The sun winks low in the sky. The Ferghana Valley is the most densely populated area in Central Asia, boasting fertile soil and flat land in a region of mountains and steppe. Many of the Silk Road's most historic cities are located here, at the end of the bottleneck on the road to China. Five miles to the south-east is the Kyrgyz border, where the trouble kicked off a few weeks ago. Five miles to the north-west is Uzbekistan. This has historically been the richest, most industrialised part of Tajikistan, and where the communist ruling elite came from.

The petrol station is deserted apart from a small Opel Corsa, which flashes its lights. Two men jump out to greet me, all smiles and handshakes. They introduce themselves as Meghan's husband, Timur, and her brother, Bahodir, who also worked in China, where he went by the name of Ben.

The sun has set by the time we arrive at their home. Apparently, word of my arrival has slipped out – around ten schoolkids are sitting in the porch and immediately begin bombarding me with questions: 'Who is your football team? Who is your new king? Which university is the best? Can I have your Instagram? Will you play football with us tomorrow?' Once they secure my signature for Proletarsk FC, Meghan chivvies them away and introduces me to her own three children.

Meghan hasn't changed much since China; she still wears a headscarf and a bright, formless dress. But while it was she who extended the invitation, it's clear that Timur is in charge of entertaining the guest.

'Tonight, we will go to Ali Baba's,' he declares. The children scramble to their feet, looking delighted. It's the best kebab house in town, or so they tell me. There are certainly some impressive specials on the menu: I munch on a cow's tongue salad as I tell them about my journey; a metre-long shish ends up being the main course.

'You drink, Joe?' asks Ben.

'Sure.'

He pours some vodka into my mug – the same kind of thin, ceramic number used for tea in Tashkent. He serves far more than a double measure. I try not to look too surprised. Everything I've heard about the Ferghana Valley has led me to believe that it's one of the most conservative places in the region. Has Ben just poured this because he thinks that's how Europeans drink?

'To our guest,' says Timur, promptly quashing my fears by downing his whole mug in a fluid motion that betrays a lifetime of practice. Ben and I follow suit. It isn't the worst vodka, even if it is from a mug. Ben refills the glasses; I'm clearly dealing with professionals. The women and children continue chatting to each other as though this is a perfectly normal thing for the blokes to do.

Once we've had a few drinks, the topic of the recent conflict between Tajikistan and Kyrgyzstan comes up.

'It wasn't so bad here,' says Meghan. 'They all know that this is an Uzbek village, and both countries have every reason to avoid upsetting Uzbekistan.'

'Did you hear the fighting?'

'Maybe the odd boom,' she shrugs, 'but the main problems were at least twenty kilometres away.'

This doesn't sound like a particularly reassuring distance, but in valley terms perhaps it's far enough.

'It's all quite sad,' says Meghan. 'Our grandmother was born in Isfara; it's a city that today is in Kyrgyzstan, but back then it was just like going to another village – no borders, no nothing. Slowly, maybe over the last four, five years or so, they've started increasing the infrastructure around there, now it's not easy at all to cross – it's what creates all these tensions and affects everyday life. We're very worried about winter, the price of coal has gone up four times as it's hard to get it across the border. Anyway, let's not worry about all that – tomorrow we have a busy day! It's Khushbaht's birthday.' She points out her middle son. 'Plus, Joe is coming to the school to give a talk.' She looks at me anxiously. 'You will give your talk, right?'

I nod vigorously, although privately I'm a little nervous. Meghan had vaguely mentioned that I might like to talk to some children at her language school about studying in England, but she hadn't given specifics. 'How many people are coming?'

'Oh, I don't know,' she says airily. 'Maybe twenty families.'

Twenty families . . . I try to do a quick calculation, people have a lot of kids here . . . Ben has filled up the vodka again, he's setting quite a pace. Let's say six kids per family . . .

Ben puts his arm round me, he's looking pretty schlonged as well. 'You will have a good time in Proletarsk,' he grins.

I grin back. 'I thought people in Tajikistan were Muslims?'

'We are Soviet Muslims,' says Timur, reaching for the vodka and filling our mugs once more. 'We call this drink white tea.'

*

The next morning I'm not given a second to wallow in my hangover. Timur is insisting on showing me the bazaar. He's wearing his smart black shoes and best jacket as we flag down a microbus heading south-east, towards the rising sun. Microbus is the most common way of travelling around the valley. It's barely my height but still manages to hold around nine people.

After five minutes shuddering along under our weight, the bus comes to a halt and a policeman squeezes aboard, sitting up front with the driver. We move onward for around half a mile, at which point the driver hands over some money to the officer, who hastily disembarks. No one else seems perturbed by the behaviour of this uniformed Dick Turpin.

'Does the driver pay the passengers here, not the other way round?' I mutter to Timur.

'Best not to ask questions,' he winks.

Cars are piled pell-mell into the parking bays outside the Ashrof Bazaar. The suits and ties of Dushanbe have been left well behind. Here people are dressed smartly in defiance of their poverty – many have patched-up jackets that have lasted a lifetime and wear shoes worn thin with polishing.

Bazaars are one of the great draws of Central Asia, where the tradition of shopping with local sellers still thrives. Even so, I can't be the first person to question the sanitary standards. We bat away the flies as we stop to munch on a *samsa* or two.*

The plague of corruption isn't far away here either. 'Each seller has to pay for their stall, so the owner of the bazaar ends up being a very powerful man,' Timur explains. 'Everyone wants to be in his good books, and they are always finding new ways to "persuade" him to let them have the best spots.'

Timur knows all the salespeople and introduces me to them like a proud uncle. 'Try this, Englishman!' the sellers say, offering me dates, nuts, apples, apricots and watermelon. It's a marked contrast to the circus tent shopping mall in Astana, with its impersonal brands and shop assistants whose presence you barely notice.

---

* A *samsa* (same etymology as samosa) is essentially a Central Asian pasty.

That said, by the time Timur has introduced me to the seventeenth stallholder, a wheezy man who insists that I try his dates – 'The best in the valley!' – I start to think that maybe the anonymity of the mall has its advantages. Young people across Central Asia have embraced mall culture for similar reasons: in societies where drinking isn't that common, and the tea house is a male-only zone, often it's one of the few places where it's safe to go on a date away from prying eyes. Still, the bazaar brings a different kind of romance. It's a very personal affair, many of the stallholders have grown the food themselves or have brought it from farms in their village. They exchange the weekly gossip with their customers, making a trip here as much a social event as a shopping trip.

Not before time, Meghan calls, jolting Timur out of his rounds. He looks at his watch in alarm, and to my relief we hurry back to the bus stop.

Before long we arrive at Millennium School, which Meghan set up earlier this year to help young students improve their language skills. Schools are not great in Tajikistan. Population growth in the country has been spectacular, almost doubling every twenty years since 1950, and educational resources have struggled to keep up.

'Children don't spend enough time at school. In ordinary schools, there are so many children that they have to be taught in two shifts: children are either taught in the morning shift or the afternoon one, and they spend the rest of the time at home,' she tells me. 'Even then there are more than thirty kids in each class.'

This is where Meghan's language school idea came in. 'I graduated from Khujand State University in 2008, majoring in Teaching English Language and Literature. Then I found this opportunity in China, so I went there for a few years, and with the money I made there opened this school with my husband. We now have a hundred and eighty students and six teachers,' she says proudly.

The Millennium School helps cover gaps left by the state system. 'Parents have to work, so it helps that we can provide schooling when their kids are at home. But I can't show you everything now; they're waiting for you!' She ushers me towards one of the classrooms, where every chair in the building has been moved to accommodate the children and parents.

'Well, everyone,' says Meghan, stepping ahead of me with the air of an apparatchik about to announce an extra-special fulfilment of the Five-Year Plan. 'We've got a very special guest from England today, who is going to tell you all about how to study abroad in Great Britain.'

A little background. When I was in China, it had been to set up a business helping students with their university applications – choosing courses, language classes, helping write their letters of motivation . . . things like that. It was reasonably rewarding – Chinese students work hard, and occasionally I even convinced a couple of them that they'd be better off studying something other than Business, Economics or Maths. But there's a reason I set up this business in China and not in Tajikistan. Not only is the average Chinese richer than the average Tajikistani, but China has the exact opposite population problem. The one-child policy has meant that a given Chinese child is often the sole descendant of both their parents and their two sets of grandparents. This brings with it a fair amount of pressure, but on the plus side, the combined savings and material resources of all six people are available to invest in that child's success. In short, Chinese students are well backed financially; even middle-class Chinese can afford to shell out upwards of $50,000 per year for the best courses that Western universities can provide.

With a GDP per capita of just $900, Tajikistani parents are less able to afford such sums, particularly when the culture here is to have large families, making it more difficult to spread around equally. So it's with a sense of despondency that I seat myself in front of the expectant rows of students, of a similar age and with the same dreams as those I had helped in Beijing. I go ahead with the speech, full of vapid clichés about the benefits of British education, the spirit of free enquiry that it encourages, the kinds of subjects that can be studied, the historic places – Oxford's dreaming spires, the famous labs of Cambridge, the Harry Potter film sets . . . I feel increasingly disgusted as I continue, Meghan translating everything I say. I do my best to pass on what Farangis told me about the scholarship options, despite being keenly aware of the long odds. There are so many eager eyes on me and there's little that I can offer them.

'Are you all right, Joe?' Meghan asks when the talk is over. I give her some initial ramblings on the injustices of the world. Meghan is understanding. She has also been to China, after all.

'What these kids need is a bit of inspiration. To know that there are things going on outside this valley and that there are other things to do in life than work as a migrant on a construction site. They might not achieve their dream, but at least it gets them learning English, taking their education seriously. I didn't expect my life to have taken the course it has. But we built our house and this school on the back of my studying hard at English.'

Sadly, many Tajik parents have no option but to work abroad for long stretches of their lives. The worst story I heard was that of a Tajik taxi driver in Warsaw, who found out about his wife's death from cancer while he was working in Poland. His wife was survived by five children for whom he was now the sole breadwinner. 'There was no way I could go back,' he told me, sadly. 'I wouldn't have been allowed to return to Poland due to the Covid restrictions on foreigners. I'm sure Allah will understand. My wife understood. We said goodbye on video call.'

At the end of my lecture on university life in England, I had asked for a show of hands from the students. 'Who has a parent who is working abroad at the moment?'

Almost three-quarters of the room put theirs in the air.

'Where are they working?'

'Kazakhstan,' says one small boy.

'Qatar,' say a couple.

But they were the exceptions. 'Russia, Russia, Russia,' most shouted.

One great irony of the Soviet collapse is that far more Kyrgyz, Tajiks and Uzbeks now live and interact with Russians than was ever the case in the Soviet era. Like many of the world's great cities, a large part of the Muscovite economy runs on the back of immigrant workers. Supermarkets, taxis, bars and restaurants can all work round the clock due to a supply of dirt-cheap labour from the former Soviet space.

While living in Moscow I met Central Asians who told me that they sleep twelve to a room, who are often there illegally and overstay their visas. They fear deportation, not so much because they won't be allowed to return but because they'll lose a month's worth of work while they arrange for a new passport (often fake) to be produced.

As with large-scale migration anywhere, local resentments and prejudices are never far away. Every single person I've encountered in the former USSR has told me that they have experienced racism in Russia.

This isn't to pigeonhole Russians as uniquely bigoted – some lame, lazy tropes are depressingly ubiquitous. And while we might expect the police and security services to be prone to such sentiment, these kinds of insults often go right to the top of public discourse. Alexei Navalny, the man whom some see as the martyr of Russian liberalism, was not averse to using nationalism to score points in the run-up to the Moscow mayoral election in 2014. During the 2008 Russian invasion of Georgia, he was also on record as describing Georgian people as 'rodents'.* Meanwhile it was only in 2021, when Russia's most popular online property website, Cian, was listed on the New York Stock Exchange, that it banned users from writing 'Slavs Only' on property rental advertisements.[8]

At Khushbaht's birthday, the rules are stricter than under the most oppressive authoritarian state. Everyone has a role they are expected to fulfil – the man is front of house, he does the entertainment and storytelling; the woman is back of house, ensuring infinite supplies of food; and the children are the servants, waiters and dogsbodies. The guest is bound by the rules of hospitality as much as anyone else. It is a requirement that he has a good time.

These social roles do not change at birthday parties. Timur ushers the men towards the dining room, which has been set for a banquet. The diners consist mainly of Timur's family and close friends and we sit hierarchically. At the head of the table is Timur's old commander from his days in the Soviet Army, his skullcap perched precariously atop his greying head.

---

* This is a pun – the Russian word for Georgians is *Gruziny*, whereas *gryzuny* means rodents.

Opposite me are Timur's brother-in-law and two other former comrades-in-arms. Most men in the USSR, regardless of which republic they came from, did two years' military service, often in mixed ethnic battalions. The bonds formed during these formative years are long-lasting. In Astana, I bumped into some Kazakh veterans celebrating the Soviet Paratroopers' Day on 2 August. The day is generally an excuse for old military types, all wearing *telnyashkas* (blue-and-white undershirts donned by the navy and airborne units), to go out, get hammered and start fights with passers-by. It surprised me that this was still a thing given the ongoing conflict in Ukraine. Most citizens of Astana gave them a wide berth, but I still thought it right to wish them a happy holiday. They thought it right to tell me to fuck off.

The older chaps have whipped out the vodka once more.

'You drink, Joe?' asks Timur's commander.

'I promised the kids I'd play football later,' I say sheepishly.

'That's fine, we'll play too!' says the commander, giving me a generous top-up. Without an excuse, I pull the mug towards me.

The next morning is not enjoyable. I barely register the leftover *plov* that I'm given with my morning cuppa. Dazed, I bid farewell to the family while Timur stands outside to flag down a bus. I'm grateful that he'll be accompanying me as far as the border.

'We were really happy to have you in our family for a while,' says Meghan. 'Our homes are small, but our hearts are big! Just try to come for a longer period next time!'

It's easy to be harsh on Tajikistan. Independence has been, by most measures, a disaster. Hemmed in by mountains, bordered by a ruined Afghanistan to the south and overlooked by an initially indifferent China to the east, Tajikistan faced enormous geographic constraints on top of the post-Soviet turmoil. All this, compounded by civil war, meant that Tajikistan has endured perhaps the harshest independence experience of all. Even peace was costly, with 'stability' coming in the form of a corrupt dictatorship and a ruling family that dominate political and economic life.

Like Uzbekistan, the country's wave of young people brings immense potential, but without jobs many turn north for work. And while we might scorn Moscow for its rights abuses and racism towards migrants, at least it lets them in – providing an umbilical cord for a country with few other opportunities.

Yet sitting here, full of *plov* and broken by endless toasts, it's hard to dismiss the country as hopeless; my enduring memories of the place will be of impossibly warm hospitality.

The whole family watch as Timur and I squeeze into the back of the microbus. As we drive off, I distinctly see each of them stoop down and throw something in our direction.

'We have a tradition when we say goodbye to people,' says Timur. 'People throw stones after you as you leave.'

'Why?' I've got one last myth in me.

'No idea,' he laughs.

I sigh with relief, sink into my corner of the bus, and begin to fall asleep.

9
TURKMENISTAN
THE REPUBLIC OF THE GREAT LEADER

As things turn out, it takes a couple of years and a lot of persistence before I make it to the final Central Asian state – a country that even former Soviets seem to view with a kind of awe.

'Is it true that women there are not allowed to wear make-up?' Farangis asked me back in Dushanbe.

'Didn't their leader order a golden statue to be built in his image?' I was asked by one Armenian.

'I thought he named the days of the week after his mother!' his friend chimed in.

The Russians too were wary – 'I heard there was a place in the middle of the country called the "Gate to Hell".'

There are so many legends about Turkmenistan that it was difficult to know where to begin. If Carlsberg did post-Soviet republics, this, it appeared, would be it. It had the oil and gas of Russia; the dynastic ruling family of Azerbaijan; the wacky capital city of Kazakhstan; the dodgy roads of Tajikistan; the slave labour of Uzbekistan; a police state and internet censorship more repressive than any of the above; and a visa policy that had exasperated, befuddled and amused me for most of the past three years.

The first time I thought it might have just been bad luck. The application for a transit visa at Turkmenistan's London embassy, a nondescript house in Shepherd's Bush, was oddly intimate. I had a pleasant chat with the consul himself, who was delighted that I planned to visit his home town of Turkmenbashi. He showed me some pictures and was only too keen to offer travel tips. But this was in March 2020: Covid began, and I never heard the result of my application.

Two years later I applied again, this time at the embassy in Tbilisi. After I'd given the intercom a solid five-minute workout, a tall, suited man opened the black gate an inch or two.

'The embassy is closed today,' he said gravely.

'Why? It's a Monday morning?'

He shrugged. 'What do you want?'

'I want a visa to Turkmenistan.'

'Where are you from?'

'Great Britain.'

He considered for a moment. 'Turkmenistan is not open for foreigners at the moment.'

'Why?' I asked again. The country had been closed since the onset of the pandemic, but even China had opened its doors by now.

The diplomat smiled wryly. 'It's not my job to know why.'

Three months later in Tashkent I was informed that the embassy was not open because the ambassador was attending a conference. In Dushanbe, I was once again invited in by the bored consul. 'Do you want a tourist visa or a transit visa?' he asked me, sipping his tea under the unsmiling portrait of the president.

'Either, but a transit visa would be best.' Tourist visas meant you had to travel everywhere on a guided tour; a transit visa permitted you less time in the country, but you were left to your own devices.

'Well, we're not offering tourist or transit visas at the moment,' he said conversationally, leaving me wondering why he'd asked the original question at all.

'Are you offering any other visas?'

'Driver's visas. For truckers.'

'Right. If I arrived in a lorry then, would you give me a visa?'

To his credit, he did actually smile.

Then, out of the blue, word spread that the government was reintroducing tourist visas in the middle of 2023. As I said, these tourist visas aren't ideal – the travel agencies who sponsor them place you in needlessly expensive hotels and fill your timetable with banalities designed to suck money out of you and prevent you from interacting with ordinary people.

For a couple of months I held out for an alternative. When none seemed forthcoming, I took the plunge. All communication with the tour group was done by email: there is no WhatsApp in Turkmenistan. It appeared that there were no banking services either as they didn't even ask for money upfront. I was just told to board a flight from Turkey, bringing as many dollars with me as I could. Someone would be waiting for me at the other end. They did not give me a number. As I flew blindly out of Istanbul into the dark night, unbidden, the voice of Captain Barbossa came swimming into my mind.

'You're off the edge of the map, mate. Here there be monsters.'

Ashgabat

Out of the aeroplane window, the dark void of the desert is suddenly illuminated by an orgasm of light: neat grids of purples, greens and blues flash merrily, beckoning us out of the sky. We taxi towards a gleaming airport, built in the shape of an eagle.

I set off on a quick march through the terminal. The tour agency did give me one helpful tip before take-off: 'Make sure you get off the plane before everyone else. Every thirty seconds you waste disembarking will lose you about fifteen minutes at customs.' But even as I hurry, it's hard not to notice the fantastical opulence. The ornate ceilings are twenty feet high, the floors glossy-white and the walls bedecked with gold. There's the odd soldier here and there, but otherwise not a soul. My feet echo along the endless, empty corridors.

The driver is waiting for me at the airport. He looks a little grumpy; the flight is late and the poor guy probably can't wait to get back to bed. In Turkmenistan, however, the flights (like the police) only ever come calling in the wee hours before dawn. As we speed into the city, Ashgabat's illuminated buildings shine even brighter up close. LED horses gallop along the facade of the national stadium, laser shows dazzle on the tallest of towers, but the capital's sweeping, five-lane boulevards are deserted.

'Is it always this empty?' I ask the driver.

He gives me a sidelong glance. 'This area is new,' he explains. 'It was built for the indoor Asian Games of 2017.'

These games, from what I understand, were the biggest event in the country's history. I had a friend who was flown out to work there; the job entailed standing around and lending a British accent and a white face of respectability to proceedings. He was paid $10,000 for his efforts, an enormous sum for a bloke who would be the first to admit that he doesn't exactly look like David Beckham.

'Did you change money at the airport?' the driver asks.

'Nope.'

'Good. You know the situation with money in our country?' he continues, giving me another sidelong glance. 'About the exchange rate?'

'I heard there's an official rate and an unofficial rate.'

'Yes,' he says, a little too quickly. 'The official rate is three and a half manat for one dollar. Do you know what the unofficial rate is?'

I decide to play dumb; suddenly I've got an inkling as to why this guy was happy to get up at 4 a.m. for the airport transfer.

'I can offer you fifteen manat for one dollar,' he blurts out.

I think about it. Is this a trap? People warned me that undercover operatives would be everywhere. I decide to exchange $30. This would have got me 105 manat at the airport. The driver promptly hands over 450. The atmosphere in the cab relaxes palpably as we drive through the bizarre, empty city, secure in our black-market complicity.

After just three hours' sleep, I'm jerked awake by the bedside telephone.

'Get up!' a voice snaps. 'I'm Mai, your guide for today, you need to come to breakfast.'

I heave myself out of bed with immense reluctance and stumble into the lobby, which, like everything else thus far, is enormous, white and empty. In the centre is a pearly grand piano. The marble floor squeaks underfoot as I advance towards the hall's lone occupant: a small, squat woman bouncing impatiently on the balls of her feet.

'Where is your companion?' she asks.

'No idea, I only got here a couple of hours ago,' I say grumpily, sinking into a luxurious green armchair.

For the five days that I'll spend in Turkmenistan, the tour agency has partnered me with a travel companion, a French guy called Emmanuel. It already sounds like the beginning of a bad joke, doesn't it? 'An Englishman, a Frenchman and a Turkmenman walk into a bar . . .' But if I was expecting someone insufferably chic, Emmanuel is a pleasant surprise. Halfway through breakfast, a dark-haired, scraggy-bearded chap appears on the other side of the hall. He's wearing a polo shirt, shorts and a pair of shoes that are dilapidated well beyond the realms of acceptability. As he shuffles over, his dying footwear flapping as he walks, he's staring at his phone with an obsessive longing through glasses that magnify his eyes threefold.

'Do you have internet?' he asks, by way of greeting.

'Haven't checked.'

'Don't bother, the connection here is a disgrace. Nothing works, even with a VPN. I've just been in Iran where my VPN worked fine; here I can barely get anything.'

I was prepared for this. A fun stat that I read before arriving was that Turkmenistan has blocked three times as many websites as China. Intrigued, I get hold of the Wi-Fi password and give WhatsApp a try. Nothing. The same for Facebook, Instagram, Telegram and even WeChat. All foreign media seems to be banned – the *New York Times*, the *Guardian*, the *Telegraph*, Al-Jazeera . . . I even try the *Newcastle Chronicle* – no good. Unfazed, I turn on my VPN only to find that it too has been blocked. I have a backup, but when this too doesn't work I give up. My initial assault on the Turkmen firewall has been swatted aside.

'You can still use email,' says Emmanuel. 'Google Maps, Gmail and Microsoft's servers all work. And I've been using L'Équipe to check the football results. Otherwise, nothing.'

Emmanuel, it turns out, is a veteran traveller, somehow already having managed to squeeze trips to 180 countries into his thirty-three years on this earth. He's just starting to tell me about his recent stint working at a business school in the Congo when Mai, who has been watching our conversation for ten minutes or so, steadily becoming more agitated, finally loses patience. With a military snap she stands up, chivvying us into the waiting car for our city tour. I get the impression that deviation from the timetable is not an option.

Sometimes it can be difficult to think of dictators as ordinary human beings with the same foibles and frailties as you or I. We don't imagine Hitler with a headache, or Pol Pot going for a poo. But we can only assume that Saparmurat Niyazov, the first president of Turkmenistan, was as wary of having his teeth done as the rest of us, because before long his personal dentist, Gurbanguly Berdimuhamedov, began to acquire enormous amounts of power. He rose to become health minister, and then, upon Niyazov's death, got hold of the top job itself.[1]

Upon attaining it, Berdimuhamedov did exactly what we would expect a dictatorial dentist to do. As we drive, the streets quite as empty as they were in the small hours, it's impossible not to notice that, like the airport and the hotel, every building, every car, every street lamp is uniformly, gleamingly white.

'Yes, it was ordered so by the president,' says Mai cheerfully when I put this to her. 'You cannot drive a car into Ashgabat unless it is white, or maybe silver.' A sop to the fillings industry, perhaps.

'In Turkmenistan, white is a sacred colour,' Mai continues. 'In fact, when wishing someone well on their journey, instead of saying "Have a nice trip" we say *ak yol*, which means "white road".'* She beams at us from the front of the car. 'Colours are very important in Turkmenistan. You can tell a lot of information about people through what they wear. Schoolgirls all wear green dresses, and girls at university all wear red.'

We pass a group of these girls waiting in identical bottle-green dresses at a white bus shelter.

'Bizarre,' breathes Emmanuel. 'What do boys wear at school?'

'Black suits, of course,' says Mai, as though this were obvious. 'Women also wear specific hats depending on their marital status. Married women wear a shawl, whereas unmarried women wear a little skullcap.'

---

* Travellers are also wished a 'white road' in the Kazakh and Kyrgyz languages.

We're driven to a museum complex above the city, where a trio of galleries introduces visitors to the three great, tragic events of modern Turkmen history. The first commemorates the Battle of Geok Tepe of 1881, decisive in the Russian conquest of Turkmen territory. Until this point, the Turkmens had long roamed the Karakum Desert, living by their horses, trading, raiding and often enslaving people from the local settled empires – the Persians to the south and the Uzbek khanates to their north and west. The child in me is imagining Tatooine's Tusken Raiders on horseback.

Such a lifestyle did not go down well with the Russians once they began to move into the region in the mid-nineteenth century, and was used as their excuse for invading. Geok Tepe was the Turkmens' last stand. In the museum there is a panorama depicting a desert fortress, surrounded by model tsarist soldiers and artillery. Mellow classical music plays as the figurines of Turkmen horsemen are mown down by Russian rifle fire. A group from a local university watches alongside us. A substantial number of the female students already don the marriage shawl.

The next museum pays tribute to the fallen in the Second World War – it's a standard Soviet affair with an eternal flame, a granite statue of the unknown soldier and vast lists of casualties from battles thousands of miles to the west. Finally, there is the earthquake museum, commemorating those that died in a 7.3 Richter Scale quake in 1948, which, Mai informs us, killed almost 10 per cent of the Turkmen population. The exhibits show images and artefacts of old Ashgabat, which was levelled by the seismic shockwaves. It seems to have been a handsome, unremarkable colonial outpost. One of the few buildings to survive was a legendary clock tower, which still stands in the city today.

These tragic events of the 1940s left indelible marks on the childhood of Saparmurat Niyazov, the country's first president, one of the biggest oddball leaders to come out of the post-Soviet space. Niyazov's father died fighting the Germans in North Ossetia in 1942; his mother and two of his brothers perished in the earthquake six years later. As a result, like Uzbekistan's Islam Karimov, like so many of the post-war generation, Niyazov would grow up in an orphanage. Whether or not this experience scarred him is unknown; what we do know is that, blessed with a newly independent country to run and plentiful reserves of oil and gas with which to run it, Niyazov's rule quickly took a dystopian turn. Styling himself Turkmenbashi (the Head of the Turkmens), he built golden monuments to himself all over the country, including one that turned to face the sun throughout the day. Months of the year were renamed – January became *Turkmenbashi*, April became *Gurbansoltan*, after his mother. For good measure, he renamed the word 'bread' after his mother as well, making a loaf of *Gurbansoltan* a mouthful in more than one sense.

Then came a list of prohibitions to maintain the 'purity' of the Turkmen culture: ballet, long hair and gold teeth were all forbidden; dogs were expelled from Ashgabat (he didn't like the smell), and after undergoing heart surgery in 1997 and being advised to give up cigarettes, Turkmenbashi decided that the whole country should join him in abstinence. You might think that he had his citizens' health in mind, but this is difficult to square with the fact that he closed every hospital outside the capital in February 2005. Other facets of his rule, such as employing the same forced labour in the cotton harvest as neighbouring Uzbekistan, or the fact that anyone who disagreed with him met the predictable fate of arrest, show trial and disappearance, seem almost prosaic by comparison.

He also wrote a book, the *Ruhnama* (Book of the Soul), which became the Turkmen equivalent of Mao's *Little Red Book*. It was made a compulsory part of the national curriculum, university admissions tests often consisted of questions on the book, and public readings of it were common. As you can perhaps imagine, Waterstones isn't currently stocking any copies, so I went to the British Library before the trip and managed to churn through fifty pages or so. It turned out to be a rather rambling screed. At times it reads like scripture: 'Turkmens will be civilised, clean, attractive and useful individuals,' comes an injunction within the opening pages. There is also an attempt to create a national identity and historical narrative, with Niyazov likening his book to a ship, 'chartered to bear the news of the past to the future over the vast sea of Turkmen history'.

But overshadowing it all is Turkmenbashi's own personality and determination to write himself a legacy. 'The burden of the responsibility of taking my people from the last years of the second millennium, in which things did not go well, to the summits of the third millennium, fell onto my shoulders,' he states, ever so humbly.

Fortunately, for those who thought that the third millennium wasn't going particularly well either, Niyazov died in 2007. You might think that the madness would have ended there, and while it was true that some of the more egregious policies were changed – the days of the week reverted to normal, hospitals were reopened and the giant, rotating statue was removed – the system remained the same. And the system demanded a similar leader.

So the Turkmens were lumped with the dentist and his fussy white city. Mai is delighted to show off the newest part of it, the so-called government district. We drive past the foreign ministry, which is in the shape of a globe, and the education ministry, in the shape of a book.

'And these buildings,' she chimes. 'Look, these buildings are *not* white! The houses and offices here have red roofs, this signifies that they are places to live for engineers.'

'Why red?'

'It is the colour of energy and strength.'

'*C'est ridicule*,' says Emmanuel, shaking his head.

Once the dentist got comfortable in power, he clearly felt he deserved some monuments of his own. We drive past a twenty-foot-high golden statue of a dog, positioned at the centre of a roundabout. 'The Alabay shepherd dog is the president's favourite breed,' says Mai.

Later we pass another even larger statue – also gold – portraying the dentist himself, riding a horse.

'Is that the one he fell off?' I ask, having seen a clip of the president falling from his steed in front of a stunned hippodrome.

'The president did not fall off a horse,' Mai laughs.

'He did,' says Emmanuel. 'It was on the news in France.'

'You must be confusing him with another president,' says Mai dismissively.

'Nope, it was definitely him,' I say. 'I saw it on YouTube.'

'You are mistaken,' she says coldly.

In any other country, I would have taken out my phone and shown her the video. Unfortunately, this is not an option in Turkmenistan.

*

Friendly as Mai is, there's no escaping the fact that we are chained to her. The first thing she did that morning was confiscate our passports, telling us that they were needed for 'registration', whatever that meant. That was just the beginning. In the bazaar, she insisted on doing the negotiating for us; in the museums, she panicked every time one of us lingered too long on an exhibit; in the restaurant, she ordered the food; all the while ushering us between the car and the sights like a mother duck.

By mid-afternoon I'm ready to rise up in rebellion against my smothering overlord. Mai wants to take us to visit the ruins of Nisa, an ancient Parthian city destroyed by another earthquake 2,000 years ago. Considering that our upcoming itinerary is already teeming with ancient ruins, I decide to bunk off and head into the city. I try to get Emmanuel in on the act as well.

'Let's go and see what it's really like here! What is an ancient temple going to teach us about the country?'

'I guess that's the idea,' he says. 'They don't want you to see anything.'

'That shouldn't stop us trying!'

'She won't let you,' he says stubbornly.

Unexpectedly, Mai does let me. She just looks surprised that anyone would want to travel anywhere alone. 'Please stay safe!' she implores. 'Don't talk to strangers!'

'Yes, Mum!'

'And don't take any pictures of any government buildings,' she calls after me as I head out into the glorious white afternoon. I try one last time to persuade Emmanuel to join, but he just mutters something about 'sticking to the schedule'. I mutter something about 'collaborationist instincts'.

In the centre of the older, Soviet part of town the buildings are still white, but at least have an air of utilitarian sanity. This doesn't last long, though, as I quickly come across the walls of the presidential palace. There is a lot of construction going on – the modern khans of Central Asia might be compared to the leaders of early modern Europe, each building their own Versailles or Escorial. The president has a sign outside his walls, warning drivers not to beep their horns. Best not to disturb the serene confines of his majesty.

There is now a third president of Turkmenistan. As in Azerbaijan, the son has inherited his father's throne, although in this case the old man is still alive, presumably content to pull the strings from the shadows. Portraits of the youthful president, Serdar Berdimuhamedov, loom down from every public building. He even has the air of a puppet: his blank, glazed eyes gazing on a blank, glazed city.

Further down the road, I'm surprised to find that there is still a Lenin in Ashgabat; it's a rather cute sight. He's mounted on a massive plinth (maroon and gold – breaking with the local tradition), but the statue itself is almost comically small. Rather than being imposing or commanding, this dinky Lenin's hand is open rather meekly, as if suggesting a path, or maybe offering a look back. From what I've seen today, the totalitarianism of the late Soviet period does seem prudent by comparison. A couple of blocks down from Lenin is the US Embassy, which, in a turn of events almost too good to be true, is located on 1984 Street. Until recently this road was named Pushkin Street, but it's refreshing to see the name updated to reflect the current state of affairs.

A new guide is waiting for us the following morning. Wearing tracksuit bottoms and a hoodie, Eziz waddles towards us, the walk of a man raised in the saddle. He has a slight lisp and the air of a petty officer in the army, but his English is impressive.

'Joe, Emmanuel . . .' he begins, waiting for our acknowledgement before continuing his rendition. 'Do you know what happens if you spend four hours in forty-degree heat in the desert?'

'You get thirsty?'

'No.' He expects us to keep guessing, despite the blatantly obvious answer.

'You die?' Emmanuel says eventually.

'Yes!' he says triumphantly. 'You die! In Turkmen language we only have one word for traitor. This word is *dönük*. It is the worst word in our language. The only way for the Russians to cross the Karakum Desert to attack us was if they knew where the watering holes were! Who told them about the watering holes, eh?'

'*Dönüks?*'

'Precisely! Water is so sacred in our country that the last Sunday of May is a holiday called the Water Holiday.'

Today we're leaving the abundant fountains of Ashgabat behind and striking into the desert, towards the second city of Mary (pronounced ma-ree). Once out of the city, we pull in for petrol, where it costs just eighty-six manat to fill the sixty-three-litre tank of our (white) Nissan Pathfinder. At my new conversion rate of 19.4 manat to the dollar, which I'd found at an illicit money changer yesterday evening, that's an entire tank of petrol for $4.43. This is a new level of cheap.

Eziz laughs when I tell him this. 'Yes, you pay too much in Europe. And tax. You pay too much tax! But Turkmenistan is sitting on oil and gas. After two years of our independence, our first president did a deal with China to export gas. They drive a hard bargain; very difficult to do business with them. After three years they tried to change the negotiation terms from sixty/forty in our favour to fifty/fifty. We froze that project and put the gas into underground storage.' Eziz is overcome by a coughing fit. 'We are in a difficult neighbourhood. It is hard for us to develop, especially because of Russia. They are our political ally but economic rival, they don't like that we have so much gas. It gives us agency.'

This agency has not been directed towards the country's intercity highways. Barely 30 miles outside of Ashgabat, the surface begins to disintegrate. It's obvious why we need the Nissan's four-wheel-drive. After 5 miles listening to the dull rumble of the tyres passing over the uneven surface, I give up any hope of conditions improving.

'Think of it as a free back massage,' says Eziz cheerfully.

Every 50 miles or so we're given a brief break from the spinal torture as police pull us over for spot checks. On each occasion, the driver refastens his seatbelt to pretend he's been wearing it all the time. I expect the police to extort bribes, but they can find nothing wrong with his documents.

As we plough on, Eziz tells us about his childhood. 'I grew up on the Afghanistan border. They were just on the other side of the river. When I was young, we would always hear gunfire and bombs over there, but thanks to our president and our military, they never came over to us.'

'Were they ever likely to come?' asks Emmanuel.

'Yes, they wanted to bring drugs across, to go to Russia. We stopped them coming, so now they go through Tajikistan and Kyrgyzstan instead. This is why we have to thank the first president; without him it could have been chaos. Instead, I got to enjoy a normal childhood.'

'What did your parents do?' I ask, foregoing the chance to ask which word he used for bread during this 'normal childhood'.

'My dad was a teacher of Russian language; we were a very educated household. He would always push us to learn more languages.'

'As a Russian-speaker, do you have a positive attitude towards the Soviet period?'

His brow furrows. 'We hate the Soviets! At school, all the textbooks wrote about how the Soviets had "civilised" us, as though before them there was nothing. There was not one page about the glories of medieval Merv, about ancient Nisa, about Konye-Urgench . . .'

'Joe skipped the ancient Nisa tour,' Emmanuel smirks. 'He said it wasn't interesting.'

Eziz clicks his tongue disapprovingly. 'The Soviets also destroyed our traditions; they took our horses and turned them into sausages!'

'They eat horses in France don't they, Emmanuel?' I say loudly.

'You eat horses in France?' Eziz looks horrified. 'In Turkmenistan the horse is a sacred animal, we would only ever eat them on very special occasions. We produce the best horses in all of the former Soviet Union. You know, in 1958, Khrushchev gave an Akhal-Teke horse as a gift to Queen Elizabeth of Great Britain. They are beautiful, elegant, golden horses. After the end of the war in 1945, they found horses from all around the world for Marshal Zhukov's parade, but none of the horses could march in time to the music. Finally, an Akhal-Teke horse did it and they were all amazed. That sums up what the Russians think about us; they didn't even consider that a Turkmen horse might be worthy of consideration. However . . .' He begins coughing again. 'However, the Soviets did build the Karakum Canal, which is the main source of water for Ashgabat and most of the country. As I said, water is life; water is the father of the harvest . . . without the Soviets we would not have any of this. So perhaps it is difficult to judge history.'

'It doesn't look like things have got much better since the Soviet period. Look at the state of the roads,' says Emmanuel bluntly.

Eziz waves his hand dismissively. 'You expect too much of us. As a country we are like a child; right now, we are crawling, why are you already expecting us to fly?'

If the roads before lunch belonged to a country that is crawling, that afternoon they become positively foetal. At times there's little more than a rough gravel track. It's left to each driver to forge his own path. It doesn't really matter which side of the road you're on, or if you're on the road at all.

'At least we're getting the train on the way back,' Emmanuel mutters.

'The train is much more dangerous,' says Eziz. 'In summer, when it's really hot, the rails expand and become soft, so lots of trains crash. They're forced to travel with a lighter load, either with fewer carriages or less cargo.'

'I guess we'll just have to have a few drinks on the train then,' I say, trying to sound undaunted.

'Oh, you can't do that,' says Eziz. 'It's illegal to drink on trains here.'

'Yeah, but what they don't know won't hurt them,' says Emmanuel.

I'm reminded of a Russian phrase used to justify rule-breaking when out of sight of the authorities. 'God is high above and the tsar is far away . . .'

Eziz does not smile when I tell him this. 'In Turkmenistan, the tsar is everywhere.'

We take a detour before Mary. Eziz wants to show us two of Turkmenistan's ancient UNESCO heritage sights. We stop to pick up his friend Akmuhammad, who will be accompanying us to a Bronze Age city called Gonur Depe. Akmuhammad had been part of the archaeological team that had uncovered the site. He left soon after the discovery, though: 'We heard the howling of wolves during the night as we were excavating, but found no footprints the next day. Then one of the diggers became ill with white blood disease. When I told my mother about this, she refused to let me work there any more.'

Little is left of Gonur Depe apart from the mounds of fortifications. These have still allowed Akmuhammad to piece together some of the idiosyncratic features of life in the city over 4,000 years ago. Horses were buried in their own graves, while servants would be buried alongside their master when he died.

'They put the servants to death?' asks Emmanuel, alarmed.

'Of course,' says Akmuhammad.

We walk a little further on.

'This here is the plague pit, they put people here when they died of a serious illness,' says Eziz, who is translating, before he breaks off, coughing again.

'Ten manat if you push him in the plague pit,' Emmanuel mutters to me.

We then drive on the dusty, ruined roads to another dusty, ruined city: this time the ancient capital of Merv. It had once been the richest city in the medieval world, the centre of the late Seljuk Empire that stretched from Uzbekistan to the Levant. In 1156 the kingdom split upon the death of Sultan Ahmad Sanjar, before it was devoured by the Mongols in 1221.

'Those Mongol animals killed everyone,' says Eziz. 'We think that somewhere between 1.2 and 1.5 million people were killed here.* Before that time, Merv was famous all over the world. People called it "The Great Merv".'

'Did people in Merv also build golden statues to their leaders?' Emmanuel asks.

'Of course not!' says Eziz, shocked. 'They were Muslims! In Islam, you cannot build icons.'

'How come leaders today build huge golden statues? Are Turkmens not Muslims now?'

'Ahh, well we are *Soviet* Muslims,' says Eziz, echoing what Timur had told me in Tajikistan.

It's nevertheless encouraging to see the ruins of these ancient cities. The rulers of Merv and Gonur Depe, masters of all they surveyed, splurged

---

* The figures I read later put it closer to 700,000.

their wealth on monumental mosques and mausoleums. All that is now unrecognisable, swallowed up by the sands of time. It's comforting to think that the same fate will likely await Ashgabat someday.

We leave the ancient cities behind and bump and buck our way towards Mary. As in Uzbekistan, there are fields and fields of cotton by the roadside. Tractors laden with the fluffy stuff trundle along the shitty roads. Lines of women farm them methodically, garbed in colourful dresses and masks that cover their faces.

'Did you ever pick cotton?' I ask Akmuhammad.

'Every year during the Soviet period,' he smiles reminiscently. 'We did it for three months: September, October, November. All the schoolchildren did it, they preferred us to pick it because children have softer hands, so we were less likely to damage the cotton.'

'That has now changed though,' Eziz interjects. 'These days there is no forced labour in Turkmenistan. That's a relic of Soviet times.'

At this precise moment we turn a corner and come across two dozen children standing in the cotton fields, their faces blackened by the sun. They look up from their work and stare at the car as it goes past. They are beyond poor: hungry, short and malnourished. Eziz chooses this moment to have another coughing fit.

The sandstorm that's been brewing all day is thick by the time we arrive in Mary. The hotel balcony is well on its way to becoming a beach and there's an acrid smell in the air. We take shelter in Mary's regional museum where we examine another collection of shields, daggers, bones and thimbles, mercifully away from Eziz, who has succumbed to his worsening cough and remained in the car. There is also a small room with a craven exhibition to the second president. A series of photographs show the dentist riding a horse, driving a rally car, playing football, and in all manner of silly poses that you might expect from a gap-year Instagram post from Thailand.

The sandstorm has abated by the time we exit. Eziz is still out for the count, so he lets us have a wander for the evening. Despite police manning every intersection, Mary is more relaxed than Ashgabat. Groups of kids are packed outside malls, and there are signs of private entrepreneurship with little businesses and restaurants. There's even the odd red car. But these green shoots of development sit aside conspicuous poverty. We have around five hours before the train, so head out for a bite at a kebab house. The serving staff are entirely male. In fact, I only discover that there are females present in the building when I ask to go to the toilet – I'm sent through the kitchen to find around six women working in there, their flamboyant dresses looking very out of place. We order two kebabs, but no sooner do they turn on the grill than the whole restaurant runs out of power, plunging us into darkness. The smiling son ushers us helpfully to the door.

Mary station, like every other public building in the city, has the portrait of the princeling president, Serdar Berdimuhamedov, gazing impassively over the entrance. The train is late, and there seems to be some confusion as to when it's actually going to turn up. I get chatting to a kid who's going to Ashgabat so he can catch a flight to Russia, where he'll begin his studies at the University of Tomsk. His mother and sister have come with him to say goodbye. He won't see them for three years.

When the train finally arrives, Eziz panics when I pull my camera out. 'Stop, stop! You cannot film this!' he snaps, his voice reverting to petty officer mode.

'Why not?'

'Mai should have told you this yesterday,' he says irritably. 'No taking pictures of government buildings or critical infrastructure.'

We board the piece of critical infrastructure, whose creaking carriages are fresh out of the 1970s. There are neither plug sockets nor air con and it stinks of cigarettes. In the summer it must be unbearable. Still, we've got a *kupé* compartment to ourselves and, given the length of the day, I quickly drift off to sleep to the sound of Eziz coughing.

Eight hours later, we get picked up by a new driver at Ashgabat station. '*Uran shad!*' he says, shaking hands. 'Very glad to meet you. I'm Muhammad.'

The road through the desert – that is to say, the country's main north–south highway – is another lunar landscape of rutted rubble. Muhammad drives us through it with the confident piety of a Georgian and the hopeless nihilism of a Russian, weaving through the potholes like moguls on a ski piste. He farts constantly and seems unable to keep his voice down, rabbiting away to Eziz in Turkmen, only slowing down for the occasional herd of camels traipsing by the roadside – and for the inevitable police checkpoints every 50 miles or so.

By mid-afternoon, our bruised buttocks crying for mercy, we make it to Turkmenistan's most renowned tourist attraction. The Darvaza gas crater is about 200 feet across and 100 deep, and would not be particularly remarkable had its insides not been wreathed in flame for over fifty years.

We feel the crater before we see it. A hot wind lashes our faces, trumping anything the elements can throw at us. We follow the source of the warmth to where the air ripples over the desert, the stench of methane growing with every step. Soon the vast maw spreads below us, its walls on fire, its surface crackling, the rocks within it smouldering. The low purring of a giant, slumbering beast.

There are no records detailing how the fire began. None that are publicly available anyway. Eziz tells us that Soviet scientists were trying to stop the spread of poisonous gases, so decided to burn them off, only to massively underestimate how much gas there was.* Others believe that something more sinister is at work – the 'Gate to Hell' is how the crater is often named. It's a label that has made Darvaza famous. For the first time since arriving in Turkmenistan, we see other tourists – big gangs of us in pickup trucks, all here to meet in the middle of the desert. The only Turkmens present are the guides. A makeshift camp of yurts has been created, giving you an authentic camping experience to go with your trip to hell.

We spend a good hour gazing into the hypnotic flames. There's nothing

---

* You might think this amateur, but it doesn't even come close to the time in 1966 when Soviet scientists resorted to using an atomic bomb to extinguish an out-of-control fire at the Urtabulak gas field in Uzbekistan.

else to do, after all. I can't shake the sense of feeling somehow cheated. I wonder if the authorities have encouraged the mystique around the 'Gate to Hell' for precisely this reason: 'Here, stare at our big fire and our shiny white city while we bleed the rest of the country dry, while children pick cotton in the fields and villagers still ride mules.'

Turkmenistan takes things to extremes – a kind of cartoon caricature of Central Asia. But it only exaggerates themes that are present across the region: the ruling khan in his palace, the statues to the Great Leader, the importance of bloodlines, and the desire to keep power concentrated within the ruling family. Not to mention the decided lack of sentimentality: Central Asia's capitals think nothing of bulldozing the past as soon as the money becomes available, producing public spaces with all the tacky bling of an Essex mansion.

While the Caucasus has been defined by ethnic conflict, most Central Asian countries avoided large-scale bloodshed following independence. In these less democratic societies, nationalism has been channelled into symbols: flags tower absurdly high above public squares, complete with ceremonial guards, and each country celebrates its literary and historical heroes with immense pride.

Then there are the great paradoxes: young, urban, Russian-speaking Central Asians increasingly employ the language of Western postcolonialism to disparage the Soviet period as one of Russian oppression, while the rural poor, more likely to speak their ancestral tongue, flock to Russia for work, their remittances providing a lifeline to their communities. Older generations, who grew up in the USSR and saw the occasional benefit, are more nuanced, but more fatalistic.

Today, Russia is no longer the only power here. Two huge stories are likely to define Central Asia's future as it relies less and less on a distracted Moscow. The first is China, which asserts itself gently, as it has done over the previous chapters, only surfacing to build a road here, a palace there, buying the region's resources and loyalty in exchange. The other is Islam, which has seen a resurgence over the last three decades, particularly among its young, impatient population. Central Asian governments welcome investment from the former, and warily shackle the latter.

But for all its similarities and shared experiences, Central Asia is anything but homogenous. There are exceptions to most of the points made above: Tajikistan has seen war; Kyrgyzstan has not yet sunk to building craven monuments; and Kazakhstan, fat on its oil wealth and with a now-established tradition of technocratic governance, is more developed than any country we've been to so far. There is also hope in Bishkek and Tashkent that their countries might be on the brink of an economic boom. Tajikistan and Turkmenistan have, sadly, sunk into stagnation under their ruling families.

This has not dulled Eziz's enthusiasm for his country, however. 'Tomorrow, I will show you something special at Konye-Urgench,' he tells us excitedly.

'Isn't that another old city?' asks Emmanuel.

'Yes, unfortunately it was destroyed by Tamerlane. He was jealous of us. He stole all of our architectural ideas and took them to Samarkand. If you look at the buildings there, you will see that they are all Turkmen designs. Obviously in Uzbekistan, Tamerlane is a hero, but here we see him as a monster. But one very important shrine did survive: the tomb of Seyit Akhmed,' says Eziz reverentially. 'You must pass around it three times and make a wish.'

Emmanuel looks unconvinced. 'How far is it to Konye-Urgench?'

'Oh, maybe four or five hours' drive.'

'I know what I'm going to wish for,' says Emmanuel gloomily. 'Some decent roads for Turkmenistan.'

Eziz laughs uproariously again, before the laugh turns to a cough.

EUROPE

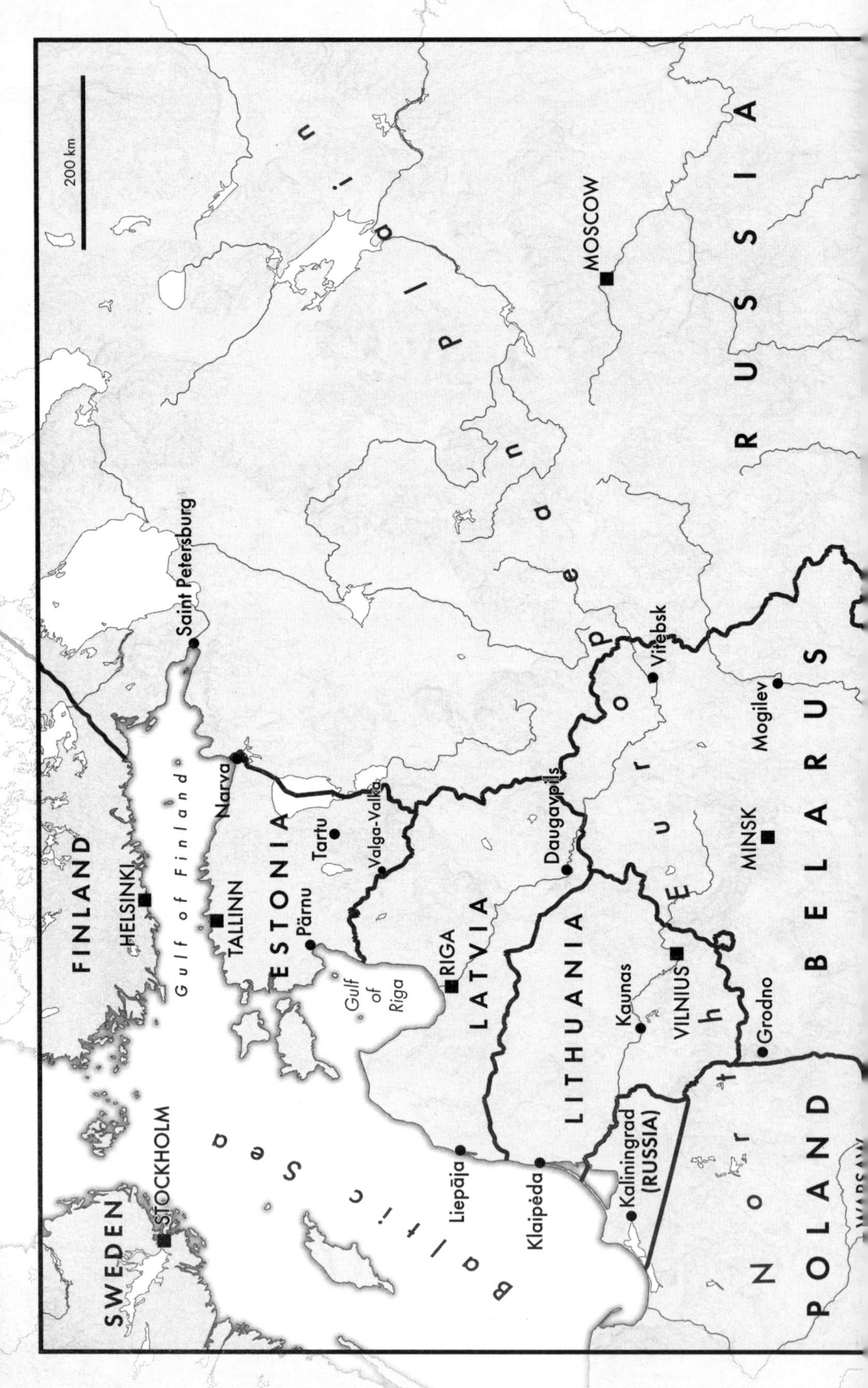

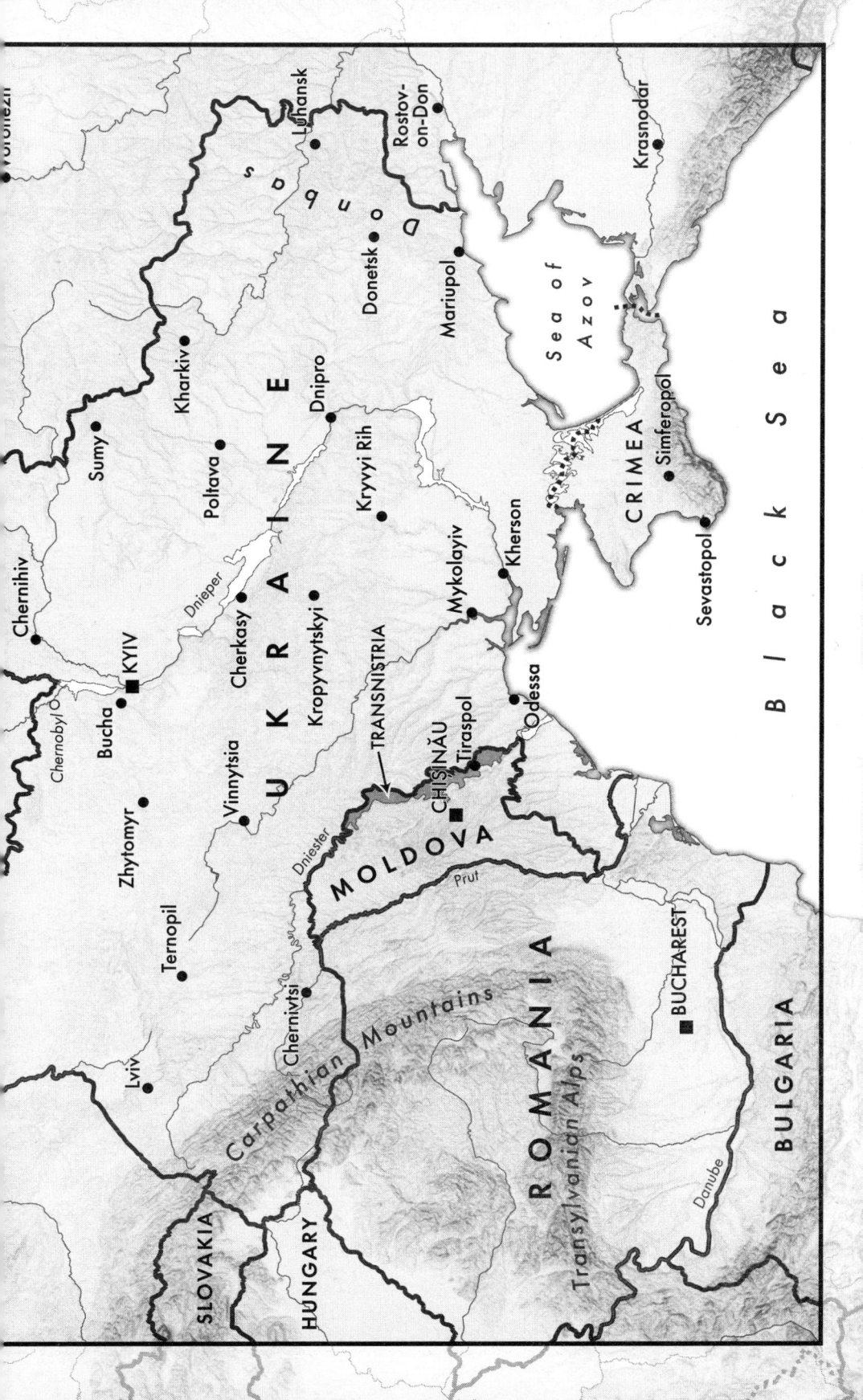

10

BELARUS
THE REMAINER REPUBLIC

Belarus doesn't exactly have a cuddly reputation. In May 2021, a Ryanair flight from Athens was flying over Belarusian airspace, en route to Vilnius, Lithuania. Just as the plane was about to begin its descent, local air traffic control warned the pilots of a bomb threat on board and instructed them to divert to Minsk. A Mig-29 fighter jet appeared alongside the aircraft, making it clear that compliance would be sensible. Upon landing in the Belarusian capital, security services boarded the plane but were unable to find evidence of any bomb. Conveniently enough, however, they did discover that two opposition journalists, wanted by the government, were among the passengers. Both were swiftly bundled away and into jail.*,1 The incident provoked international outcry. Europe had long turned a blind eye to goings-on within Belarus, but plucking a plane full of Greeks and Lithuanians out of the sky just to settle a political score had few international precedents.

Belarusians have spent almost three decades under the rule of Alexander Lukashenko, a mercurial, moustachioed strongman for whom hijacking budget airliners is just a minor footnote on the CV. For years he has been known as 'Europe's Last Dictator'. It's a label he's apparently comfortable with – when Germany's openly gay foreign minister used this epithet to describe Mr Lukashenko, the president shot back, 'I'd rather be a dictator than a queer.'[2] But his regime took a hard turn towards full-on autocracy in 2020, when a rigged election brought out mass protests. These were put down with extreme force amid an internet blackout, with thousands of

---

* In a further interesting insight into Belarus's justice system, both received presidential pardons within two years. One of the kidnapped journalists, Roman Protasevich, now hosts a TV show on Belarusian state television.

people facing arbitrary arrest. The fear induced by such brutality caused 200,000 Belarusians to flee the country. I've met several of them over the course of this trip in the Caucasus and Central Asia; few had any desire to return. Many had been left broken by the failure of the revolution and seemed bereft of hope about the future.

'All the talented people have left,' Andrei, a coffee shop owner in Tashkent, told me. 'It's just the thugs and yokels who live there now.'

Terespol, Poland

Two miles separate Terespol station from Belarus, which we'll be entering through its western border, near the city of Brest, before taking in Minsk and exiting north-west towards Lithuania. The southern frontier with Ukraine is closed for obvious reasons, while Russia to the east we have already covered.

Gusts of October wind tug at my hair and a splitting hangover pounds my head from within. I spent last night in Warsaw with some friends from the Polish foreign ministry, which involved predictable amounts of *wódka* with even more predictable consequences. One of these friends had been stationed in Minsk for two years by the ministry. He wasn't reassuring. He advised me to delete all the notes from my laptop about my trip and warned me with a straight face that I should not be surprised if I was followed around by the secret police.

'Should I check if they've bugged my room, too?' I joked.

He didn't laugh. 'I would just assume they can monitor your communications and act accordingly.'

So it's with no small amount of dread that I come across an ancient bus with the sign 'Brest' in the front window. A small group is milling around it; several are brandishing Ukrainian passports in the direction of the driver, who is checking each carefully before allowing anyone aboard. Eventually we move forward. It's like the scene in *Billy Elliot* where the strike-breaking miners head back down the pit. There's total silence among the passengers as we leave behind the quiet, ordered prosperity of the EU. Polish troops in balaclavas wave us over the narrow bridge that traverses the Bug River, a reminder that we are also bidding farewell to NATO's protective embrace.

On the Belarusian bank the bus is boarded by a lean youth barely out of his teens, his military fatigues comically oversized. He's evidently been sent as a scout to give everyone's documents a cursory glance. Once we've proven that we all have passports, we're allowed to advance another 200 yards before being ordered to disembark once more. We enter a large, deserted hall, our feet squeaking on the floor. This time it's a proper passport control, with an officer in a smart green uniform and a wide-brimmed commissar's hat. The line of Ukrainians in front of me is subjected to interrogation, which, in the silent hall, we can all hear. Each is asked the same questions.

'What are you doing here? How did you leave your country? Do you plan to go to Russia? Are you sure you don't plan to go to Russia?'

Belarus and Russia form part of what is called the Union State and have removed border checks with each other, meaning that the Belarus border is effectively the Russian border. Presumably the last thing Belarus wants is to be accused of allowing Ukrainians free passage into the Russian Federation to cause trouble.

When it's my turn to hand my passport over, my palms are sweaty. If they'd given the Ukrainians a grilling, I wonder how many questions they're going to ask a Brit. Remarkably, there are none.

'Irish?' the officer smiles encouragingly. I wonder if this is a trick or just more illiteracy. I give a half-shrug, which seems to be the correct response. The officer looks at my visa, tells me to make sure I'm not here for longer than eight days, and gives me a stamp. I'm relieved to have entered hassle-free, but as we drive past the epic line of cars waiting patiently at border control on the other side of the road, it doesn't escape my notice that the queue to get out of Belarus seems far longer than the one to get in.

Next day, the turnaround is almost biblical. The clouds disperse, the wind drops, and a golden dawn greets Brest. The smiling manager at the Hotel Bug waves me out of the door with such enthusiasm that I'm even tempted to reconsider my plans to spend the whole day making Bug-related puns (yes, I did check the room for hidden cameras). Besides, the frowning, Soviet city of my imagination is nowhere to be seen; in fact, Brest old town is something of a gem. There are dinky little cafés, brick-built churches, and on some streets even old-fashioned gas lamps. It's mid-autumn, unseasonably warm, and the trees have come out in some beautiful reds and ochres. Small armies of orange-bibbed workers scuttle up and down every avenue with rakes, pulling the freshly fallen leaves into neat piles before adding them to bin bags. Indeed, the streets are conspicuously clean and litter-free, a fact that is probably more noticeable after months spent in Central Asia. I'm also surprised by the lack of police. Law enforcement presence was ubiquitous in even minor Central Asian towns, with loudspeakers attached to their cars so they could harry the hard-pressed populace. Their absence here is quite startling, given my friends' insistence that this is a fearsome authoritarian state.

The pedestrianised Sovietskaya Street, in the centre of town, is flanked by bars and cafés that spill onto the pavement. Brestovians are gregarious and quick to welcome a stranger. In one bar I meet Ksenia, who is keen to shatter these initial positive impressions. 'Oh don't worry, if you go just a couple of kilometres up the road, you'll see that everything is grey and communist,' she drawls.

Ksenia works in a British software company. 'IT is a big industry here, one of the success stories of this country over the last few years. Lots of foreign companies outsource work to us. Of course, the problem is that it means exposing Belarus to the outside world quite a lot, so the government needs to decide if it prefers to have money or to be a closed country.'

I'm unsurprised by this; I tell her that most of the Belarusians that I've encountered on my travels have been IT workers.

'Yes, lots of people left,' she says sadly. 'That's always an option for me too, I suppose, but there aren't that many places that will take us. Georgia, Turkey, Poland maybe ... But I like it here. I'm close to my parents and the cost of living is quite low. It's enough to afford a decent car and lifestyle.'

'You don't worry about the politics?' I ask, deciding to chance my arm.

'I don't see what I have to worry about. It doesn't affect me too much. I don't support the president, but I also get nervous about some of the things the opposition want.'

'Like what?'

'Their big policy is to restore the Belarusian language and make it the country's only language. But most of us don't want to learn Belarusian. It's like in Ireland: just because someone from Dublin speaks English, it doesn't mean they aren't proud about where they're from.'

Ksenia, as you might have guessed, is speaking Russian. In fact, around the city today I haven't heard a single conversation that isn't in Russian. I know I probably shouldn't celebrate the successful crushing of a culture, but it has made things a lot easier.

'Is Brest a particularly Russian-speaking region, or is the whole country like this?'

'Some cities in the north-west are Belarusian-speaking; there are also lots of Poles there. But apart from that, you'll only hear Belarusian in the countryside, and more so in the west than the east.'

'So in Minsk they'll all speak Russian?'

Ksenia laughs. 'If you speak Belarusian in Minsk, people will look at you like you're an alien.'

From the bars on Sovietskaya, it's just a short stroll back to the Hotel Bug, which is located at the northern end of Lenin Street. Yes, it is still called Lenin Street. Having already travelled to seven countries that have gone to great lengths to rename anything associated with Vladimir Ilych, it's rather charming to be walking through public spaces that don't declare that the past never happened. And it's not just Soviet nostalgists that can bask in this refreshing glow of honesty. Many of Brest's streets sport smart brass plaques that go back even further, detailing their various historical names, as well as the dates they changed.

On Lenin Street, the sign reads:

Бульварный проспект: XIX–нач. XX	Boulevard Avenue: 19th–start of 20th century
Романовский проспект: 1913–1919	Romanov Avenue: 1913–19
Ul. Unji Lubelskiej: 1919–1939	Union of Lublin Street: 1919–39
Улица 17 сентября: 1940–1948	17th September Street: 1940–48
Улица Ленина: с 1948	Lenin Street: 1948–

The nearby square has suffered similar identity alterations, leapfrogging between:

Ратушная площадь: XIX	Town Hall Square: 19th century
Думская площадь: XIX–нач. XX	Duma Square: 19th–start of 20th century
Plac Ratuszowy: 1919–1935	Square of the Town Hall: 1919–35
Plac Piłsudskiego: 1935–1939	Piłsudski Square: 1935–39
Площадь Свободы: с 1940	Freedom Square: 1940–

These name changes, as well as the variations in script, can tell us much about Brest's past. In some ways, Brest might be considered *the* crossroads of Eastern Europe. There has been a castle on the island where the Bug River meets the Mukhavets River for over six centuries, one of the few defensible positions in a country with fewer contours than the proverbial crêpe. The castle has nevertheless changed hands dozens of times, variously being claimed by Swedes, Russians, Tatars and, for much of the last millennium, Lithuanians and Poles. Belarus has long been the ground for other states' clashes and has long suffered for it: it lost around half its population between 1654 and 1657, when the Polish Commonwealth, which ruled Belarus at the time, was invaded simultaneously by Sweden and Muscovy.[3]

But perhaps it is this slippery nature that has also made Brest a place of treaties. Brest was the spot where, in 1596, Orthodox Christians in the Polish-Lithuanian Commonwealth accepted the authority of the Pope. In 1918 it was the site of the Treaty of Brest-Litovsk, where the Bolsheviks signed away much of their Eastern European territory to buy off a rampant

German army. And twenty-one years later, in September 1939, Brest was where Berlin and Moscow's forces met once more, having each invaded Poland from opposite directions.

The Germans organised a parade in Brest for the handover to Kremlin control (the Molotov-Ribbentrop Pact, signed a month earlier, had stipulated the Bug River as the dividing line between the Nazi and Soviet spheres of influence). There's surreal footage of this parade on YouTube, with Nazi and Soviet troops, once sworn enemies, marching alongside each other.[4] When pressed on the outlandishness of this alliance, the Soviet foreign minister, Vyacheslav Molotov, is said to have quipped, 'Fascism is a matter of taste.'

But the fortress has not become the city's most visited tourist attraction because it's a convenient place for Germans and Russians to sign treaties and go on parade together. On 22 June 1941, Operation Barbarossa began. Eight million German soldiers swept into the Soviet Union, overrunning hundreds of miles of territory within the first three days of the invasion. Stalin was reportedly so shocked that he remained out of reach in his dacha for three days.

At Brest, however, the Soviets found their first wartime propaganda story. Even as the Wehrmacht advanced on all fronts, the 6,000 or so defenders at Brest Fortress stood their ground. Although they died almost to a man, it took the Germans eight days to seize the citadel, and some members of the resistance were still fighting in the stronghold's many tunnels a month later. The title 'Hero Fortress' was bestowed upon the site in recognition of the defenders' bravery.

The fortress complex is a mile or so from the city, nestled behind thick brick walls painted Bolshevik red. Everything here is designed to awe. You approach along a wide pedestrianised avenue, neatly trimmed grass on either side. The gate is an enormous concrete slab stretched across the path, with a five-pointed star carved out of the centre. As you pass through, the Soviet military anthem, 'The Sacred War', roars over the loudspeakers. Inside, the courtyard is strewn with mammoth granite sculptures of fallen warriors, their faces set, their shoulders and square jaws immovable. An eternal flame flickers in the wind.

The USSR lost over 20 million citizens during the Great Patriotic War, and of all the republics Belarus was the worst affected. As well as the carnage on the battlefield, there was also plenty of resistance to German occupation by partisan fighters, which was countered with devastating brutality by the Nazis, who subjected whole villages to collective punishment. The once-substantial community of Belarusian Jewry was annihilated. In all, around a quarter of the population died during the war.*

This trauma of conflict has fostered a modern Belarusian identity that is focused on peace. The first lines of the Belarusian national anthem are: 'We Belarusians, are peaceful people'. Indeed, one of independent Belarus's first major foreign policy steps was in 1993, when it gave up the nuclear weapons it had inherited from the Soviet Union without any strings attached.

'People say we are the same as Russians,' Ksenia told me. 'But one big difference is that Belarusians will not tolerate war. Some people say Lukashenko is going to call up people to fight alongside Russia in Ukraine; I don't think he would survive that.'

I'm up early the next morning and sleepwalking towards the station, where the 6.30 train to Minsk awaits. Brest station is a trainspotter's paradise, and one of the rare places in the world where trains exchange bogies.

No, you did not read that wrongly. Bogies are the equivalent of the axle of a train. They need switching because the rails in former Soviet countries are set 8.5 centimetres further apart than their European counterparts. Where the two gauges meet, such as at Brest, we get a bogie exchange: each carriage of the train is lifted off its axle and fitted with a new set of wheels for its onward journey. It's a bit like a Formula One pit stop, but instead of three seconds it takes three hours.

---

* Anyone with an interest in the Belarusian wartime experience would do well to watch *Idi i smotri* (Come and See), a visceral 1985 film described as one of the greatest anti-war works of all time.

The 'Warsaw Side', which uses the four-foot, eight-and-a-half-inch Stephenson Gauge, is the more modern part of the vast station complex. It has an arched glass-and-steel roof covering the platforms, designed for trains that once travelled all the way to Berlin. Since the onset of the pandemic and Belarus's subsequent political isolation, no passenger trains have passed this way. But Brest's bogiemen have still been kept busy: neither plague nor war have prevented tonnes of Russian freight continuing to roll through here towards the West.

The huge, classical station building is in the centre of two sets of platforms. At the ticket office, I'm pleasantly surprised not only by the price of a ticket – one-way to Minsk is 25 Belarusian roubles (£7) – but also that I'm allowed to purchase it without handing over my passport for scrutiny. The walls may be adorned with hammers and sickles, but this is the first place in the whole former USSR that hasn't required me to identify myself to move around the country.

I head to the 'Moscow side' of the station, with its 1,520mm Russian Gauge rails, and board the morning commuter service to the capital. I go to the end of the carriage and order a coffee. As compensation for the bitter, instant filth she pours into the cup, the carriage attendant is delighted to aid me on my linguistic quest to discover how Belarusian differs from Russian.

'Oho! So many differences!' she smiles. 'Food and clothes are often different, but you should look up the months of the year.'

Set on the right track, I discover that the old Slavic calendar – still followed by Poles, Ukrainians and Belarusians – has distinctive names for each month that coincide with the seasons. For example, in Belarusian, February is *Liuty* (the fierce month); August is *Zhnivień* (reaping month); and November is *Listapad* (leaf-falling month). The Russian language forsook these names, replacing them with the Roman equivalents at the dawn of the eighteenth century during Peter the Great's 'modernisation' drive. This is why the Bolshevik takeover in 1917 is referred to as the *Oktyabrskaya Revolutsiya* and not something sweet like the Mushroom-picking Putsch or the Conkers Coup.

Armed with these new words, I begin to feel slightly guilty about dismissing Belarusian. It's sad to see an old language squished under an imperial steamroller, no matter how convenient it might be. Mind you, much of the steamrolling appears to be self-induced. Census data from 2019 suggests that although 60 per cent of people consider Belarusian to be their mother tongue, only 32 per cent speak it at home, compared to 64 per cent who speak Russian.[5]

Natallia, a Belarusian I met in Georgia, told me how she and a group of friends had tried to start a language meet-up – a get-together where Belarusian exiles could gather to practise their own language.

'They tended to last about five minutes, and then someone's discipline would crack and we'd just end up speaking Russian,' she told me sadly. 'How can we regain independence if we can't even speak our own language?'

Belarus is often dismissed by Western commentators as being somewhat of a Russian client state – still lumbered with Soviet street names, speaking Russian, and reliant on Moscow for oil and foreign policy direction. Personally, I think this is a little harsh, and there is nuance beneath the surface. Indeed, I've come here seeking to test my hypothesis that Belarus is essentially like modern Britain: a country that chose to become independent, but with a population that didn't know what independence meant, and a political class who lacked the vision to carry it out.

Like Britain, Belarus was one of the richer and more successful republics of the union to which it belonged. It had seen a post-war boom, centred around heavy industry and high-tech machinery; there was even an automotive sector: the Minsk motorbike and the Belarus tractor were popular across the Eastern Bloc. Belarus was also a key refining point for Soviet oil. Faith in the USSR among Belarusians remained strong, even after the Chernobyl Nuclear Disaster in 1986, which disproportionately affected Belarus as northerly winds carried radioactive fallout from nearby Ukraine. A 1989 poll showed 69 per cent of Belarusians identifying as Soviet first, Belarusian second. In contrast, in Armenia the number seeing themselves as Soviet first was a mere 8 per cent; in Estonia, just 3 per cent.[6]

So when the USSR's collapse came, many of the conditions were already in place for what we might call a 'Soft Belarexit'. Without cheap Russian fuel to lubricate it, Belarus's heavy industry quickly became a heavy burden. Unemployment piled up. Inflation rocketed. All the while, superficial changes came to be seen as examples of petty nationalism: the Belarusian language was imposed in schools, causing resentment among Russian-speakers, and the reversion to the old white-red-white tricolour flag got the same sneering response that the return of blue passports received in Britain. 'What about the price rises?' people asked instead. 'What about the red tape? What about the families divided? What about our jobs?'

Unlike many other republics, which held some sort of pre-emptive referendum in 1991 on whether to secede, Belarus did not put the question to its people. Legally, the collapse of the USSR made independence inevitable, but the absence of a referendum left the new government without the popular mandate that other republics enjoyed. This legitimacy gap was worsened by delaying the first election until 1994, presumably in the hope that things would improve before voters went to the polls. But by the time it came round, the old communist elite who had inherited the country were tearing themselves apart, setting the stage for a young populist to enter the political fray who would mould Belarus in his image for years to come.

It's funny how the most oppressive post-Soviet leaders come in pairs. Russia and Azerbaijan have both been run by KGB operatives, Turkmenistan and Uzbekistan by graduates of Soviet orphanages. Belarus, like Tajikistan, found salvation in the form of a former director of a state farm.

Admittedly, Alexander Lukashenko was a pig farmer, which is probably a little haram for Tajik tastes; on the other hand, he did share with Emomali Rahmon the advantage of being an outsider who could profit from the infighting between the former Communist Party elite. In the 1994 presidential election campaign, he railed against corruption; against inflation that averaged 40 per cent a month; and above all, promised closer ties to Russia.[7]

In Belarus's first (and last) free and fair election, Lukashenko won a crushing landslide, and quickly sought to reverse some key steps towards independence. A referendum in 1995 saw Belarusians vote in large numbers to reintroduce the Soviet-era flag, to give the Russian language equal status to Belarusian, and to move Independence Day to 3 July, the day of the liberation of Belarus from Nazi Germany in 1944.* The process of renaming streets and removing statues, which had only just begun, was also put on hold.

Lukashenko also signed a treaty that would create the Union State of Russia and Belarus. This removed borders between the two countries, but more importantly unlocked the supply of Russian oil at rates far below world prices. This allowed Belarus's state-owned oil refineries to roar back into action and make billions for the state, helping Lukashenko to restore some Soviet-era prosperity. In effect, Russia's cheap energy would subsidise the Lukashenko regime's social policies. Over the following three decades, incremental tweaks were made to align Belarus with its big brother: Russia was permitted to place its military on Belarusian territory; and between 2011 and 2014, the two countries began coordinating their time zones – Minsk's clocks now move in lockstep with Moscow.

However, while Lukashenko has often danced to Moscow's balalaika, he has never quite given Russia an excuse to abolish his state entirely. He refused to support Russia's recognition of South Ossetia and Abkhazia as independent states, just as he baulked at Putin's annexation of Crimea. Meanwhile, the Kremlin's attempts to force Belarus into paying higher prices for Russian gas often result in Lukashenko adopting a more accommodating policy towards the EU. He is, if nothing else, a wily operator. Along with Comrade Rahmonov, he is the longest ruling post-Soviet leader. Indeed, helped along by the post-Soviet incumbent's usual bag of thuggish tricks, the two farmers recently overtook Joseph Stalin's record of twenty-nine years in power.

The brief Indian summer is over already. Minsk is cold and blustery, with clouds that are toying with the idea of unloading upon us. Come-and-have-a-go-if-you-think-yer-hard-enough sort of weather. No sooner have I registered these stern omens than I'm whisked by the crowd of passengers

---

* The original date, 27 July, was the day the Belarusian parliament declared its sovereignty from the USSR.

down into the warren of tunnels beneath the station. Passengers also pile in from the adjacent platform; the train from Moscow has just arrived from the east. A group of young Russian women are ahead of me, eagerly discussing the first stop on their shopping trip.

'What's the name of the mall?'

'Zamok, I think. It's right next to the Marriot.'

'And our cards will work here, right?'

'Should do. Maybe we should go for coffee to test them.' They erupt into excited giggling.

Since the outbreak of the war in Ukraine, many foreign brands have left the Russian market, and Belarus has done a decent bit of business as a middleman. Russians who can't necessarily afford to fly to Dubai or Turkey have started taking advantage of the open border to do a little holiday shopping. They are likely to feel right at home. Minsk residents will be tired of hearing this – but the capital does look like a mini-Moscow. Eighty per cent of the original city was razed to the ground in the Second World War, and the rebuild drew heavily on the neoclassical structures, almighty squares and broad, arrow-straight streets that came to define late Stalinism. Here too the streets bear the names of communist idols – the British Embassy, for example, is located at the junction of Lenin and Marx Streets.

But this evening I make a beeline for another of His Majesty's outposts. Anyone who has been on the road for a while will understand the feeling; constantly getting used to different foods, languages and customs can take its toll. Sometimes on a Wednesday night you miss those times where you can head down your local, order a pint and get the football on the telly. Fortunately, Minsk has a place that fits the bill. On the train I discovered with a flush of patriotic pride that there is an establishment in this city called the Vinnie Jones Pub. The name is not as outlandish as it sounds – Guy Ritchie films set in the 1990s involving guns and gangsters have become immensely popular in these parts. Presumably they struck a chord.

After a day wandering around some of the museums, I head to International Street and spot the neon sign above the door – Vinie Jones Pub – even more beautiful because it's been misspelled.

'Pint of the black stuff, please, guv'nor,' I say, taking a seat at the bar. I'm promptly served their house stout – a Vinie Dark. Next to me is a thickset bloke in his late thirties. We get chatting after Newcastle take the lead against Everton; it turns out Denis is a Spartak Moscow fan.

'You don't support Dinamo Minsk?' I ask him.

'No, no,' he says firmly. 'Spartak until death.'

It would be easy to dismiss this as another example of Belarusians' lack of national identity, having so little sense of self that they even support Russian football teams, but Spartak Moscow actually have a strong following across the former Soviet space.

In the USSR, football sides, like everything else, needed to be approved by the authorities. Successful teams enjoyed powerful institutional backing from one of the ministries that represented a sector of the Soviet economy or society. You can usually guess which industry a team represents by its name: we have already noted Cotton Picker FC in Tashkent, but the variety is endless. In Ukraine it's Shakhtar Donetsk (The Donetsk Miners); in Moscow the Soviet Ministry of Transportation's side was Lokomotiv, and the military was represented by the Central Sports Club of the Army (CSKA). Meanwhile Belarus's most successful team in recent times has been BATE Borisov. BATE is short for the Borisov factory for Automotive and Tractor Electrical equipment. You can see why they went for the acronym.

Then there was Dinamo, sponsored by the secret police, which became an association of clubs across the USSR and the Eastern Bloc. These became some of the best in the country, with Dinamo sides from Kyiv, Moscow, Tbilisi and Minsk all competing in the Soviet Top League.

One team, however, began without any state backing. Spartak Moscow, founded in 1921, was a team of ordinary, talented people who originally funded themselves through the suspiciously capitalist means of selling tickets to matches. At the core of their team were Nikolai Starostin, the captain of the Soviet national side, and his three brothers. Eventually their performances and popularity earned them backing from the Food and Meatpackers Union (hence their nickname of *Myaso* – meat), but for ordinary people they weren't seen as representing any special interest, instead being viewed as the people's team. By the end of the 1930s, Spartak rivalled Dynamo

Moscow as the most successful side in the USSR. Unfortunately, the late 1930s was a bad time to be a rival of the Soviet secret police. Led by the football-mad Lavrentiy Beria, the secret police were ordered to compile files on the Spartak players. For Starostin, let's just say Siberia beckoned.

For once, though, this story has a happy ending – such was his fame that Starostin was treated well by the Gulag guards and his fellow prisoners, even serving as a coach in the camps. Upon his release, a compromise was reached between his secret police enemies and equally influential friends, and he was allowed to move to the Kazakh SSR, where he founded the team that is still the biggest club in Kazakhstan today: Kairat Almaty (The Almaty Braves).

The Spartak–Dynamo rivalry has lasted almost one hundred years, and Spartak have remained the people's team.

'Has football got worse since the Soviet times?'

He laughs. 'Grisha!' he shouts to the barman. 'The Englishman wants to know if football here has got worse since the Soviet times!'

The barman shakes his head. It was a leading question, I admit. I've been to a couple of games so far, one in Tbilisi and the other in Almaty. The first was watched by around twenty people, and the second had more police in attendance than supporters.

'No one cares any more,' says Grisha. 'The matches are shit; the players are shit. The whole thing is just a playground for oligarchs. Who wants to watch Belarusian football?'

'It actually became popular in England during the pandemic,' I say.

'Yeah, because no one else was playing except us.'

Denis decides that I need to see more of Minsk, so we bid goodbye to Grisha and head back into the misty night. The pedestrianised Zybitskaya Street has bars that are open round the clock, even on a weekday. But Denis takes me back along International Street, where we stand outside a hole-in-the-wall metal dive called Rock n Rollshik so he can have a smoke.

Our football chat is quickly interrupted as Denis catches sight of two figures approaching from the other end of the street. His face grows pale.

'Come on, inside!' he hisses. Bewildered, I get my first, briefest glimpse of two policemen, clanking up the street like a pair of Cybermen in full body armour, before I'm dragged within. Denis keeps his eye close to the steamy window to ensure they have passed.

'OK, safe now,' he says. 'Leave your drink here.'

'What was all that about?' I ask once we step outside once more.

'You can't drink on the street here. Usually it's not a problem, the police will normally just ignore it, but I don't want to give them any excuses to arrest me again.'

'Again?'

'I was picked up earlier this year; I was part of a group of people, and someone shouted a chant against the president. They started arresting us all at random.'

'Arrested you for what? Shouting something?'

'Article three hundred and forty-two of the Belarusian criminal code, organising actions that grossly violate public order,' Denis reels off in a bored voice. 'You can get three years inside for that; luckily they let me out after fifteen days.'

'Not sure I'd call fifteen days in jail *lucky*.'

He gives a hollow laugh. 'It wasn't nice. At first the cell was very cold, but then more and more people were arrested, and it just started filling up, and we had the opposite problem. There must have been twelve of us in there, slowly stewing in this small room, for two weeks, none of us knowing what was going to happen to us. Eventually they let us all go. But as you can tell, I'm not that keen on going back any time soon, even if it's just to the Sizo.'

Sizo is the Russian acronym for Pre-trial Detention Centre. It's a mark of honour among many opposition activists to have ended up here at one point or another. They tend to be used by the authorities as a holding pen for people involved in protests while they work out what to do with them. Usually stints inside them aren't long, but they can occasionally turn out to be quite brutal. In the summer of 2020, thousands of people were arrested while protesting against the results of the presidential election, which were widely seen as fraudulent. Many of them suffered grievous injuries while in detention. Most infamously, the Okrestina Detention Centre on the outskirts of Minsk became associated with mistreatment of detainees, who were packed into cells, refused access to the toilet and arbitrarily tortured, including several being hospitalised with injuries consistent with being raped with a police baton.[8]

'What are your memories of those protests?' I ask Denis.

His face relaxes into a vague smile. 'I have only good memories. Obviously, towards the end we worried; we feared for ourselves and our friends. But I'll never forget the unity, the purpose we all had. The music. The hope. Whatever happens, they'll never be able to take that memory away.'

I had seen the protests on the news. Tens of thousands of people in Minsk, all singing the *perestroika* anthem 'Khochu Peremen' (I Want Changes) by rock group Kino.

'We used to go to a bar called Karma,' Denis continues. 'It was a hub for the opposition movement. But then the crackdown happened; half of my friends chose to flee the country. Karma closed down eventually; they moved to Kyiv instead.' He gives a short bark of mirthless laughter. 'That didn't go too well for them either. They're in Warsaw now.' He sighs, deeply. 'We're peaceful people here in Minsk, Joe. That's all any of us want. As Pushkin said: a bad peace is better than a good quarrel.* I've seen the pictures of this city after the war with Germany. There was nothing left. When we see what is happening over in Ukraine . . . Just remember the First World War started with a single shot. Who knows how far this could escalate?'

This has taken quite a decisive turn away from Soviet football.

'Do they keep a low profile now, the opposition?'

He looks at me appraisingly. 'I suppose so, yeah.' He glances up and down the road once again. Not a cosmonaut in sight. 'There's a place I can show you.'

He takes me down a nearby set of steps at the foot of which a stocky man is standing guard; he nods surreptitiously at Denis before rapping

---

* *Khudoy mir luchshe dobroy ssory* (literally – a thin peace is better than a good quarrel) is actually an old Russian proverb, although Pushkin does say it in *The Captain's Daughter* (1836). Ironically enough, this was six months before Pushkin himself died from wounds sustained in a duel.

three times on the black metal door behind him. It opens from within and muffled jazz echoes up the passage. Inside the speakeasy, everyone seems trendy. There are beards, topknots, leather boots and whisky. People seem to know Denis.

He introduces me to a raven-haired woman named Alina.

'What are you up to in Minsk?' she asks me.

'Trying to find the difference between Belarus and Russia.'

'Oh, good luck with that.'

Denis frowns at her. 'You need to have some of our food,' he says, 'then you'll get a real taste of the country.'

'Oh god, don't put the poor guy off forever,' mocks Alina.

'I wouldn't mind some restaurant recommendations actually,' I say. 'It's been a while since I had something Slavic.'

'OK, well, let's hang out tomorrow night,' she says, without a moment's hesitation. 'I'll show you somewhere fun!'

'Somewhere fun' turns out to be a daunting building on Independence Avenue. Its facade has classical columns painted an anaemic yellow. There's very little adornment; it's an austerity that fills the onlooker with dread. The wide pavement makes it impossible to walk up to it without being conspicuous. Perhaps it's just me, but I get the sense that people speed up as they pass. No one looks at it. Nobody seems to be going in or out.

This is the headquarters of the Belarusian Committee of State Security; this is a literal translation of its Russian name, *Komitet Gosudarstvennoy Bezopasnosti*, but in both languages it usually goes by its acronym, the KGB. Belarus is the only former Soviet state whose secret services have retained the name. Opposite the building is a park that leads to the Dinamo football stadium, it's named Dzerzhinsky Garden after the founder of the original Soviet secret police – the Cheka. Dzerzhinsky's statue, standing at the park's entrance, gazes across the street at the stomping ground of his successors. There is a freshly laid bouquet of flowers at the foot of the plinth.

I check my map once more. Worryingly, the directions to the restaurant where I'm set to meet Alina are telling me to proceed directly towards the dread edifice. My mind jumps to all the spy literature, all the Bond films... surely I hadn't fallen for the oldest trick in the book, the KGB honeytrap?

I reach an unremarkable door in the south-eastern wing of the building and push. There is indeed a restaurant within. No one grabs me; no one places a sack over my head. Alina bursts out laughing when I suggest she might be a police agent.

'No offence, but trust me, the government has much bigger problems policing its own people to be worrying about foreign tourists.'

'I'm not a tourist; I'm a writer,' I say, nettled.

'Well, if I *were* a government agent, you'd have just given yourself away right there!' she grins. 'Admitting to being a writer in the middle of KGB HQ! Anyway, let's order before it fills up in here. Last night, you told me you wanted to eat something traditional. Something Slavic, you said.'

We now come to the most important linguistic difference between Russian and Belarusian: the former imported the German word for potato (*kartofel*), whereas Belarusians say *bulba*. And there's a very good reason that Belarusians have their own special word for the humble spud: Belarusians are, per capita, the largest consumers of potatoes in the world. A study from 2017 found that the average Belarusian gobbled down 178 kilograms of *bulbas* a year – *half a kilo every day*.[9]

Many people find this amusing. A Ukrainian friend, upon hearing that I was going to Belarus, commented, with a hint of a sneer, 'Cool, have fun in Potato Land.'

There's also a Russian phrase, 'Love is not a potato, you can't just chuck it out the window' – the implication being that a potato is prosaic, bland, common as the muck it's dug up from.

I find much of this snootiness unfair. I tell Alina that I associate potatoes with honesty, solidity and reliability.

'You don't need to patronise us,' she smiles. 'We know we eat too many of them, OK? I'm sure we'll all be eating couscous and drinking oat milk like you guys soon enough.'

'OK, well until then, what do you cook with all these potatoes?'

She frowns, as though trying to decide if I'm being serious, and then seemingly gives me the benefit of the doubt. 'OK, first, I'm going to make you try *draniki*.'

'I've heard of those, they're basically hash browns, right?' I try to sound enthusiastic but can't help feeling a little underwhelmed to be dining right under the KGB's nose and only ordering hash browns.

'They most certainly are *not* hash browns!' says Alina, looking scandalised, before embarking on a long explanation of the intimate differences between *draniki* and hash browns. I quickly zone out. I'm beginning to see what my Ukrainian friend meant – these people take their potatoes seriously. For those who are curious, I suppose *draniki* are more like potato pancakes or Jewish latkes than hash browns. Another difference is that whereas in Anglo-Saxon nations hash browns are generally a small part of a larger breakfast, here *draniki* are the main event, eaten in huge quantities, along with sour cream.

'They're also the world's best hangover cure,' Alina concludes, which is convenient, because at that moment the waiter arrives with a large, ornate carafe filled with a curious amber liquid. To add an air of menace to the picture, he plonks a shot glass down in front of each of us.

'What's this?' I ask warily.

'*Krambambula*. It's our national drink.'

I eye it suspiciously. 'Dare I ask the ingredients?'

'Well, each recipe is different, but it generally involves red wine, gin, rum, sometimes some vodka too.'

'Jeez, so you *are* trying to poison me?'

'It has some honey and spices too!' says Alina defensively. 'Anyway, what shall we toast to? Potatoes?'

'To Walter Raleigh.'

I down my glass of Lukashenko Iced Tea and feel my throat ignite. I immediately see the need for *draniki* to absorb the attack. I lather them in sour cream and, once I've dried my eyes and taken several swigs of water, wolf them down – meagre compensation for the ordeal I've just put my insides through. That said, I've had few things perk me up faster.

I ask her what brought her back to Belarus after living in America, and discover that – ironically – it was in part due to the relative freedom there during the pandemic.

'So you think Lukashenko did the right—'

'Ssshhh!!' she hisses, alarmed. 'Don't say his name!'

I laugh. 'Who is he? Voldemort?'

'You just don't want to draw attention to yourself, we just call him The President.'

'Remind me what you were saying about Belarus being freer than America?' I grin. She doesn't smile.

This is a phenomenon that you will see across former Soviet countries – an oddly impersonal relationship with the head of state. In Russia, Azerbaijan and across Central Asia, 'The President' is marked by the lowering of one's voice – perhaps in reverence, often warily. But this is the first time I've been actively told not to say the leader's name.

'We sometimes call our president "*Batka*"; it means father in Belarusian, so you can say that if you prefer,' says Alina in a low tone. 'But do try to remember where you are! You know right next to this restaurant is what we call the *Amerikanka*. It's a Sizo where they hold important political prisoners. It's actually one of the first prisons the Cheka built here. Unless you'd like to spend the night there, I suggest we talk about something else.'

'Fine,' I say, trying not to smile. Alina's lips are twitching too.

I hadn't known what to expect from Belarus. I'd come here wondering what distinguished this country, or whether it was indeed a country any more, rather than a place that turned its back on independence to become a mere offshoot of Russia. But it's this lack of nationalism that is the most charming feature of Belarusians, and is ironically something that marks out a Belarusian from the average Russian. Belarusians are not in your face about every historical grievance; they don't see their neighbours as potential threats; they don't view everything as a conspiracy theory; nor do they try to police your language or rip down every statue that doesn't suit the nationalist narrative. Still, many argue that Belarus's failure to fully expunge the legacy of the USSR has caused the worst elements of it to linger. The warnings I received about an all-encompassing police state, where people are afraid of strangers and of speaking their mind, seem overblown in hindsight, but there is nevertheless a chill one feels when dealing with the authorities, and the stories of Denis and his friends seem to fully justify that.

So despite the cultural differences, in political and economic terms, bound by Moscow's institutions and abetting its war, the client state characterisation is probably fair. More than anywhere else, Belarus's farewell to Russia was less a 'goodbye' and more a 'be right back', leaving little room for true independence, at least from the current Kremlin administration.

Alina is keeping up quite a pace as we bar-crawl along Zybitskaya. Before long I've had too much and begin worrying about waking up in time to catch my bus to Vilnius in the morning. We start to head back to the hotel, pleased that wisdom has prevailed for a change. But as we're about to exit the street, I spot a sign outside a cocktail bar that's offering two-for-one on margaritas. I catch Alina's eye. The establishment's name is Uno Más. Seeing as this is Europe's last dictatorship, we take this as an order.

11

THE BALTIC STATES
THE STRAIGHT-A REPUBLICS

This book has had its fair share of corruption, war, ethnic cleansing, inequality and dictatorship. The Baltic States – Estonia, Latvia and Lithuania – are something different: Baltic GDP per capita dwarfs other former Soviet countries; their educational standards are higher; they are less corrupt; their infrastructure is better; the air is cleaner; people live longer; and there have been no wars.

Was this just luck? What has gone so right in these countries that everyone else has missed?

Back in London, I put some of these questions to Mart Kuldkepp, a Professor of Estonian and Nordic History at University College London, beginning with these key questions of identity. I know that there are people from Estonia, Latvia and Lithuania who will object to being included in a book about the former USSR. As a general rule, people from the Baltic States *hate* being described as being from a post-Soviet country, so I start off by asking Kuldkepp why that is.

'Well often it serves no useful function!' he says. 'Like you take a random article about, I don't know, Estonian e-governance or Latvian tourism or Lithuanian tech startups. And then you see this label, "oh, the small Eastern European, post-Soviet country . . ." applied in a context where it doesn't contribute anything, people quite strongly react against being associated with this label. You wouldn't say that France is an ex-Nazi country, even though France was occupied by Nazi Germany during the Second World War. It's more than thirty years now since the Soviet Union ceased to exist!'

I wonder if it would be churlish to point out that a four-year wartime occupation is a bit different to half a century of Soviet rule, but Kuldkepp hasn't finished.

'Another reason why people don't like it is because the Baltic States were independent countries in the 1920s and 30s,' he says, referring to their successful break from over a century of tsarist rule in the aftermath of the Bolshevik Revolution. 'They were then illegally annexed by the Soviet Union, an annexation that was never recognised by most of the Western world. When the Soviet Union collapsed, people didn't see their countries as new states, they saw a lifting of the occupation and a restoration of the state they used to have. So being labelled "post-Soviet" all the time, people feel like it gives too much credence to this idea that they are new states, which they don't want to be. They want to be old states who have regained their pre-war independence.'

Vilnius

A dull dawn presides over the cobbled streets and terracotta roofs of Vilnius old town. The Lithuanian capital is an undeniably pretty place, but it's also expensive. It comes as a shock to be paying €20 a night for a hostel bed beside the musty bus station. Perhaps I've become too used to how far my money has gone thus far on my travels, but it's certainly a shock after cheap and cheerful Belarus, just 23 miles to the south-east. Still, the prices are accompanied by a certain level of quality. There's an affluence, a self-confidence, and I'd go so far as to say a smugness about Vilnius. The narrow streets are home to innumerable bars, antique stores and bookshops. There are cafés with people beavering away on Macs, beanies worn so high they're almost a kippah; e-scooters whizz up and down the streets; and the level of English is excellent – or 'super-good', as people here say.

On the corporate front, it's clear that Vilnius has been showered in foreign investment, and from more niche areas than we might expect. The banking sector has been gobbled up by Swedish giants Swedbank and SEB Group; meanwhile Hesburger, a Finnish fast-food chain, seems to be going toe-to-toe with America's finest. Other than that, the Lithuanian capital has all the accoutrements that a tourist in Eastern Europe might expect. The young are kept occupied through the provision of free walking tours and pub crawls, Kalashnikov shooting ranges and vodka-tasting sessions. For the culture vultures there are innumerable overly restored churches, a KGB museum that details the atrocities of the Soviet era, including the deportation of 130,000 Lithuanians to remote parts of the USSR, and a Jewish Museum that pays tribute to the rich history of Lithuania's Jewish community, 90 per cent of whom were massacred in the Second World War. Despite this, it's the KGB museum that has adopted the moniker 'The Museum of Occupation and Genocide'.

On the more original end of the scale, there's a nifty bar area that has been created from the bowels of a former prison called Lukiškės. There's also the Republic of Užupis, an 'independent territory' proclaimed by a group of anarchists on April Fool's Day in 1997. It's a chilled, bohemian part of town. Pimple-faced, baseball-capped students, nattering loudly in Spanish and German, queue up to read the republic's constitution printed in forty-odd languages on a wall in Paupio Street. It contains such inanities as 'Everyone has the right to live by the River Vilnelė, and the River Vilnelė has the right to flow by everyone' (I thought back to the chains of razor wire on the Belarus border) and 'Everyone has the right to be unique' (naturally there's a queue of people ignoring this right by lining up in front of the constitution to take *exactly* the same selfie). At least they're making the most of Article Nine: 'Everyone has a right to idle'.

More discerning visitors buy handmade postcards from artists' studios, or loaf around drinking on the cobblestones in front of Špunka, a craft beer joint. All in all, it's a merry, peaceful part of town; almost as if Lithuanians are trolling the other former Soviet states. 'Look, we've even made a success of a self-proclaimed republic in our midst.'

I had hoped to be reunited with some of my old university friends in Vilnius. Unfortunately, this being a weekend in late October, one of them is out in the countryside, picking mushrooms with her family, a fascination that the entirety of north-eastern Europe seems to share. The other, Elena, is occupied by something even more stereotypical – she works in London. However, she does a sterling job of acting as a digital co-pilot, guiding me to restaurants and insisting that I try *šaltibarščiai* (cold beetroot soup) and *cepelinai* (potato dumplings that get their name from being shaped like a

Zeppelin airship – read the word again and you'll see why). Finally, there are *bulviniai blynai*, which turn out to be the same potato pancakes that we tried in Minsk. I gobble all of this up, and apart from one rather unappetising experience with a pig's ear, it goes down very well.

Their absence is a shame because, for all the city's aesthetic charm, I find it hard to meet people. I wander around, exceptionally well fed and watered, but rather lonely. Locals seem less inclined to chat with strangers than in other post-Soviet states. Perhaps this is because foreigners are less exotic on the Western side of modern Europe's iron curtain, although it may also have something to do with where I'm from. In the countries I've travelled to thus far, the English are viewed quite favourably. People in the Baltics are more likely to have seen the reality. Tens of thousands of Estonians, Latvians and Lithuanians moved to work in Britain once permitted to do so without a visa in 2004.[1] In return, tens of thousands of Brits came to the Baltics on cheap flights looking for cheap booze. So when a Lithuanian meets a tourist who starts speaking to them in English, there's not only a lack of curiosity, I suspect there's also wariness. They know the odds of you throwing up over the cobblestones within a couple of hours.

That said, I've been advised by Elena that speaking English is by far preferable to Russian.

'It's much safer, especially when talking to younger people. Only switch to Russian if they tell you they don't speak English.'

This makes sense; we've already talked about what the Balts think of Russian occupiers. It's a feeling that has only been enhanced since the Ukraine war began. There are Ukrainian flags on every street; local buses move around town with 'Vilnius ♥ Ukraine' written on them; there are even billboards seeking volunteers to cold-call people in Russia, asking them to protest and end the fighting.

All this to say that my usual tactic of walking into a bar and canvassing local opinion doesn't seem to be bearing much fruit here.

Fortunately, some of the museums here are very good, particularly the Centre for Civil Education, part of the Presidential Museum. Civil education is not a concept I have yet come across in the former USSR: the museum explains the different arms of government and how they work; it also talks about what it means to be a member of society. In another daring departure from the post-Soviet mindset, the centre has embraced interactive exhibits. As I've got so used to visiting museums whose purpose is not to encourage thought but to tell the 'correct' story of a country's past – usually emphasising the victimhood – I find this trust in the visitor rather refreshing.

In one exhibit, visitors are given an iPad and offered a chance to take a 'corruption test', in which they are presented with a series of shady situations and offered various options. Some of the examples of corruption seem mundane – 'Would you pay your driving teacher to pass you?', or 'Would you share the exam questions with friends if you got hold of them before the test took place?' – but they make the point that corruption always begins at the lowest level. As I have seen on my travels thus far, while people may indict leaders for corruption, it often reflects a wider societal problem.

The Soviet system, with its centralised control over all aspects of society, allowed the very worst kinds of cronyism to prosper. In most countries it continues to this day: in Azerbaijan, we saw Eldon paying the examiner to secure top marks in his sociology exam; we had the disappearing funds for the Astana light railway in Kazakhstan; and that's not to mention the trail of greased palms I left behind me after my own years in Moscow. Overcoming corruption is no mean achievement. Georgia took some steps towards it in Mikheil Saakashvili's first term, although it has been backsliding ever since. But in the three Baltic States, the vision of themselves as Western countries gave them huge impetus to make the changes required to join the EU, including tackling corruption.

'The idea of having been in the West and needing to be reintegrated was embedded in this idea of restoring our inter-war statehood,' Kuldkepp tells me. 'The Baltic politicians in the late 1980s and early 1990s were adamant that we were members of Europe and a part of the West.'

One of the first objectives was to join the EU, which meant adopting Brussels' *Acquis Communautaire*, a hulking body of law and institutional standards that binds the EU members together. To make the necessary changes, the Baltic States implemented drastic reforms in the 1990s, keeping government debt low, while going further than even the IMF and World Bank had suggested in order to steer the economy away from Russian influence.

'There was this saying of "We're willing to eat potato peelings if we have to, only so that we become free again," and this was quite universally shared,' says Kuldkepp. 'There was a sense of needing to make sacrifices and people were ready for that. They had an idealised view of the West as well, obviously, because they hadn't had that much actual contact with it. They tended to think that everything will be fine once we are in the West . . .'

All three countries were accepted into the EU in 2004, but their progress has not slowed since then. Lithuania now sits thirty-fourth in Transparency International's World Corruption Perception Index, ahead of countries like Spain, Italy and Portugal. Estonia, meanwhile, is an amazing twelfth, higher than Britain and France.[2] Meanwhile, Lithuania's elections have all been conducted smoothly and deemed free and fair by international observers. Transitions of power have occurred without incident. Even when, in 2003, the Lithuanian presidential election was won by Rolandas Paksas, a man who *did* turn out to have connections to the Russian mafia, his impeachment was swift and constitutional once these links were discovered. Perhaps we might view this as only right, but it's worth stopping to consider how unusual this is. Orderly transitions of power have been far from frequent in the former USSR; every other country we've been to either languishes under a dictatorship or has been forced to remove lousy governments through revolution.

Along with this iron political discipline at home, some credit must go to the EU for setting the institutional standards for these countries to follow. But this presents us with an irony: in order to become successful independent countries, the Baltics have been forced to outsource much of the government's power: their central bank is based in Frankfurt, while many of their laws are made in Brussels and upheld in courts in Luxembourg. It's as though, having fought so hard to be free, they've taken another look at governance and chosen the option that says 'Essential Cookies Only'.

On the north bank of the Neris River are the beginnings of a more modern Vilnius. Glass office blocks hosting the likes of Radisson Blu and KPMG have begun to sprout up overlooking the old town. Crouched beneath them, along the highway leading north out of the city, is a brick wall painted in the colours of the national flag. Humanoid figures have been carved out of the wall, which stretches for around 150 feet. Many of the bricks have names written on them. According to a plaque beside it, the monument is called Road to Freedom: 'A sculpture built to commemorate the 20th anniversary of the restoration of the State of Lithuania and the Legendary Baltic Way'.

For those unaware of the legend, the Baltic Way was a human chain stretching over 400 miles from Vilnius to Tallinn. It comprised around 2 million people, all of whom had come to demand an end to the Soviet occupation of the three Baltic States. The date chosen was 23 August 1989 – fifty years to the day since the signing of the Molotov-Ribbentrop Pact, when the decision to annex them was agreed by Stalin and Hitler. In the Soviet Union, a country that frowned on any form of mass protest, bringing 2 million people together like this was a stunning achievement. What with the mass protests that had convulsed the Caucasus a year earlier over the issue of Nagorno-Karabakh, it began to make Soviet authority in the outer rim look decidedly weak. It would not immediately bring freedom – many Lithuanians died defending the Vilnius TV tower from Soviet special forces in January 1991 – but such was the elation brought by this powerful, visual symbol of defiance that it stands out as a major step on the road to independence.

It was also a high point in Baltic unity, something that has been on the wane ever since. This is important, as another label that tends to infuriate people around here is referring to Estonia, Latvia and Lithuania as 'the Baltics', as though they are one country, which I suppose I have done for most of this chapter. This does a disservice to the history and culture of all three nations. Linguistically, the Estonian language has more in common with Finnish than Lithuanian and Latvian.* The latter two are members of the curiously isolated Baltic language family. Both languages have almost identical words for things like earth, fire, sun, day and night.† They also share the same word for 'hi' – *sveiki* (pronounced svay-key), which you can use when going into any restaurant or bar in both countries. I briefly dated a Latvian once upon a time and used to wake her up in the morning by saying *sveiki wakey* – needless to say the relationship didn't last long, but I've found it a useful mnemonic nonetheless.

Indeed, back in the early Middle Ages there was probably little between the Latvians and Lithuanians. They both worshipped pagan deities with names like Dievas, Perkunas and Velinas. Incidentally, one thing that you will quickly notice in Lithuania is that many words seem to end in -as. I arrived in Vilnius from Minskas; and other major world cities include Tokijas, Berlynas and Niujorkas. The fondness for this particular suffix even extends to words that already end in -as: if Elvis had been Lithuanian, he would have sung 'Viva Las Vegasas'.

However, following the marriage of Grand Duke Jogaila to Queen Hedwig of Poland in 1386, Lithuania was dragged irresistibly into the Catholic world, bringing an eventual end to the era of -as worship. The Polish-Lithuanian Commonwealth developed into one of the largest states in Europe, with Polish becoming the language of the elite in multi-ethnic Vilnius, and Lithuanian mainly surviving in the countryside among the peasantry. Meanwhile Latvia and Estonia were dominated by Baltic-German merchants and clerics, with Riga, Tallinn and other cities along the Baltic seaboard becoming outposts of Lutheranism after the Reformation.

These differences may seem trivial to outsiders but have nevertheless bred proud, distinct cultures that were only really brought together by Russian imperialism. As Estonian President Ilves said in a 1999 speech, 'What we [the Baltic States] have in common almost completely derives

---

* The Finnish and Estonian anthems, incidentally, have almost exactly the same tune.
† For those interested, earth is *zeme* in Latvian, *žemė* in Lithuanian; fire (*uguns/ugnis*), sun (*saule/saulė*), day (*diena/diena*) and night (*nakts/naktis*).

from shared unhappy experiences imposed upon us from outside: occupations, deportations, annexation, Sovietisation, collectivisation, Russification. What these countries do not share is a common identity.'[3]

But I'm going to disagree with the president. I feel these countries are united by more than calamity. The Baltic States have followed an almost identical institutional trajectory since regaining independence: they joined the EU and NATO together in 2004; they joined the Schengen Zone together in 2007; and, although joining the euro was more staggered, they had all adopted it by 2015. Granted, you could say similar things about other Eastern European countries – the pattern described above also applies to Slovakia, for example. But the EU is also heavily invested in Baltic unity. The iron successor to the Baltic Way's human chain is a project called Rail Baltica, which seeks to connect the three capitals by high-speed train. It's a link that has been mooted for decades but, as in Central Asia, these are the kinds of epic projects that small nations struggle to finance. The tsars and the Soviets never viewed linking the cities as a priority, preferring to build lines that tethered each of them to a Moscow-centric network. However, the EU does see the strategic benefit of linking up its member states and has provided 85 per cent of the $6 billion funding for the project. The new train will cut the journey from Vilnius to Riga to just ninety minutes, and from Riga to Tallinn to a little over one hundred.

As it is, Rail Baltica has barely broken ground, so I'm stuck with taking the four-hour Flixbus on a rain-lashed journey north. I loiter for a few days in Riga before boarding a train north-east. My destination is Valka, a border town in the quite literal sense, straddling the Latvia-Estonia frontier. A place where we can truly explore the extent to which European integration has blurred the lines between the Baltic nations.

Valga-Valka

By the time we pull into our destination the weather has become genuinely bleak, the temperature hovering around one degree. The station, whose neoclassical design could place it in any small town from Odessa to Vladivostok, has one distinguishing feature. Written on the frontispiece, where a hammer and sickle doubtless once stood, are the words 'Valga-Valka – One City, Two Countries' in several languages. The slogan is no joke. Since 2007, this city has gone further than perhaps any other in pursuing the Brussels dream of a United States of Europe. The station is on the Estonian side. A police patrol is waiting at the end of the platform, casually glancing at identity documents, but other than that checks are minimal. The walk from the station towards the centre is undeniably ugly. A towering factory looms over the railway tracks, the pavements are uneven, and several of the apartment blocks seem abandoned. The clammy mizzle suits the town well.

I head to the city museum, where I hope to learn a little about how the idea of 'one city – two countries' works in practice. Unfortunately, I'm left disappointed. The museum's permanent exhibition has a lot of information on former Estonian residents of the town, on the Estonian victory over the Red Army at the Battle of Paju in 1919, and on a former Estonian theatre that was once located here, but I learn little about the presence of others. As far as the museum is concerned, this could just be any old provincial town. I put these thoughts to the lady at reception. I want to know how deeply the concept of a shared Estonian-Latvian town has taken root.

'Do the two parts of the town have a joint mayor?'

'No, we have separate ones.'

'What about schools?'

'We have separate schools too, Latvian schools on the Latvian side, Estonian on this side, but sometimes we hold common events together. Actually, they don't mix so much as older generations. People over forty or so, because we all studied Russian at school, we all have a common language. Now, kids don't want to learn Russian, and the level of English isn't so high in Latvia as it is here in Estonia – so they have no real way of communicating with each other.'

'Do you not learn each other's languages at school?'

'Why would we learn Latvian?' she says, with a hint of a sneer. 'We've always used a third language to communicate, either Russian or English. In fact, back in the old days people used German. We don't see language as a barrier really, I still go to the Latvian side pretty much every day. Things are cheaper there – my aunt lives in the Latvian part of town and she has to live on a crazy low pension of just two hundred and fifty euros a month. Can you imagine? In Estonia, pensions are double that! But she can't afford to move here because she can't sell her house. So she's ended up stuck, like a lot of people,' she tails off sadly before being struck by a sudden thought. 'Here, let me put you in touch with someone.' She scrawls an email address on a piece of paper. 'Talk to Rainer Kuutma, he used to work on cross-border relations between the two sides. He should be able to tell you more. And try the Latvian side; you'll see the difference.'

I head out into the drizzle, through the quiet, worn-out Estonian streets, wondering how bad Latvian Valka must be if this was the nice part of town. I come across the border rather suddenly. There's little to signify that this is an international frontier between two sovereign nations. On the Estonian side, the same two policemen from the station are sitting in an unmarked Škoda, watching a troop of teenage skaters scythe across the main road. An angry mother on the school run blares her horn at them. The police are unmoved. The kids may have begun their antics in Estonia, but they are in another country now, out of reach of the law. Telecoms companies are less easy to elude. 'WELCOME TO LATVIA' comes the message from O2 around twenty seconds after my incursion south-east.

The border itself has become a tourist attraction. The banks of the river (Pedele in Latvian, Pedeli in Estonian) have been redeveloped into a park spanning the two countries. There's even a love swing so you can swish from one to the other. On either side the architecture is identical, and the miserable autumn air equally cold; my nose has started to stream.

However, it's noticeable that certain industries have sprung up on the border's edge, giving solid form to each government's tax policies. Mammoth warehouses feature prominently on the Latvian side. Their names – AlkoShop, SuperAlko, Alko1000 etc. – should give you a general idea of their line of business, and judging by the number of cars parked outside they're doing a roaring trade. Curious, I poke my nose inside one of the megastores and am confronted by mountains of beer and wine; a whole aisle is reserved just for cognac, while vodka has three all to itself. People buy in such quantities that the staff go around with forklift trucks to assist thirsty customers.

Dining options are pretty thin on the ground, but Latvia does at least boast the charming Café Walk. I've only just grown accustomed to using the Estonian greeting '*tere*', so it's disconcerting when the barista greets me with a cheery '*sveiki*' once more. People are far more personable out in the sticks and no sooner have I ordered an *alus*, which is the Latvian (and Lithuanian) for beer, than I end up chatting to a woman called Madara, who is Latvian but lives in Estonia.

'I'm just heading back to Riga to get a new ID card,' she tells me. 'I drive through Valka all the time on my way back from Estonia. I've always thought it looked like one of those small, sad towns with nothing much happening, but I decided to give it a chance to see if I was wrong – turns out I wasn't!'

I look at the menu, which is in Latvian and English.

'You should try the *kartupeļu pankūkas*!' Madara tells me. 'They're a traditional Latvian staple.'

I order them and the waitress arrives with . . . can you guess? Yep, it's a plate full of potato pancakes.

'So you're a Latvian, living in Estonia . . .' I ask Madara. 'What do Estonians think of Latvians?'

She laughs. 'The classic thing they always say is that Latvians have six toes; they seem to feel we're some kind of mutants.'

'What do Latvians think of Estonians?'

'That they're slow as fuck,' she grins. 'It's just our little joke about them. I have no idea where it comes from, just like no Estonian can explain the six-toe thing. But we just have these endless jokes of how anything that happens doesn't reach Estonia until the next day, or how they take forever to complete a task. The biggest irony is that they are always ahead of us in most things and that annoys us even more.'

'How are they ahead of you?'

'They're just more advanced; they have more money, a better education system and stuff like that. Whenever the Latvian government has a project, we aim to be, if not better, then at least on the same level as Estonia and Lithuania. Whereas Estonians see Finland as their benchmark.'

'How do you feel about Lithuanians?'

'Well the language is more similar; we call Lithuanians our brothers and vice versa. But mentally we are more like Estonians. I think the best way to think of the Baltics is as three sisters who have this sibling rivalry and get annoyed by each other, but at the same time will stand up for each other and stick together without a doubt.'

I head down to the Latvian version of the Valka Museum, which costs just €2. In true Soviet fashion, I'm given a free guided tour from a smiling, middle-aged woman called Inese. I learn that Valka was once a small market town in the Russian Empire called Walk (pronounced Valck), populated predominantly by German merchants and Latvian tradesmen. Walk became a railway hub at the end of the nineteenth century, which brought local Estonian villagers here in search of jobs. Walk's inhabitants rubbed along fairly well until the Russian Revolution, which was followed by Latvia and Estonia's successful struggles for independence. In 1920 the two new nations set about trying to form a border, with both claiming the town. They needed some kind of referee, and so, naturally, an English knight was brought in. Sir Stephen Tallents opted for the stock British solution: partitioning the town on ethnic lines according to who made up the majority in each area. Two-thirds was awarded to Estonia and the remainder to Latvia. Walk became two separate towns in two separate countries; border fences came up in the centre and its population shrank as trade collapsed.

That might have been that, but unlikely champions of the town's unity were found in the form of Nazi Germany and the Soviet Union, who both presided over a united Walk. The Soviets reopened the vital rail link with Russia and the town became a hub for producing agricultural machinery and textiles, as well as a base for around 3,000 Red Army soldiers.

Inese seems to feel that Valka saw better days in the Soviet era. As with many small Baltic towns, independence dealt it a significant economic blow. The soldiers left, industry collapsed, and the once-bustling centre took on a dilapidated mien.

'Obviously the soldiers were not well loved, especially in the early days, but later on ... I won't say we got along, as we never stopped resenting them being there, but many lived here with their families; the theatres were full; the town felt like it had life. We had industry here too. The sewing factory employed over a thousand people. Today I'm not even sure if it employs a hundred.'

This highlights an important caveat to the Baltic success story. For all the undoubted progress that they have made over the past three decades, their populations have shrunk dramatically, and not only due to the departure of Soviet garrisons. All three countries are hampered by low birth rates and young people flocking west for work. This is a trend that can be seen across the non-Muslim states of the former USSR, but it has hit the Baltics particularly hard.* On the eve of independence, the combined population of the three countries was around 8 million; it's now a little under 6 million. Latvia's population has decreased by over a third. Lithuania hasn't fared much better, losing almost a million residents since independence, seven times the number deported by the Soviets after the war.

At the same time, within all three countries a familiar capitalist dynamic has emerged: major cities have received the lion's share of investment as the new service industries and government administrations are concentrated there. This has transformed Tallinn and Vilnius in particular into vibrant, wealthy capitals that are now almost unrecognisable as former Soviet metropoles. But such growth comes at the expense of the regions. The vast majority of towns are less peopled than they once were. Valga-Valka has been hit particularly badly: from a peak population of 26,558 in the early 1980s, the town's combined population is now just 16,755.

Next day I'm venturing up to Narva, a city in the far-north-eastern corner of Estonia, on the border with Russia. The weather is even fouler than yesterday, turning my last glimpses of Valga into a grey, sludgy blur. The one element of colour is offered by the train to Tallinn, which is bright orange. With its sleek sliding doors and fancy on-board ticket machine, it feels like an emissary from the twenty-first century sent to dazzle the hackneyed inhabitants of this little old town, harvesting them one by one

---

* The Islamic countries, as we saw in Tajikistan with kids crammed into schools, have the opposite problem.

from their half-abandoned housing blocks. Inside, the train is warm and modern – more than could be said for the ancient Latvian banger that hauled me up here. After a couple of hours' respite from the elements, staring at the bleak, boggy countryside rushing by, I alight at Tapa for the connection to Narva. It's even colder this far north, my breath rises in spouts in front of my nose as I step outside. Even on a sunny day, there's not much to recommend Tapa. Its name hardly inspires confidence – in Estonian it means 'to kill' – perhaps this is why the Red Army decided to establish an airfield here in 1939. The Soviets are long gone of course, but the base remains. It now houses new guests, who have brought with them a certain amount of geopolitical tension.

It's part of Russian foreign policy lore that the West made a promise to Mikhail Gorbachev, ruling out the expansion of NATO after the collapse of communism in Eastern Europe. A range of figures, from Margaret Thatcher to François Mitterrand, Helmut Kohl to US Secretary of State James Baker, all intimated that Soviet security interests would be respected if Moscow peacefully let go of its hold over the Eastern Bloc and accepted a reunified Germany.[4] 'Not one inch eastward' was Baker's formulation.

The view in Moscow is that Gorbachev was betrayed. Far from being disbanded, NATO quickly began to gallop towards the borders of the new Russian Federation. East Germany, Hungary, Poland and the Czech Republic had joined by 1999. In 2004 there followed a cascade of new members: Bulgaria, Romania and Slovakia completed the entire set of Warsaw Pact countries, and they were accompanied by the Baltic States, which had been part of the Soviet Union itself.[5]

From the Baltic perspective, joining NATO was *the* most important guarantee of their renewed independence. The anti-corruption drive, aligning their economies to EU standards, the euro, the borderless Schengen zone, all meant nothing if there was no military protection for these gains.

The Soviet experience has left the Baltics with a level of Russophobia unlike anywhere else I've been, even more so than Georgia. For the past three decades, the Baltic States have been the loudest in predicting that they will be next on the Kremlin's territorial shopping list. They point to Vladimir Putin's desire to undermine NATO, to create a land bridge to its enclave of Kaliningrad via the Suwałki Gap,* and more generally, in the words of the Lithuanian foreign minister, to 'rebuild the Soviet Union 2.0'.⁶ Indeed, there has been a definite 'told-you-so' air about many of their leaders and public intellectuals since the Ukraine invasion. Thus the chance to nestle into the bosom of the world's most fearsome military alliance was welcomed almost unanimously. As soon as the Baltic States joined NATO in 2004, the alliance began patrolling its newly acquired airspace from Šiauliai airbase in Lithuania. Ten years later, after the Russian annexation of Crimea, more aircraft started operating out of Ämari airbase in Estonia.⁷

Getting boots on the ground has proved more complex, and from the Baltics' perspective, the alliance's presence here is alarmingly small.⁸ Each country plays host to a NATO battlegroup: Lithuania and Latvia host multinational forces led by the Germans and Canadians respectively, whereas Estonia's defensive contingent is largely made up of British soldiers, based in Tapa. In the face of a full-blooded Russian invasion, these forces are likely to act as little more than a speed bump, and as with any alliance – it's only an alliance on paper until the fighting starts. The world waits to see if Russia is prepared to call NATO's bluff by triggering the infamous Article 5 – which compels all members of the NATO alliance to come to the aid of a country under attack.

The article has only been triggered once before, by the USA in the wake of the 11 September attacks in 2001. This led to the subsequent NATO invasion of Afghanistan. The Baltic States joined NATO three years into this war and were under pressure to prove their worth to the alliance. They therefore committed troops to the war in Afghanistan, putting these countries in the unique position of having invaded Afghanistan twice in little over twenty years, first under the Soviets and then under NATO. But Afghanistan is a different proposition to war with Russia. The question that hangs over the alliance remains: when the threat of

---

* A strip of land where the borders of Poland and Lithuania meet. The gap – 65 miles wide at its narrowest point – separates Belarus from the Russian exclave of Kaliningrad.

nuclear war is placed on the table, will French, Spanish, Italian and, most importantly, American soldiers be sent to protect little Lithuania and tiny Tallinn?

Narva

Friends from Tallinn have been less than complimentary about Estonia's easternmost city: 'Narva can be a dangerous place, you ought to watch your step,' was a comment I'd heard on more than one occasion. I figure I've been to plenty of places about which similar remarks could be made, so generally brush them off. Still, comments like this shape how we see our physical environment. The silhouettes of Soviet towers seem somehow intimidating as we approach the station. The elements too are aggressive: what was mizzle in Valga has now become sleet. Still, the town does at least have some mod cons – a Lidl, a Hesburger and, best of all, Bolt e-scooters scattered everywhere. However, there is one large difference. It was noticeable on the train as we skipped eastwards into the onsetting dusk, but here it's unmistakable. All the street signs, and many of the shop names, are in Estonian, but everyone is speaking Russian.

The slight snag with all this Baltic Russophobia is that Russians (or Russian-speakers) still represent around a quarter of the population in both Estonia and Latvia. When the Baltics regained their independence in the 1990s, there was a debate among the new authorities about whether to grant citizenship to those who had arrived from other parts of the USSR during what they saw as the Soviet occupation.

'By international law, they had no right to be there,' Mart Kuldkepp told me. 'If we conceive of the Estonian state as having been illegally occupied and annexed, they could be considered agents of a foreign power rather than people who were there for legitimate reasons. Some forces in the liberation movement wanted to extend citizenship to everyone who was a lawful resident of Estonia, whereas others – and this was the policy choice that won out – wanted to restrict citizenship only to people who either themselves had been citizens of the pre-1940 Estonian state, or whose parents or grandparents had been citizens.

'The same thing happened in Latvia; it got both countries a huge amount of international criticism, because it was framed by Russia and by well-meaning people in the West as basically a form of Russophobia. They said things like, "How can you punish these poor, innocent people who haven't done anything wrong except move to a different part of the Soviet Union? How can you now leave them without citizenship?"'

I hate to be grouped in with well-meaning people from the West, but these do strike me as legitimate questions, especially when the full implications of this citizenship policy become clear to me later in the evening.

For a large town, Narva's nightlife is disappointing. I try most of the central bars around Peetri Plats (Peter's Square). There's an Irish pub with very little atmosphere and no seats at the bar (so not an Irish pub); a restaurant called Old Trafford that isn't showing the Man United game; and a craft beer place with a confederate flag on the ceiling and a barman with a ten-inch knife in his back pocket. The latter proves most fruitful. A young bearded chap named Gleb overhears me ordering the bar's own brand of honey beer, which seems to be enough of an excuse to start a conversation.

'What brings you to this dump?' he asks, shifting his stool closer to mine.

'Seeing the sights,' I shrug. I'm unsure how convincing this sounds, but Gleb doesn't comment. He's here from Tallinn to visit his family.

'So you're from Narva originally?' I ask.

'I was born here, yeah, but moved to Tallinn as soon as I could, like anyone with a brain.'

'What makes you call Narva a dump?'

He raises an eyebrow. 'Have you seen it?! There's nothing to do here, all the factories have closed, the border with Russia is getting increasingly difficult to cross, half the houses are empty too.'

I ask him about the non-citizen situation.

'Oh ho, so you know about that? I guess that's what Narva is famous for these days,' he says darkly. 'OK, so here is my personal situation. I was born here in Narva in 1988, my parents both came here from Ukraine in the Soviet period. So you'd think that, OK maybe my parents are "occupants" or whatever, coming to work in land that had been illegally annexed – not that they knew anything about that, my dad just got offered a job on the power plant; but still, let's call them occupants. But my sister and I, we were born here. I didn't choose to come, it's just where I happened to come into this world. So what exactly am I occupying? A hospital bed?'

'So you couldn't get Estonian citizenship?'

'Nope! And you know the hilarious thing? They don't consider me Ukrainian either. They consider me Russian, because in their heads everything that is bad has to come from Russia. They gave out these grey passports, which is basically a residency document that allows us to remain in Estonia – kind of them, I know! – but for international travel it isn't accepted by the rest of the world, only by Russia and Belarus. Does that sound fair to you?'

I'm unsure if he wants me to answer this. Even the European Court of Human Rights and the Council of Europe have expressed concerns regarding the treatment of stateless individuals in Estonia and Latvia.[9] The situation has improved in Estonia in recent years, while the Ukraine war has been used by the Latvian government to justify stricter measures towards Russian-speakers.[10] These days, around 48 per cent of Narvans are Estonian citizens, 36 per cent have a Russian passport, and about 14 per cent have no international passport at all, so are legally regarded as stateless.[11]

Whatever his origins, Gleb certainly sees his future as part of Estonia. 'It's all I know!' he says.

Most of the borders I've crossed on this journey have been innocuous, with lines seemingly drawn arbitrarily. Lithuania and Belarus, for example, demarcated their border using the boundaries of collective farms. But the Estonia–Russia border is epic. On either bank of the Narva River is a towering medieval fortress. On the Estonian side is the Danish-built Narva Castle, over 150 feet high and festooned with Estonian, Ukrainian and EU flags. Opposite is the Russian-built Ivangorod Fortress, slightly squatter, its thickset walls imposing. The road bridge that forms part of the Tallinn–Saint Petersburg highway crosses beneath these two keeps. There is a reasonably steady stream of traffic, although there are increasing signs that the border may close soon. I get talking to an old man who is also propped against the railings, looking across at Russia. I ask him about life in Narva; the conversation quickly takes on a familiar tone.

'There used to be people here,' he tells me. 'Now it's all empty. There's no work for anybody.'

'When did you move here?'

'In the seventies, I came to work at Krenholm; it was a famous factory once. All closed now.' He gestures towards the south, where there looms a massive nineteenth-century brick edifice. I went round it earlier; it appeared, like much of the city, to be in a state of decay. The glass was missing from the windows, and the surroundings were overgrown. I was reminded strongly of Pripyat – the abandoned town in the shadow of Chernobyl. Every entrance was sealed shut. Once, during the tsarist period, Krenholm was the largest cotton factory in the world. It was still a powerhouse in the Soviet era – I have a suspicion that much of the cotton farmed by the slave labour of Uzbek children may have ended up here.

'Why did it close?' I ask the old man.

'The EU.' He shrugs. I decide not to challenge this assessment; I've seen Brussels blamed for less likely things.

'Did you consider going back to Russia when it closed?'

For an answer, he points across to the opposite bank. 'Over there, people receive maybe a hundred to a hundred and fifty euros a month for their pension. Here I receive five hundred euros.' He seems to feel that this is all that needs to be said.

'Do you not feel discriminated against in Estonia?' I ask when he doesn't elaborate.

'Discriminated? How?'

'I don't know . . . they don't let you vote . . .'

'Vote?' he laughs. 'The Soviets didn't let me vote either. And Putin? You think Putin will let me vote?'

He leaves soon after and I'm left contemplating the border and the Baltics' journey of independence. We began by asking how these countries have been so disproportionately successful in comparison to the rest of the former Soviet Union. Sure, it helps to have nice neighbours. Who wouldn't want Finnish fast-food chains and Swedish banks next door? But it seems to me that these countries had a political class with a genuine vision for independence and were ready for it when the time came. This vision, combined with a spirit of sacrifice in the 1990s, saw them weather the harshest of economic shocks. In Estonia especially, investment in education and technology has yielded impressive results with world-famous companies such as Skype, Bolt and TransferWise all founded here.

Then there is their canny diplomacy. These three states have voluntarily chosen to hand over their currency, their borders, their national security and much of their lawmaking capacity to foreign powers, whether in the form of NATO or the EU. This seems to have worked, allowing slimmer states, and making the countries safer for investment, while foreign soldiers protect them. On the other hand, it has meant that much of the success has been concentrated in the major cities, and it is also notable that millions of people have chosen to leave their homeland altogether in search of better prospects overseas.

But the most chilling conclusion from the Baltic States' success is that systematic ethnic cleansing and disenfranchisement works. This part of the world was once a diverse collection of ethnic groups. The twentieth century saw the region's Jews exterminated by the Nazis, in many cases helped all too enthusiastically by the local population. The Germans and Poles who once lived here were also booted out in the war's wake, with many of Lithuania's Poles also 'repatriated' to Poland under Soviet direction – a policy that Lithuanian officials were not unhappy to see carried out. These losses were partially replaced by an influx of migrants from other parts of the USSR who, in Estonia and Latvia, now find themselves denied the right of citizenship and are deemed to have been occupants, even if they were born there. This has resulted in the creation of what have been termed ethnic democracies – polities that have managed to create a unified political culture by pretending that a substantial proportion of the population does not exist.

But perhaps this was the least bad option. 'If they had given everyone citizenship,' says Mart Kuldkepp, 'it is quite likely that Estonian and Latvian politics would have looked different. Citizenship comes with the right to vote in the national elections, and there would have likely been a much stronger pro-Russian political force in each country. It could have meant no integration with the EU or with NATO, and everything would have developed in a different way.'

To see just how differently things might have developed I'm next heading to Moldova and Ukraine, where debates over Russian-speaking communities have dominated politics for the past three decades.

12

MOLDOVA
THE REPUBLIC OF REUNIONS

'Moldova is a landlocked country between the Prut and the Dniester rivers, we have Ukraine to the north and Romania to the south,' intones Olga. 'Everyone learns this at school!'

Olga is an old friend from the Moscow days, but it's fair to say she's not entirely satisfied about having returned to her home country.

'You're really not selling it well,' I say. 'You need to emphasise the good things about Moldova. *In the plains that roll out from the Carpathian Mountains, where every village is overflowing with vineyards* . . . that sort of thing.'

'You really should have come in summer,' she sighs. 'This country is a bit shit in January.'

'I can't visit everywhere in May or September! Some country had to get January; I guess Moldova drew the short straw.'

'Moldova always draws the short straw,' she sighs gloomily.

The cards are stacked against Moldova in many ways. As Olga says, it's landlocked. Its main port is the Ukrainian city of Odessa, which has been under an intermittent Russian blockade for the past eleven months. Moldova's electricity and gas supply also largely comes through Ukraine. The country's biggest export partner is Russia, which is now under sanctions. And what's worse, Moldova was the poorest country in Europe *before* all of this kicked off.

For all that, there's a bleak midwinter charm about Chișinău (pronounced Kish-in-ow), the nation's capital. Snow can hush the hum of even the busiest city, but when a place is as much of a backwater as this its effects are positively eerie. Skeletal trees, stripped naked by the season, look forlornly on the quiet streets, which are flanked by two-storey houses and low-build hotels. If it weren't for the weather, the city might have a Latin feel. The word for street is *strada*, as in Italian, and on almost every *strada* is a wine bar with gregarious groups milling outside, smoking and drinking. Meanwhile the police are called the *carabinieri*, and in front of the city's history museum someone has even plonked a statue of the Roman Lupa, with Romulus and Remus sucking at her icy teats.

Chișinău is built on a gradual slope. I'm staying near the top, a short walk from Stefan Cel Mare Park. Stefan – Stephen the Great in English – is the country's national hero, having ruled the medieval principality of Moldavia for almost fifty years in the late fifteenth century. He came to power shortly after the fall of Constantinople to the Ottomans in 1453 and spent much of his reign steering a middle course, fending off the predatory intentions of the sultan, as well as the kings of Poland and Hungary. Stefan was successful in the main, but in the final years of his life gave in to Ottoman overlordship. The Moldavian principality spent the next 300 years being bounced around by the Turks, the Poles and Austrians until, in 1812, the Russians arrived on the scene.

Chișinău was considered even more of a backwater in those days. The poet Alexander Pushkin was exiled here, taking up residence in what he termed 'the only house in the town that is not made of clay'. It has since been turned into a museum, a quiet poke around which reveals few tourists but several enthusiastic babushka-guides who press-gang me into sitting in on a recital of his poetry. I begin to remove my coat before taking my seat, but one of them stops me. 'Keep it on! It's cold here!'

It turns out that much of the city is similarly chilly. Moldova is currently going through one of its periodic gas crises. These usually happen when small European countries do something that upsets their main supplier – Russia. Moldova's generally pro-European government, led by former World Bank economist Maia Sandu, has vehemently criticised Russia for its invasion of neighbouring Ukraine; she has also promised to drag Moldova out of Russia's economic orbit, and has banned their military symbols and TV channels. The Kremlin's initial reaction was to cut gas supplies by 70 per cent, and then, just as winter was drawing in, to zero. Meanwhile electricity, much of which had been imported from Ukraine, began to falter as the Ukrainian energy grid was targeted by

Russian bombing. This has meant that evenings in Chișinău are spent in semi-darkness: street lights are intermittently turned off to save electricity – as, on occasion, are traffic lights.

Moldova's opposition figures have condemned the government's confrontational line towards the old master, and the winter has seen rolling protests calling for a rapprochement with Moscow. Many of these have been led by parties linked to Ilan Shor, a Moldovan-Jewish oligarch who stands accused of a billion-dollar bank fraud and is currently in exile in Israel. Olga has invited me to an upmarket restaurant, Atypic. It does steaks. Naughty, juicy ones. She has brought her friend Adrian along too.

'He knows much more about Moldovan politics than me,' she says.

Adrian turns out to be shaven-headed with a scraggly beard and a cardigan, and his English is excellent.

'*Noroc*,' he says as we chink glasses.

'I'm presuming *noroc* is the word for cheers in Romanian . . . or Moldovan?' I add quickly.

'I call it Romanian,' says Adrian.

For decades, Moldovans have been struggling to agree on what language they speak. Depending on whom you ask, the official language in Moldova is either Romanian or Moldovan. Amazingly, this isn't just a matter of individual preference; even governing institutions have disagreed on it. The 1991 Declaration of Independence, for instance, stated that the national language of Moldova was Romanian, whereas the 1994 Constitution declared it to be Moldovan. The Supreme Court ruled in favour of Romanian in 2013, but a year later, when Moldovans were asked to name their mother tongue in the 2014 census, 53 per cent of people claimed to be Moldovan-speakers. Here's the thing – Moldovan and Romanian are *exactly* the same language. Which one you call it is often seen as a political statement: those who say that they speak Romanian also tend to consider Moldova a lost province of Romania and dream of one day reunifying the Romanian principalities; those who claim to speak Moldovan are more likely to have a stronger emotional connection to the Soviet past.

To cut a millennia-long story short, the almost simultaneous collapse of the Russian, Ottoman and Austrian Empires in 1918 saw an enormous power vacuum around the lower reaches of the Danube. This set the stage for the completion of the Romanian nationalist dream that had begun in the nineteenth century: unifying the Romanian-speaking principalities of Moldavia, Wallachia and Transylvania. As in the Baltics, nationalists in the Russian-ruled part of Moldavia (called Bessarabia) grabbed their chance swiftly. Initially declaring independence, they then invited the Romanian army to take over and annex the territory.*

Greater Romania did not last long: following the agreement between our old friends Molotov and Ribbentrop, Stalin was in a position to demand the return of those territories he considered to have been Moscow's all along. In 1940, with just a day's notice, the Romanian forces were asked to vacate lands beyond the Prut River as the Red Army moved in. The region was laid waste during the back and forth of the Second World War, with Romania joining the conflict on the Axis side. Finally victorious, Stalin installed a puppet government in Bucharest while, in the Moldovan SSR, Soviet propaganda did not let people forget the Romanian association with fascism. Instead, they tried to create a distinctive Moldovan identity as part of the USSR, changing the name of the language to Moldovan and converting it to the Cyrillic script.† Meanwhile, radio broadcasts and television from Romania were banned and border crossings were strictly limited. But the idea of a Greater Romania did not die.

In 1989, the fall of Nicolae Ceaușescu's regime at the hands of a Christmas Day kangaroo court made Romania seem like a place of new possibilities. On the eastern bank of the Prut, the Moldovan Popular Front came to power, openly calling for 'reunification' with their fellow Romanian-speakers. They saw Germany as their model. Moldovans and Romanians saw the river as a kind of liquid Berlin Wall. On 6 May 1990, the Popular Front organised the *Podul de Flori* or 'Bridge of Flowers',

---

* The annexation was never recognised by the Soviet Union, nor, incidentally, by the USA.

† There was a certain amount of historical justice to this, as Romanian itself had been written in Cyrillic until the mid-nineteenth century.

opening all the bridges across the river. Half a million people participated and threw flowers into the water, obscuring the gap between the two lands. By 1990, the Germans had overcome the deep scepticism of Britain and France and unification became inevitable; many in Romania and Moldova assumed the same.

And yet, over thirty years later, there is still a country called Moldova, and the Prut River still marks the point where Moldova ends and the EU begins.

'What stopped the reunification?' I ask Adrian.

He snorts, 'The Russians, basically. But it's become less important over time. The border crossing is quite smooth, and a lot of us have Romanian passports anyway. They're quite easy to acquire. The idea of two states doesn't matter so much if you have a passport for both. But it's also a matter of whether they want us,' he adds. 'I went to university in Cluj, it's the capital of Transylvania. It's a really great city, and if you ever get the chance to go, they have an awesome jazz festival. Anyway, when I was there, studying Literature, one of our teachers was also an immigrant from Moldova. She started publicly shaming me in front of the rest of the class about how awful Moldovans are, how we cheat, lie etc., and I'm like, *you're Moldovan!!*

'One day she made me stand up in front of the class and read the preface of an old Moldovan-Romanian dictionary; everyone could understand it obviously, but I was the only one who could read it as it was written in Cyrillic. And she was treating me as though I was some sort of exotic species for everyone to laugh at because I could do this. Can you imagine being *shamed* for having a talent that no one else has? It was bizarre. So I guess my point is: whether we want to be part of Romania or not, they have certain attitudes towards us that are hard to shake. If you drive to Romania and police see you with Moldovan number plates, they're guaranteed to pull you over.'

There's hope in some quarters that the war in Ukraine might finally push Moldova into the arms of its Romanian brother. This has certainly been the case with energy – one thing that has staved off an even more acute crisis this winter is the Romanian decision to supply Moldova with electricity at a vastly reduced rate. The EU has also provided €250 million to support the Moldovan economy.

'What do you think of all this?' I ask Olga, who has remained quiet so far. 'What do you call your mother tongue, Moldovan or Romanian?'

She grins, 'My mother tongue is Russian.'

'Does that not annoy people?'

'Some people maybe, but this is my country too; I was born here so I don't see why I should be forced to speak a different language,' she shrugs, reminding me strongly of people I'd encountered in Narva.

'But you can speak both?' I ask Adrian.

'As the Georgians say, we speak the language of the stupidest,' he says, flashing Olga a grin.

A couple of days later I meet Adrian and Olga once more, this time in Adrian's house. None of the lights are on and a T-shirt hangs over the chandelier in the living room.

'I'm epileptic, so these power cuts aren't good for me,' he says drily.

Adrian is midway through roasting his own coffee beans – he's recently purchased a roasting machine and driven it back here from Berlin.

'This is the only place I can find decent coffee in the whole country,' Olga laughs.

'I thought Tucano was OK,' I say, referring to a coffee shop I'd been to that morning. They both give me looks verging on the contemptuous.

'I guess he has just been in Uzbekistan,' Olga mutters to Adrian.

I want to protest. Tucano had treated me well, but I can feel that the delicate bubble of sophistication that Soviet people tend to perceive around British travellers is on the verge of popping, so I keep the enthusiastic review of my caramel cappuccino to myself. This is a shame, though, because Moldova is not known for its range of worldwide brands, and Tucano Coffee has been a bit of a success story, first opening here in 2014 and now with franchises popping up in seven countries over two continents. But neither Olga nor Adrian seem interested in Moldova's successes.

'Why don't you like this city?' I ask them.

'Why?! Because it's disgusting!! Look at this shitty architecture!' Adrian exclaims, gesturing out of the window.

'There's some decent stuff,' I say. 'It's the capital after all.'

'Capital punishment,' grimaces Adrian. 'OK, maybe you're right. I'd think it was a fine city if I wasn't from Moldova. But when you have to experience it every day, and you see that nothing improves, and the standard of public services is so bad . . . Look at the healthcare service, where you have to bribe people just to get anything done. People here have no imagination, they just run on impulses – greed mainly. They're like birds born in a cage. Now the cage is gone, but they don't know how to fly.'

'Nothing ever gets built here,' Olga chimes in. 'All the infrastructure, all the roads, the trains . . . that was thanks to the Soviets. In thirty years, people here have built nothing.' She takes a look at Adrian. 'This is why I think it's ridiculous when you say that the Soviets were entirely bad. Before them, people in this country were just peasants. There was nothing but farms. No one got an education. The Soviets built all this . . .' She gestures outside the window at the hulking grey masses surrounding the frosty, half-lit park. Adrian shakes his head and drinks more wine.

'You might argue that the twentieth century built all that,' I say carefully. 'Most countries in 1900 were full of uneducated peasants.'

'Maybe,' says Olga sceptically. 'I still think we should be grateful for what we had. This is what working in Russia taught me. When I lived in Moscow, working for an oligarch wasn't the difficult part. It was the city in general. As soon as people found out that I was from Moldova they would look at me differently, looking down on me as though I was some sort of immigrant criminal. That's what's happened to this country in the last thirty years.'

'This is what they want you to think,' sighs Adrian. 'That we are worthless people who can't survive without big brother Russia. Who do you think has caused all the instability that stops us growing?'

Adrian does have a point. There is often little that a small country can do to resist the corruption stemming from its much larger neighbours. This isn't merely a post-Soviet problem – look at how middle-class cocaine users in the USA have almost single-handedly scotched any prospect of political stability in Latin America – but in this region a reasonably rich oligarch who has made his wealth in Russia can wield a disproportionate influence. Ilan Shor's billion-dollar bank fraud represented 12 per cent of Moldova's entire GDP in 2014, while his Russian backers have given him powerful political capital.

It can therefore be tempting to see post-Soviet politics as a bunch of corrupt oligarchs on the one hand, all of whom are pro-Russian, and the good, freedom-loving, pro-European people on the other. The temptation is understandable – Moscow thrives when dealing with individual interests who can be easily bought, and indeed plays host to such a system of nepotism itself. Meanwhile, the EU has strict rules for entry, many of which have been designed to promote transparency and limit corrupt interests, the success of which we saw in the Baltic States. However, oligarchs are first and foremost businessmen, and the EU is a far bigger pie than Russia. While Ilan Shor might be a prominent pro-Russian figure, other oligarchs-cum-politicians, most notably Vlad Filat and Vlad Plahotniuc, have run and supported parties that are avowedly pro-European.

What is clear, however, is that these individuals' business interests have had a disorientating effect on the country's politics. Since independence, Moldova has had sixteen prime ministers, each lasting an average of 1.4 years, as well as nine presidents. In fact, Moldova is the only former Soviet country to re-elect the communists. The Party was banned in the 1990s, but under the leadership of Vladimir Voronin it won 71 of the 101 seats in the parliamentary election of February 2001. Voronin was more of an old-fashioned authoritarian populist than a man promising a return to the good old days of the hammer and sickle, but his election proved the rule, truer in Moldovan politics than elsewhere: change is the only constant.

'What do ordinary people do about this?' I ask Olga and Adrian. I'm expecting them to tell me that people leave, that people just try to get on with their lives. But there is a glint in Adrian's eye.

'We still care. We're not stupid. We protest when we can.' He pulls out his phone and shows us a picture of himself, photographed at the time of the revolution of 2009. A red shirt covers his nose and mouth while a fire blazes behind him.

'Are you in retirement now?'

'It's winter; I'm in hibernation.' He opens the fifth bottle of Floricica. 'If you really want to understand the romance of Soviet alcoholism, Joe, you need to read *Moscow-Petushki* by Venedikt Yerofeyev. It perfectly sums up the end of the USSR – lies, grey buildings, a police state, a land where alcohol was the only truth.' He pours three glasses of wine and raises them for a toast. 'And this is why I'm quite proud to be from Moldova: at least our alcohol is good.'

Transnistria

While many Moldovans dream of reuniting with Romania, a thin strip of land on the north-eastern bank of the Dniester River is more likely to express a desire to rejoin Russia. Transnistria, 120 miles long and just 5 wide at its narrowest point, straddles the border with Ukraine, and declared itself independent from Moldova during the collapse of the Soviet Union.

Like Estonia and Latvia, Moldova was also home to a large Russian-speaking population on the eve of independence. With Romanian nationalism gaining ground in both Bucharest and Chișinău, many of them worried about being absorbed into a larger Romanian state. They therefore declared the territory a separate republic and fought a successful war to defend this independence in 1992 – with no small help from Russian soldiers and volunteers. After thirty years in isolation, it presents an intriguing prospect for a visitor, given its depiction as the Soviet Union frozen in time.[1]

Olga and Adrian are not complimentary about their breakaway region when I tell them where I'm going. 'My epilepsy medication got seized there once,' growls Adrian. 'You think Moldovan corruption is bad, wait till you get a taste of the Transnistrian version.'

'You don't want it back as part of Moldova then?'

They laugh. 'Transnistria is like our Romania. They were part of us once; but right now, I'd be thrilled if we gave them their fucking independence.'

'Enjoy your trip to the zoo,' Olga grins, a twinkle in her eye.

*

Winter has not done the land any favours. It looks yellow and defeated. Thankfully it's not long before the rugged *marshrutka* from Chișinău splutters to a halt at the border, although border might be too grand a term. There are no exit checks. I guess this makes sense as, in the eyes of the authorities, we're not leaving Moldova. On the Transnistrian side we disembark and line up outside a small hut for our passports to be inspected. I'm not given a stamp, just a slip of paper permitting me to remain for seven days in the Pridnestrovian Moldavian Republic (PMR) – Transnistria is the Romanian word for the land 'across the Dniester'; its Russian equivalent is Pridnestrovie, and woe betide the tourist who forgets this.

My mobile reception starts to get a little uppity after we cross the river. The air is hazy, thick with industry, powered by heavily subsidised gas from Moscow. There are Russian and PMR flags fluttering by the bridge, and Russian peacekeeping forces standing guard beside it.* Not for the first time I'm baffled by post-Soviet politics; the gas powering these factories has been sent here across Ukrainian territory, while Russian forces are allowed to amble around here while falling in their thousands across the border, which is less than ten miles away.

I'm meant to meet a guy called Valery at Tiraspol train station at noon. Valery runs the *Dom Kultury*† in the little village of Mălăiești, which lies a twenty-minute drive from the capital. A few buses are scattered around the car park in front of the empty station. Several battered old cars driven by battered old men are waiting to pick up women laden with shopping. Once they have all dispersed, a tall, silvering fellow approaches and holds out his hand. Valery steers me towards an ancient Toyota people carrier and gestures to the front seat.

---

* The border doesn't quite follow the Dniester; both the Moldovan and Transnistrian administrations occupy pockets of land on either side of it. However, the peace deal signed in July 1992 assigned Russian peacekeepers to the bridges. Also worth noting is that the troops are often local conscripts given a Russian passport, rather than regular Russian soldiers.

† A *Dom Kultury* (House of Culture) is a Soviet community arts centre, roughly akin to a village hall combined with an arts venue; many continue to operate across the former USSR.

'This is my colleague Misha,' Valery says, pointing behind him. Misha, a little man barely taller than five foot, is lolling in the back. He gives me a friendly grin.

First up, I get the Tiraspol tour. When busy conquering this part of the world in the late eighteenth century, the Russians were going through what we might call their Olympian phase, leading to a series of cities dotted around the Black Sea bestowed with the -pol suffix, among them Sevastopol (Venerable City), Mariupol (City of Mary) and Tiraspol (City on the Tiras, which is the Greek name for the Dniester).

But that is as far as the Hellenism goes. The city has an air of stale, worn concrete. We overtake creaking blue trolleybuses on the way to the town centre. We're not driving along *stradas* any more, the street signs and advertisements are all in the old imperial tongue. Twenty-fifth of October Street, named after the date of the Bolshevik Revolution, is home to most of the city's governmental buildings. Most interesting of these is the brightly coloured House of the Soviets – which now marks the city hall. On the other side of the road is an expansive Second World War memorial monument, where a cute chapel of St George is neatly juxtaposed against a T-34 tank. To complete the bizarre spectacle, the flags of other self-declared republics – Abkhazia, South Ossetia and Nagorno-Karabakh – flutter in the wintry breeze nearby.

Our first stop is the Green Market on Karl Liebknecht Street.* Housed under an iron hangar but otherwise exposed to the elements, the market is typical post-Soviet fare, although less pungent than those in Central Asia – one of the benefits of near-zero temperatures. Valery gets a whole herring, half a kilo of ham, eggs and pickles for the evening's meal. My offer to chip in is met with a snort.

'What will you pay with?' he laughs.

I suddenly feel rather stupid; I'd assumed that the Moldovan leu would be used here.

---

* Fellow travellers will be delighted to hear that Tiraspol has Liebknecht, Marx and Luxemburg streets all running parallel to each other in what locals call the 'German Quarter'.

'We have the Pridnestrovian rouble,' Valery says, holding up a tacky piece of paper.

'And I'm guessing no cards?'

'I don't think Western cards work here – certainly not in the market. And I prefer to shop in the market when I can. You see that supermarket?' he says, pointing across the street.

I follow his gesture and see a smart, mirrored glass structure with the words 'Sheriff' written on the front in Cyrillic. 'Sheriff?' I say. 'Like the football team?'

'That's the one.'

Sheriff Tiraspol had beaten Real Madrid in the Champions League little over a year ago, quite a feat for a little town like this. I found it difficult to imagine the likes of Karim Benzema and Luka Modrić setting foot inside a breakaway republic.

'They didn't play here,' Valery laughs. 'They played back in Chișinău.'

'So Sheriff is a company?' I ask, once we're back in the car.

'Sure, and not just football teams and supermarkets. They run everything – factories, petrol stations, internet – you see that hotel?' We are driving past the modern, five-storey Hotel Rossiya. 'That's where businessmen always stay – also owned by Sheriff.'

The Sheriff is a former KGB officer named Viktor Gushan who has built an empire on the back of Transnistria's disputed status and porous borders.[2] He founded the company, Sheriff, along with former KGB colleague Ilya Kazmaly. Initially, the company allegedly operated by smuggling cigarettes, alcohol and food into Ukraine, it has since then used its political connections to expand its tentacles into most fields of Transnistrian life.

We drive back to Valery's village, Mălăiești. Along the road are police checkpoints; they are decidedly not *carabinieri*. They are the PMR Militsiya, and yes, they drive Ladas.

'They'll stop you for anything. They've recently discovered how much money can be made for drink-driving fines,' says Valery.

As we exit the city for open country, a mound of earth appears on the side of the road towering over a 10-foot-wide ditch, running parallel with us for miles, like the defences of some epic Celtic hill fort.

'Ukraine,' says Valery, simply.

'Just there?' I ask, a little shocked. I hadn't appreciated how close Ukraine was to Tiraspol, nor, by extension, just how thin Transnistria was – little over five miles wide in some places.

'Yep. Right next to my village. The field next to us is in Ukraine. The nearest village, Velykoploske, is only five kilometres away. When I was a kid, boys from our village would go and try it on with the girls from their village,' he grins.

'When did they build the mound?'

'Around ten years ago, after Russia took Crimea. Ukraine's attitude towards us became less friendly after that; until 2014, you could pretty much cross at will. Still, they kept the official border open right until the war began in February.'

'Do you feel trapped now?'

'I'm old, I've done my travelling. It's the young people I feel sorry for.'

We arrive in Mălăiești as the sun is beginning to set. It's a smallish town, the roads are unmarked but smooth enough; ramshackle houses spring up every twenty yards or so, surrounded by brightly coloured wooden palisades. We park up. There's a big drive and front porch. It looks like it's been unused for a while. Valery and Misha rummage in a back room with some cables; suddenly the lights spring to life.

'This was my grandmother's house,' Valery tells me. 'We've had it in the family for ages; we never sold it – I mean, who is going to buy it?'

'Are there a lot of empty houses around here?'

'Maybe half the village.'

He lays the table and Misha sets about frying some eggs to go with our market purchases. It's not gourmet, but it goes down well, except the raw herring, which needs slicing pretty thinly.

Valery gets Misha to pour out some wine from a large plastic bottle. 'This is wine from Mălăiești,' he says proudly. We do a toast and then Valery and Misha sink their glasses of wine in one. I thought the Tajiks drinking free-poured vodka out of mugs was bad; downing wine isn't something I've done since my uni days. Olga's quip comes back to me: 'Enjoy your trip to the zoo.'

The descent is predictable and precipitous. We dine, with Valery occasionally sending little Misha to the kitchen for various extra items, each time turning obediently, like a beaming R2-D2. I ask Misha about the tattoo on his hand – it's the letter M.

'It's M, for Misha,' he explains to me.

'Why did you get it?'

'I got it when I did the national service, the guys thought I might need help remembering who I was,' he says, eyes wide and innocent, untroubled by irony.

'What was service here like?' I ask him.

'Boring. I did mine about twenty years ago, long after the civil war. We'd been at peace for eight years by then; in the end it was just the older guys giving you a hard time.'

'Did you serve, Valery?'

'Yes, but in the Soviet Army. I did two years in Magdeburg, East Germany – 1974–5. The best thing was the music,' he grins reminiscently. 'We were only about thirty kilometres from West Germany, so we were in range of the short-wave radio. I remember the songs so well. The Beatles, Led Zeppelin. Eric Clapton . . .'

'Were you allowed to listen to it on the base?'

'Of course not! Are you mad? But we would find ways.'

'What did you do after serving?'

'I got a job as a long-distance lorry driver. I'd drive everywhere. Kazan, Tbilisi, Tallinn . . . It would take six or seven days to drive to Dushanbe.'

'I imagine it was easier then than now.' Having spent the past year struggling to travel to half of these places, the vision of a borderless Soviet space seemed like paradise.

'Not always,' he grins. 'There were constant internal passport checks and police checkpoints. Your nationality was written on your passport, so as soon as they saw you were from another republic they'd look for a way to make money. Russians got targeted the most, but when people saw "Moldovan" they were usually friendly. Apart from in Turkmenistan – they'd make trouble for everyone. When I went through there, I always had two or three roubles hidden in the passport – that speeded things up.

Sometimes you'd get to know the police if you did a certain route for long enough. They'd always say "hello" in Moldovan.'

I notice he calls it Moldovan and not Romanian.

'Moldovan, Romanian,' he waves his hand in the air. 'It doesn't matter really. But yes, I call the language Moldovan. I can't read Latin script very well, for example. Cyrillic is much easier.'

After going through a two-litre plastic bottle of wine, Valery brings out a bottle labelled Kvint Divin Eight-Year-Old.

'The best cognac in Pridnestrovie!' he says proudly.

'Are you allowed to call it cognac?' I ask.

'Why not?'

I try to give him an explanation of French insistence that cognac can only come from a little village just north of Bordeaux, and that everything else must be referred to as brandy.

Valery just shrugs. 'We call it cognac. Here, try some.'

I guess if you don't recognise someone's self-proclaimed country, you can't expect them to recognise your self-proclaimed drink.

Valery wakes up feeling rather ill, a problem he solves by pouring us all a glass of cognac for breakfast. This seems to give him enough impetus to show me the *Dom Kultury*. Valery shows off the theatre hall, which is vast for such a small village.

'It seats around six hundred or seven hundred people. In the past, we used to pack it out for most events. These days, we're lucky if we can get two hundred people.'

On the wall of one of the offices there's a portrait of Transnistrian President Vadim Krasnoselsky hanging from the wall behind a desk.

'They have to put him up,' he sighs, seeing where I'm looking.

'Who is Krasnoselsky? What's his background?'

'Oh, he's a nobody. He was in the police, in the anti-corruption department; then he became friendly with Sheriff and joined their party.'

Played correctly, being the head of the anti-corruption department offers some excellent career prospects – indeed, Presidents Japarov in

Kyrgyzstan and Lukashenko in Belarus first cut their teeth in this position. The benefits are twofold: firstly, the position allows you to make a name for yourself by going after the 'bad guys'; second, you get to make highly lucrative deals with those people you'd rather not pursue. So the fact that Krasnoselsky the Anti-Corruption Crusader ended up being on the ballot paper for the country's largest monopolist should not overly surprise us.

'One of my friends ran to become mayor of this town,' says Valery. 'He knows everyone here; he's worked in the community for a long time. I actually thought he had a chance,' he laughs bitterly. 'When I arrived here to cast my vote, it was seven a.m. and his opponent's urn was already half full.'

I think back to the clichés about Transnistria as a fossilised USSR, but this is only superficially true. Ignore the nostalgic monuments to old tanks and streets named after communist thinkers, and you have a thuggish, corrupt police state addicted to Russian gas, whose leaders rail against the Romanian language and imperialism while everyone who can gets their hands on a Romanian passport. There are job advertisements for Poland, Germany and England. All the while the parasitic Sheriff organisation buys up everything, from political parties to football teams, supermarkets to banks to internet.

'How long can this situation last?' I ask Valery.

'Who knows? Right now, we can only watch and wait to see what happens in Ukraine. That's all we can do – wait.'

I head towards the train station with no trains, in the country that isn't a country, trying to spend the last of my unconvertible money before I get there. One way or the other, the Ukraine war is likely to spell the end of Transnistria. For a quarter of a century, this region has been kept on life support by a combination of Ukrainian corruption and Russia's subsidised gas and diplomatic support. Russia's full-scale invasion has finally convinced Ukraine to get serious about policing this border, which in the long run is likely to make the Kremlin-backed regime here untenable. On the other hand, if Russia manages to seize the southern coast of Ukraine, there will be little to stop them taking Transnistria along with it. Perhaps now it's about time to turn our heads to that war, and head north to Kyiv.

13

UKRAINE
THE REPUBLIC OF RESISTANCE

That morning, Valery had briefly taken me to visit his neighbour, a kindly, short-haired old woman named Grandma Vera, who, upon discovering that I would be taking the train that evening, set about creating me a hamperful of home-made food and wine for the journey. Armed with these culinary gifts, I approach Chișinău station across a drab, pedestrianised plaza just off Gagarin Boulevard. It's a stark contrast to the hubbub of the bus station 200 yards down the road. The station's splendid fresco, built by German prisoners of war in 1948, gives it an air of grandeur, but my footsteps echo mournfully around the empty atrium.[1] Not long ago, trains would run to Tiraspol and Odessa, Minsk and Moscow, but war and pandemic have severed Moldova's links to the world. Now there are only occasional international services – a couple to the Romanian city of Iași; a night train to Bucharest departing at 17.30; and my train, the 17.45 service to Kyiv.

I'm the sole occupant of the four-person compartment. I hadn't expected the train to be rammed, but the ghostly atmosphere is quite forbidding. There's no restaurant carriage, so I seek refuge in Grandma Vera's cottage cheese pie and swill it down with her home-made plonk; it's cuttingly acidic, but steadying. We begin our torpid chug through the Moldovan night, zigzagging across the country. We stop at the town of Ungheni in the west, lying across the border with Romania. I have a momentary urge to alight here, maybe head for a comfortable week vampire-hunting in Transylvania . . . But I'm distracted from my dread by a young woman knocking on the door, accompanied by the conductor.

'Excuse me,' the woman asks falteringly, 'would it be possible to switch places, I'm in a room with a man and I feel a little uncomfortable.'

I glance at the conductor, who is giving me a pointed stare. I heave myself up resignedly and traipse down the corridor to the next compartment.

It's immediately obvious why the girl had wanted to switch. I'm confronted by a bald, tough-looking chap lying on his bunk, a half-drunk bottle of Jameson sits on the table. He half rises, taking his headphones off with a quizzical look on his face. The conductor explains the situation to him in brisk Ukrainian.

The man laughs. 'Not my type. But fine,' he responds in Russian.

I hoped that he would put his headphones back in, but he sits up and extends a hand.

'Volodymyr.'

'Joe.'

'You're going to Ukraine?'

'Yeah, seeing friends,' I say vaguely. 'You?'

'I was born in Ukraine, in Chernihiv; but I live in Israel now. My family are still living there though. My mother is a stubborn woman and refuses to move, even now the war has started, so I've been coming back when I can to check on her.'

'Are they all well?'

'Sure, we stopped those fascists before they entered the city.'

'They got pretty close I heard?' Chernihiv is in the far north of the country, close to the border with Russia and Belarus, and saw some heavy fighting in the first month of the war.

'Yeah, within range of their artillery, so we were getting bombed daily. Look . . .' He pulls out his phone and shows me a ruined shell of a building. 'This was the market where my mother used to do her shopping, and this . . .' he flicks across the screen '. . . this is the hairdresser's.' Another empty concrete husk, stripped of all identifying features. I'm already starting to think I made the wrong decision back at Ungheni. The vampire-hunting is getting more appealing by the minute. But Volodymyr has reached the opposite conclusion.

'I just wish I could do more. They won't let me join the army because I am not a Ukrainian citizen.' He seems almost apologetic. 'I asked if I could join the Foreign Legion, but they said I needed to have military experience. I told them I was a surgeon, surely they needed medical people? Apparently not.'

'How long ago did you leave?'

'Oh, ages ago, right after I finished med school. This was 1995. Ukraine was a mess back then and the salary in Israel was good. I've created a life there.'

Volodymyr was not the only one. Ukraine had a population of almost 52 million on the eve of independence; by 2014, even before Crimea was occupied by Russia, that had fallen to 45 million.[2] Ukraine's Jewish population fell even more precipitously, from around 500,000 in 1989 to just a fifth of that by 2001. Meanwhile the economy experienced negative growth in every year of the 1990s, with GDP going from $82 billion in 1989 to $31.5 billion in 1999 as the Soviet system unravelled and chaotic reforms deepened the transitional shock.[3] Annual inflation reached 10,000 per cent in 1993, a remarkable figure even in the wild world of post-Soviet economics.[4] Tel Aviv did seem like a reasonable alternative.

'Have you experienced rocket attacks in Israel?'

'Sure,' he laughs. 'But nothing like this. In Israel, people are prepared; most people have a safe room in the house. And the rockets they fire from Gaza are nothing like the missiles these fascists use.'

I find it interesting to hear him call the Russians fascists while speaking Russian himself. I ask if he knows any Ukrainian.

'Not really; my whole family speak Russian, but if I could forget this fucking language I would.'

'I guess we could toast in Hebrew?' I suggest, gesturing to my plastic bottle of wine. He gives a half-smile. 'It was given to me by a woman from Transnistria,' I add, pouring him a glass. 'It's the first place I've ever been where people down wine rather than just drinking it.'

Volodymyr grunts and, apparently taking this as a challenge, sinks his own glass in one. I shake my head before doing the same. He pulls my empty vessel towards him as soon as I set it down.

'We can only toast with a proper drink,' he says, filling our glasses with a generous portion of Jameson.

'*L'Chaim*,' Volodymyr grins. 'It means "To life".'

At 3.30 a.m. there's a rapping on the compartment door. The swaying of the train has ceased, and the conductor is marching down the carriage calling, 'Moldovan passport control'. Shortly after, the train lurches back to life and we cross the Dniester into Ukraine. The knowledge that we are now deemed a legitimate target by the Russian military creeps into the carriage. Somewhere, the Eye of Sauron, far away but unresting, may even now be aware that we have crossed into his domain.

I wake to find that the view from the window, which on my last visit had resembled the golden-yellow wheat fields and brilliant-blue heavens depicted on the Ukrainian flag, is now more sombre: the ground is mustard-brown, soggy and ragged, overseen by baleful clouds. The monotony is occasionally punctuated by villages with wooden houses, inoffensive and unthreatening. It's difficult to believe that this is a country at war.

The landscape is uncannily flat, a topographical curse that generally makes the country a dream destination for an invading army. The difficulty of defending it has meant the territory has tended to end up on the edge of empires. Indeed, this is widely considered to be the root of the country's name – *ukraina* comes from an old Polish/Russian word meaning 'the borderland'.*

In its time, this borderland has been overrun by everyone from the Nazis to the Mongols, it has fallen prey to Tatar slaving parties, and suffered the attentions of the Swedes and the Poles. Even the Lithuanians once got in on the action. Save for the Carpathians in the far south-west, the Dnieper River is the only natural defensive barrier in the whole country.† The river, which on a modern map appears to be the heart of Ukraine, has served historically to divide it. In the seventeenth century, a period referred to by Ukrainians as 'The Ruin', these lands were divvied up between the Poles, who took the west bank of the river, and the Russians, who took the east.

Though the borders have never been particularly stable, this division has had a corresponding effect on Ukraine's culture, with a Russified east and south and a more European west.

This brutal history of invaders sweeping across the steppe makes the

---

* It's worth noting that in Ukraine the word *ukraina* is interpreted as meaning 'homeland'.
† Not to be confused with the Dniester River, separating Ukraine and Moldova, which we crossed earlier.

Ukrainians' defence of their homeland against Putin's onslaught even more remarkable. In the First World War, Kyiv changed hands between the Germans, the tsarist forces, the Ukrainian nationalists and the Bolsheviks as though it were a game of pass-the-parcel. In the Second World War, the city fell to the Wehrmacht within four months. But eleven months into the present war, the Russian army, with vastly greater numbers and air superiority, has barely managed to budge the Ukrainians out of the Donbas – the part of Eastern Ukraine supposedly so keen to break from Kyiv.

While much of this is due to the performances of each country's military, the Ukrainian terrain does have one trick up its sleeve. Those sticky, sodden quagmires slipping past the window may not look pretty, but they do a remarkably good job of slowing down tanks. In February 2022 these saturated bogs proved impassable to heavy armoured vehicles, causing the Russian blitzkrieg to grind to a halt. With no way to reach Kyiv save from using the main roads, an absurd forty-mile tank traffic jam formed on its well-defended approaches, providing easy target practice for Ukrainian drones and artillery.[5] It was a humiliation for a Russian army that many had predicted to capture Kyiv within days.[6] For the Russians to come undone at the hands of this treacherous terrain was ironic given that 'Marshall Mud' is credited as one of the reasons why the Nazi advance, which had swept across Ukraine so quickly, came to a standstill on the outskirts of Moscow in the autumn deluge of 1941.

The remnants of last year's battle have not disappeared. As we near the capital, we pass pillboxes and fortified positions at railway junctions; there's even a camouflaged Pepsi kiosk.

The train arrives at Kyiv station. In true Soviet fashion, it's taken us about six hours longer than it needed to, given the amount of time we've spent dawdling at each station, but we've made it here exactly when the ticket said we would. Throughout the war, Ukrainian Railways have prided themselves on sticking to the timetable, despite missile strikes and power cuts. Such timeliness has symbolic value for the state: the kind of stoic, steady reliability that you can build a defence around.

As we pull into the platform, I say a hurried goodbye to Volodymyr, who still has another five hours of northward travel to Chernihiv, and join those descending the carriage steps. There's quite a reception committee. The girl who switched places with me last night gives a little squeal and throws herself at the dark-haired man awaiting her. The rest of the train's occupants, almost all women, each have a weary-eyed boyfriend, husband, father or brother to greet them. The bouquet-sellers have done a roaring trade. This is the way all station pickups should occur: no ticket barriers, no hectoring announcements, no beeping doors. Just people. I see Mykola, who thankfully does not squeal but instead roars with laughter when he spots my home-made wine wrapped in Transnistrian newspaper.

Mykola used to live in Kharkiv in north-eastern Ukraine, about a forty-minute drive from the Russian border. The war pushed him to relocate to Kyiv, along with his marketing agency, which is doing quite well if his brand-new motor is anything to go by. He opens the boot for me to chuck my bag inside and is keen to show me two bulletproof jackets, a propane cooker, a first aid kit and a torch already residing within.

'Always good to be prepared,' I quip, couching my alarm in sarcasm. I pick up a packet of thick white tablets. 'What are these?'

'Tablets for purifying water. And these,' he points to another pack, 'are iodine tablets, in case of a nuclear explosion; they reduce pressure on the thyroid gland if you get radiation poisoning.'

This isn't a reassuring start, even Volodymyr hadn't gone nuclear. I'm half expecting an air raid siren to go off any minute, and it doesn't help that Mykola begins to point out war damage as we drive.

'That got hit by a rocket right at the start of the war,' he says casually, pointing to a navy-blue tower with a large Samsung hoarding above it. Half of its windows are missing. 'It's a shame, there was a great steak house on the ground floor.'

On the whole, though, it's remarkable how normal Kyiv looks: the traffic rumbles along, shops are open, and people walk the streets wrapped up against the elements. Its appearance is as anodyne as any other post-Soviet city on a dull January morning – until you pass the odd tank trap standing idly next to a coffee kiosk, or a pile of sandbags at a junction. As we near the Olympic Stadium a huge poster looms ahead, featuring the words 'Keep Calm and Love Ukraine – We Will Prevail'.

Given that I've eaten nothing since yesterday evening, Mykola drives straight to a place called Musafir for a spot of lunch.

'This place is quite famous; it's run by Crimean Tatars. Loads of great Turkic food here. We call it the Crimean Embassy,' he winks.

Sure enough, we're *salam alaykum*-ed through the door and led to our seats. As we recall from the first chapter, the Russians will tell you that Crimea has always been theirs, harking back in a rich historical line through Stalin meeting Churchill and Roosevelt at Yalta; Chekhov's *The Lady with a Dog*; and Tolstoy in the Crimean War. But in the tug of war between Ukraine and Russia about the rightful ownership of the peninsula, it's often forgotten that the Crimean Tartars have been there for far longer than either. The original cities were built by the Greeks, but it has been primarily Islamic since the fourteenth century.

The Tatars called their land Kirim, meaning 'The Fortress' (from which we get the Russian/Ukrainian word *Krim*, and the English *Crimea*), and it was from here that they would terrorise the lands north of them for half a millennium. Every spring, thousands of horsemen would emerge from The Fortress, raiding towns and villages and bringing captured Poles, Ukrainians, Lithuanians and Russians to the port of Kaffa, where they would be sold on as slaves to the Islamic world. It's estimated that around 2 million Slavs were captured and sold by the Crimean Tatars between 1500 and 1700.[8]

Eventually, however, with the improvement of military technology, mounted Tatar horsemen became less of a menace to increasingly well-armed Europeans, and in 1783 Catherine the Great formally annexed the peninsula to achieve Russia's age-old goal of a warm-water port on the Black Sea. Later Crimea became the Soviet riviera, a fashionable place for the rich to holiday and old sea dogs to retire. Save for the idealistic early Bolshevik period in the 1920s when Tatar culture was promoted, their presence came to be seen as a nuisance. Stalin saw them as far worse than that. Claiming that the Crimean Tatars had colluded with the Nazi invaders during the Second World War, he ordered their deportation to Central Asia. On the night of 18 May 1944, *Kara Dun* (Dark Day) as the Tatars call it, almost the entire Tatar population of Crimea was rounded up, packed onto trains and sent east. Many died en route in the cramped, stifling carriages.[9]

When hundreds of thousands of Tatars were finally permitted to return from their long exile in the late 1980s and early 1990s, they brought back with them a deep mistrust of Russia and were some of the most vociferous voices against the annexation of Crimea by the Putin regime in 2014.[10] They also brought back some new cuisine. While Musafir is famous for its traditional Crimean *yantiks* and *chebureks* (varieties of savoury pancake), there is also a large Central Asian selection on the menu: the *lagman*, *manti* and *plov* could have been pulled straight from the bazaars in Tashkent or Samarkand.

And the food is popular. It's weird, being in a rammed restaurant during a war, especially as I'm still in the waiting-for-the-missile-to-drop-from-the-sky phase of my trip. Perhaps all these diners are happily enjoying their lunch having already subconsciously located the nearest bunker.

'What happens when there's an air raid siren?' I blurt.

'You get used to it,' Mykola shrugs. 'You just become more alert. Yesterday I was having a meeting with a client when the siren sounded. We continued the meeting as usual, but then one of the other people in the room moved the sofa around behind us and it made this scraping noise on the ground, and all of us jumped at once. It just sets you on edge.'

'You don't head to the bunker or anything?'

He laughs. 'We can't stop life for every air alert. We'd get nothing done. And sometimes you can't find cover. Take me, for example: I live on the twenty-third floor. It takes me five minutes and twenty-three seconds to reach the basement from there. In that time there's a good chance that the missile will have arrived. Obviously, I haven't used the lift for six months because you never know if there'll be a power cut. And that's not a pleasant thought, is it? Trapped in a lift shaft during an air raid. The best thing is just to stay put and try to follow the two walls rule if you can.'

'Which is?'

'Make sure there are two walls between you and whatever is being fired at you. It won't save you if there's a direct hit, but it doesn't hurt your survival chances.'

I shake my head. I'd been hoping for some steadying words, or even a grand escape plan such as he had showcased in the boot of his car. But nope, his plan amounted to living your life, hoping that today was not your last day.

'How long do you think you can go on like this?'

He sighs. 'All I want is for these bastards to give me a routine. When it's an ordinary rocket, or a Shahed,* then it's OK: the air alert sounds, you know it's going to be a shitty hour or so, but then, God willing, the air defences will shoot them down and you can carry on afterwards. Sometimes, though, they fire Kinzhals – hypersonic missiles – which slip through the defences. Last Saturday, for example, I was woken up by a huge boom near my house, so loud that it cracked some of the ceiling. It was a difficult day after that. I needed several whiskies and a sauna.' He tries to smile. 'It's friends that really get you through it. Last night, one of my best friends, the co-director of our company, decided to leave.'

'Is that possible?'

'There are ways . . .' Mykola says sadly. 'You basically pay someone and they get you on the roster to be an international truck driver or something like that. Now, for the first time, I'm considering getting out of here as well. I've never thought about it before. Ukraine is my home; I love my country. But what is life without friends? Jesus, I'm an honest man, I hate it when people take short cuts in this country; the corruption is horrendous . . . and now, just to get out of here, I'd have to play the same game.' He shakes his head. 'I don't know, man . . .'

'What about your parents?' I ask him. His parents have spent the last eight years in Stakhanov,† Mykola's home town in the separatist Donbas region.

'I think this week was the last time we'll speak. My parents support the separatists, even now. They want Ukraine to lose this war. I called my father

---

* A Shahed is a type of suicide drone originally supplied to the Russian military by the Iranians, but now mass produced in Tatarstan.

† The town is named after the legendary Soviet miner Alexei Stakhanov, said to have mined fourteen times his quota in 1935, from where the word Stakhanovite is derived. The Ukrainian government changed the town's name from Stakhanov back to its pre-Soviet name of Kadiivka in 2016 as part of its de-communisation programme.

the other day and he was still talking about the fascist government we've got here in Kyiv. I'm sure he doesn't believe it, but he's too deeply invested now.'

'What about your mother?'

He chuckles darkly. 'There's no point with her, literally no point.'

There's a pause as we munch in silence on our cheesy *chebureks*.

'Do you miss the Donbas at all?' I ask eventually, causing Mykola to laugh through his mouthful of food.

'Miss it? No, I got out as soon as I could – moved to Kharkiv back in 2004. It's an interesting place though. There's a lot of coal, which means cheap energy for factories, so it's really industrial. People there are used to raw, disciplined and tough lives, but they have a very paternal view of their workplace. They expect the plant's owners, which has historically been the government, to serve them with everything – hospitals, food, places to live and extra wages as compensation for doing high-risk jobs. They had a decent life for a long time under the Soviets – working hard physically, earning a relatively good wage. When everything collapsed that all disappeared, and these people had to find a scapegoat for all their problems. Moscow lobbyists, alongside local criminals and oligarchs, were there with easy answers: "It's all because of Kyiv and the independent Ukrainian government." All the while, their bosses stole everything they could. From a social perspective I guess it's similar to how people felt in mining regions in England after Thatcher – but with a criminal, post-Soviet flavour,' he grins. 'So no, I don't miss it.'

We go in search of some drinks. Our first stop is VarVar brewery. We order a couple of milk stouts and before long are joined by Pasha and Rustam, old colleagues of Mykola from Kharkiv. Gathered together, all three of them are eager to recount their tales from the first days of the war.

'We all left around the same time. It was fucking crazy. The traffic was insane,' Mykola recalls. 'And then, from different places, we all ended up in Kyiv around May/June last year.'

'Mykola was first out,' laughs Pasha.

'That's because I had a plan!' he bristles. 'I was the only one expecting it. We went to my wife's village in the countryside on the other side of the Dnieper. And even though we were prepared – we got up in the morning and drove immediately – it still took us eight hours just to get out of the city. Everyone was trying to leave and there were checkpoints everywhere.'

'What about you, Rustam?'

'It took us a while to leave,' he says slowly. 'That was a mistake. It was just the worst experience. My son was completely traumatised by it. The bombs . . .' he shudders. 'They're in France now, my wife is a French teacher, so I guess it makes the most sense.'

'Have you seen them since the war began?' I ask, remembering the men waiting for their partners on the station platform.

'My wife came here in July for a bit, but I haven't seen my son for ten months. Every time Ukraine is mentioned he gets upset. He associates it with those times in February. I'm not sure he will ever come back here.'

'It's OK, we will win,' says Pasha shortly. 'And we'll see each other again. Anyway, Joe, how are you feeling here on your first day in Ukraine?'

'Better after a few drinks.'

'Your first day in the reality show "Crazy Neighbour from Hell",' smirks Mykola.

'Looks like he might survive the first day without a rocket attack,' grins Pasha.

'Yeah, you're lucky that we are not celebrating anything today,' says Mykola. 'Those bastards usually fire on us every time something good happens or when they think we're having too much fun. On New Year's Eve we were having a house party at my place and we could see the air defence shooting their missiles out of the sky.'

'New Year fireworks,' Rustam smiles grimly.

Our pub crawl stretches on until late evening – we stop to down a glass of *vyshnivka* (or drunken cherry, a liqueur popular in the city of Lviv) and end up watching some live music in a cramped underground bar named São Miguel. Throughout the day, I haven't been able to get over how busy everywhere is. There's a lust for life, to drink and dance. Even in wartime Kyiv has swagger: there are young, fashionable people everywhere. But then I suppose I've spent the day with Kyiv's comfortable middle classes. Civilians. People who have been affected and uprooted by war, but haven't been forced to go to the front lines themselves.

'Do you worry you'll get called up to fight?' I ask the other three.

'I think every man worries about that,' Pasha sighs. 'But we're here, and we'll do our duty.'

'The army isn't actually that big,' says Mykola. 'Maybe two hundred and fifty thousand men, and there are around ten to twelve million eligible to be called up. They tend to ask those with military experience first, plus there are plenty of volunteers.'

'Who knows how long the war will last, though?' says Pasha. 'It will be our turn one day, I expect. What's that line from *Fight Club*? "On a long enough timeline, the survival rate for everyone drops to zero" . . .'

Soon after 10 p.m. people start to drift off; a strictly enforced curfew begins in an hour. 'Looks like we're walking,' says Pasha. 'Taxi prices go up by five hundred per cent an hour before curfew.'

We pour our beers into plastic cups and head out through the deserted city.

'What happens to people if they get caught outside?' I ask the group at large.

'Depends,' says Mykola. 'Generally, the police here are human. You'll normally just get away with a fine. One of my female friends got drunk one night and got caught wandering around after curfew, but the police just drove her home. It can be annoying though. Those bastards in Lviv have a curfew at midnight. That hour makes so much difference.'

'Do any bars try to stay open?'

'Plenty do; corruption is never far away,' he shrugs. 'And obviously you can have house parties. You just can't be caught on the street, so it becomes a case of "going big or going home", as you guys say.'

We march through the eerie city, our footsteps silenced by the mist. Nearly all the street lights are out – one of countless small sacrifices Ukrainians have made to save power. We pass through Taras Shevchenko Park, named after Ukrainian literature's great statesman. There have been more internationally famous authors born on Ukrainian soil – Nikolai Gogol or Mikhail Bulgakov, for instance. In fact, football fans are more likely to associate the name Shevchenko with the legendary AC Milan striker. But none of those are revered like Taras Shevchenko. Ukrainians often call him *Kobzar*, which translates, like Shakespeare, simply as 'The Bard'.

Shevchenko's poetry, often excoriating the injustices of the Russian Empire in the mid-nineteenth century, earned him wide renown, and not only among Ukrainians. In his epic poem 'Kavkaz' (The Caucasus) he likens all nations under tsarist rule, 'from the Moldovan to the Finn', to prisoners chained to the mountains like Prometheus, with an eagle pecking at their chest.[11] It's perhaps for this reason that he has streets and monuments named after him all over the former Soviet Union. In his homeland, his poem 'Zapovit' (Testament) has historically been quoted, or even sung, by Ukrainians as a rallying call to the nation, especially in times like this. But when we come to the centre of the park I'm saddened to see that his statue has been boarded up.

'I know their aim is shit, but it would be such a classic Russian thing to do to try and bomb him,' says Pasha. 'They already turned the house where he was exiled in Russia into a car park.'*

'I guess it's his words that really matter,' I say. 'That keep people going . . .'

They laugh. 'Shevchenko's words keep us going? You've got a very romantic view of us. Did the English quote Shakespeare and Shelley to get them through the pandemic?'

'I think our prime minister did,' I smile, 'but fair enough, I won't romanticise you.'

We reach the intersection of Volodymyrska Street and Shevchenko Boulevard. 'Look how normal this place looks now,' says Pasha. 'The Russians bombed here a few months ago, they managed to kill another three people who were just innocently going about their business crossing the road.'

This sobers me up somewhat. I look at my watch.

'Just five minutes to curfew,' I mutter, quickening my step.

*

---

* The Russian authorities thought it appropriate to turn his house in Orenburg into a car park in 2015. 'The poet never lived there,' lied the Culture Ministry at the time.

Now I don't want to slag off Tatar cuisine, nor Kyiv's breweries, nor Lviv's distilleries – and especially not Grandma Vera's home-made hamper, but it's 2 a.m. and I'm currently in the hotel bathroom with severe indigestion. I'll spare you the details, and just try to focus on breathing, hoping that the worst will soon be over.

And that's when the air raid siren goes off.

It's exactly the noise I'd imagined, one that I've heard in a hundred films. The long, piercing klaxon howl, a sound that the whole world is pre-programmed to fear. All-encompassing, even from where I'm staying on the fourteenth floor of the hotel.

You'd think that it might have acted as some sort of laxative. Apparently not. If you've ever wondered what goes through people's minds at a time like this, you might imagine that thoughts drift to one's children, to family, lovers, friends. Mine drift to Elvis, perhaps the only person who might appreciate the true absurdity of my position. At that moment, my phone lights up.

'Enjoying your first air raid?' reads the message from Julia, who gave me my first tour of Kyiv all those years ago and whom I'm planning to meet tomorrow. Hilarious, these people. I just about muster a cry emoji in response.

'I hope you're down in the basement?' she adds.

'The shelter is fifteen floors down!' I respond, deciding that she doesn't need to know my precise location.

'That's kind of the idea!' This is a fair enough point.

'Are *you* in a shelter?' I ask her.

'No, I'm in the kitchen, watching TV.'

I laugh. 'What you watching?'

'*The Crown.*'

Perhaps there are worse ways to die than on the toilet after all.

'Observing the two-wall rule, I hope?' I ask her, for some reason trying to make out as though I'm an experienced veteran of a hundred air raids. One thing I will say for this bathroom is that the walls are thick.

'Yup. Anyway, I was just checking in on you. I'm going back to the TV now. See you tomorrow at 11 . . . or will I? :)'

I have a strong sense that she's thoroughly enjoying my suffering. At least she only knew the half of it. Miraculously, the siren halts after just ten minutes. In the silence my stomach gives another low, rumbling groan.

'Right,' I tell it. 'A little less conversation, a little more action.'

Kyiv's metro system is as magnificent as those in Moscow and Tashkent, and it's an even better place to be in a war. Arsenalna, 350 feet underground, may well be the deepest station in the world, providing a better barrier against an opposition barrage than a prime David Seaman. I can feel myself getting safer as I walk down the escalators, marvelling at those who have the time to do as they're told and *hold on to the handrail*. It must take five minutes of waiting before they reach the platform.

The train whisks me a couple of stops to Teatralna, and from there it's a quick walk to Idealist, a fashionable coffee haunt where I'm meeting Julia. Like the bars yesterday, it's hard to find a seat. Everyone is young and well dressed; it's a step up in class from Tucano Coffee in Chișinău. I sit waiting for Julia, and nerves that have nothing to do with the war or the hangover form in the pit of my stomach. I've spoken with her sporadically throughout the past year and can't help but wonder what a year of war has done to her.

The first thing I notice is her hair, a more subdued brown, though the smile and warm hug are the same as eight years previously. The other notable change to her appearance is that now she is sporting a fluorescent armband.

'What's that for?' I ask by way of greeting.

'For when we have a power cut. Crossing the road becomes a little dangerous in the dark.'

She takes off her coat to reveal a black jumper; emblazoned across it is 'Independence 1991'. She sits down, we look at each other for a second or two. There aren't really words. With Mykola the bravado had come easily.

'Don't suppose it's worth asking how you've been?' I say weakly.

'Up and down. I was more prepared than most as I've been working as a fixer in the Donbas since 2015 – not that you cared about it much back then.' This remark stings, but she's right. The world never really cared about the Donbas. 'So yeah, I was in the Donbas until the twenty-second of February last year, right near the front line. I was working with a team of Dutch journalists. I was in Kyiv when it all began though. Where were you?'

'Moscow,' I say quietly, 'but I didn't expect this to happen!' I feel the need to justify myself before her blue gaze. 'Did you?'

'Not really, not like this. Not even on the twenty-third. When it started, I kind of felt it was my turn to step back. I'd given so much to this struggle over eight years, now someone else could take over. I came back to Kyiv and just did nothing for two weeks. I just lay in bed listening to the explosions: my family's apartment is near one of the city's air defence systems – it can get quite noisy,' she tries to smile. 'But since then I've been keeping busy helping to organise concerts to raise money for the army. It's given me some time abroad, I spent a lot of time in Georgia, and I went to Barcelona over New Year. It's strange to be somewhere and not have to worry about rockets and war.'

We pay for our coffee and walk to St Michael's Square, where a large number of destroyed Russian vehicles have been parked. Their rusty metal hulks sit squat and shameless in front of the periwinkle-blue church with its golden domes. One of the tanks is the much-vaunted T-90, now reduced to a great lumbering toad, paraded before the people it was designed to conquer. A family poses for photos in front of it, and some young lads have managed to scramble on top.

'When they first brought them here, people could barely go near them because of the smell,' said Julia airily.

'Smell of what?'

'Burnt human flesh.'

'Oh.'

The idea that these are trophies from an ongoing war is still hard to relate to, even with the constant threat of a missile strike. These tanks are inert, their turrets point obscenely towards the city: erect but impotent. The smell has gone too, and the noise of war is non-existent. But among the tanks, the remains of a lime-green car serve to remind Kyiv's citizens just how close the Russians came to their city back in February last year. Bullet holes riddle its side, glass from the smashed windscreen litters the passenger seat and there's a pair of bloodstained jeans in the back.

'This car is from Bucha,' says Julia quietly, 'it belonged to a family who were just trying to get out of there.'

We both stand in silence. The dormitory town of Bucha is about twenty miles from the spot where we now stand. Some of the worst civilian massacres of the war occurred there in April last year.[12]

'I was going to suggest you go there, to Irpin or Bucha. It'll give you an idea of what the Russians do when they take over a place. But I suppose it's become a bit of a Disney destination now, where they take all the Western dignitaries and celebrities. Most of the other towns that we've liberated have been allowed to rebuild, but there are parts of Bucha that have deliberately been kept in a semi-destroyed state, just so people can visit.'

'Interesting choice to put it here next to the tanks.'

'Oh well the tanks are just a bit of fun,' she grins. 'We heard that Putin wanted to do a parade once he'd conquered Kyiv, so we thought we would organise one for him. We arranged his tanks all along Khreshchatyk for Victory Day on the ninth of May.* Unfortunately, none of his soldiers could make it.'

I laugh. Throughout the war, people here have made use of that greatest of weapons, the Ukrainian sense of humour. But there's still no mistaking the scarring, even if it's masked well. 'I think it will be five or ten years before I know if I'm OK,' Rustam had told me yesterday.

We take a stroll down the Alley of the Heavenly Hundred to the Maidan.

'Where it all began,' I say.

'Yep.'

Maidan. So many things about modern Ukraine can be evoked by that single word. In the Western world, Maidan is an event: the site of the 2013/14 Euromaidan protests that overthrew Viktor Yanukovych. But Maidan itself is actually a place. Today, Maidan Nezalezhnosti, or

---

* Think of Khreshchatyk as Kyiv's Champs-Élysées.

Independence Square, stands right at the heart of the city. At the square's centre is a column, 200 feet high, topped by a Slavic goddess, her arms raised aloft and golden leaves blossoming between them. At the far end, the sandstone Stalinist block of the Hotel Ukraine looms over proceedings, offering a perfect vantage point for the foreign TV crews to film the square below. And that is convenient, because until the war, the history of independent Ukraine tended to play out here. In fact, it's hard to think of a square that has so consistently been home to revolutionary activity over such a short period. Since 1990 there have been four mass-protest movements involving tens of thousands of people occupying the Maidan for weeks at a time: in 1990; in 2001; the Orange Revolution of 2004; and 2013/14's Euromaidan, which in Ukraine is more commonly called the Revolution of Dignity.*

The combatants have usually been the same as those in similar protests across the former USSR: civil society on one side, generally comprising students and the aspirational, urban middle classes; and opposing them the many-headed hydra of regime-linked vested interests. The difference in Ukraine is that civil society has tended to put up a better fight, and so, with each confrontation, the stakes have been raised. The Revolution of Dignity was the bloodiest yet.

'Do you still remember 2014?'

'Of course! I still remember the feeling that I was living in wonderful times. I was living off pure adrenaline for those weeks. You definitely notice this feeling of the masses – it's crazy, like an animal spirit. You don't feel anything except this unity . . .' she smiles, reminiscing. 'Maidan was life-changing for everyone in my generation, whether you were an active or passive participant.'

When it began, back in November 2013, Julia had still been at university. 'I was doing some lecturing and holding seminars for undergraduates

---

* The Revolution on Granite of October 1990, where students came to what was then called the Square of the October Revolution in Soviet Kiev and went on hunger strike to express their discontent about numerous aspects of Soviet rule. The Kuchmagate protests in 2001 resulted from the murder of journalist Georgiy Gongadze, purportedly on the orders of President Leonid Kuchma.

in the philosophy faculty. At some point they started to ask, "Miss Julia, have you seen what's going on? Can we go to Maidan?"'

What was going on was one of those moments in history that could have been minor, like a gunshot on a June morning in Sarajevo. Students were gathering to protest President Yanukovych's decision to back away from an Association Agreement with the EU and instead to strengthen ties with Russia. There was nothing irreversible about his choice, and elections were a mere eighteen months away, but it nevertheless seemed to many of the dismayed young people on the Maidan that their European future had been snatched from them.

'I told my students that if they felt that they needed to be there, then go. But the official position of the university was that attending the protests was forbidden and I was told to put an absence mark for them for not attending lectures,' says Julia.

'Did you not consider joining them?'

'Not at first. I wasn't against this Association Agreement per se, I'm all for cooperation with our neighbours, but I could see where it was going, and I didn't want to be part of the EU to be honest – nor a Russian union. I wanted us to try to balance somehow, to be a kind of Switzerland.'

Julia wasn't the only one unconvinced; the agreement would have committed Ukraine to wide-ranging reforms during a time of financial crisis. To complicate matters, Russia had made it clear that signing such an agreement would make it impossible for Ukraine to sign up to Moscow's own Eurasian Economic Union (EAEU) project. The Kremlin had launched a carrot-and-stick campaign of pre-emptive sanctions combined with offers of loans and subsidised gas to put pressure on Yanukovych.

Despite landslide support in parliament for a deal with the EU, ordinary Ukrainians were divided.[13] A poll undertaken by the Kyiv International Institute of Sociology showed people narrowly opting for Brussels over Moscow's EAEU by 40.5 to 35 per cent, but it also highlighted huge regional differences.[14]

Yanukovych's voter base was largely concentrated in the Russophile east and south. He traded heavily on Soviet nostalgia and had passed a language bill the previous year that gave official status to the Russian language in regions where a significant minority spoke it. It was so controversial that it had been pushed through only after a fist fight in parliament.[15] Protesters on the Maidan had also thwarted Yanukovych once before: 2004's Orange Revolution forced a second vote in the presidential election of that year, after Yanukovych had won the first edition through blatant vote tampering.[16]

So we can perhaps understand why, by the end of November 2013, the president, already buffeted this way and that by Russian and EU diplomacy, was in no mood to compromise with the small but growing student gathering. At 4.30 a.m. on 30 November he sent in the security forces to clear the square.[17] It was to prove a severe miscalculation. The riot police – a thuggish paramilitary unit called the Berkut* – dispersed the students with such brutality that it brought thousands of indignant citizens of Kyiv out alongside them in solidarity.[18]

'No one really wanted another Maidan, but I suppose every action has a reaction; in this case people came after they saw the students being beaten so savagely,' says Julia.

The Euromaidan lasted for three months, through the depths of winter. Protesters barricaded the entrances to the square, occupied the local government offices and constructed a permanent tent city as they had done on three previous occasions.

'There was also a stage, music concerts and a big screen. Veterans of the Orange Revolution would come to speak. They also showed a film from the Egyptian revolution of 2011. Then there was the Euromaidan university on the square, which gave lectures on democracy, human rights and revolutions around the world, plus practical things like basic first aid.'

'Who was organising all this? The opposition?'

'No! Definitely not. This wasn't a launchpad for anyone's election campaign! That was part of the problem actually – there was no real leader, it was unclear what Maidan wanted. There were so many people there with

---

* One for etymology fans: *berkut* is a Turkic word that likely came to Ukraine via the Tatars. It translates as 'golden eagle' in Ukrainian, Russian, Kazakh, Kyrgyz, Turkmen and Uzbek.

different motivations; but we all wanted Yanukovych and his corruption to end. I guess people just refused to move from the square.'

'And then it all became violent, right?'

Julia sighs. 'I can't explain how fast it all happened. I was volunteering in one of the hospitals. It had been pretty quiet, and then one day in February there were suddenly hundreds of people; bullets in their legs, hands, heads . . . There weren't enough doctors and nurses, so I was helping to feed patients, change their bandages and clothes. Or just entertain them with some news.'

The violence had been escalating since the start of January 2014 – in the worst instances, detained activists and journalists were stripped naked and shot at with rubber bullets before being sent out into the freezing night.[19] As the winter wore on, permanent protesters on the square became decidedly more male.

'Girls weren't allowed to be in front. We could be somewhere behind the crowd or helping in a medical centre. But boys were literally stopping girls getting involved on the front line,' says Julia.

Orange hard hats became standard equipment, as did Molotov cocktails, metal clubs and corrugated-iron shields. There were frequent sightings of protesters with light firearms such as hunting rifles or pistols.[20] As Lenin once observed, you cannot make a revolution in white gloves. In the final battles, the Maidan became a war zone as police snipers and armed demonstrators desperately sought to secure the square and its surrounding buildings.[21] Police failed to take the square while killing dozens with live ammunition.

The gun battle seemed to bring the country to its senses; an agreement was reached with the opposition to hold fresh elections and to investigate the murders by police. But Yanukovych did not hang around to see the agreement implemented; the deal with the opposition signalled to his allies in the security forces that he was ready to throw them under the bus. The fearsome Berkut, which had proved such a savage opponent to the protesters, melted away the minute the agreement was signed. The president was not far behind. He fled to Russia, from where he continued to claim that a coup had taken place.[22]

The protests were not popular everywhere in Ukraine. By January, more people disapproved of the protesters than approved of them.[23] Large swathes of the east and south saw Euromaidan as little more than a coup against a president who had stood up for their interests. They pointed to the questions about the legality of Yanukovych's removal.[24] Russian media enthusiastically fanned the flames by pointing to EU and US involvement,[25] as well as the far-right elements that had gained prominence as the protests continued[26] – the presence of which was also documented by Western media at the time.[27]

'Did any part of you worry about the legality of overthrowing the president?' I ask Julia.

'Not really. When parliament announced that he had fled, everyone started to cry and clap. It was a wonderful moment. Kind of like a relief. Then when I came back home, I began to question myself, what would be the consequences of all this . . . but I didn't worry about the legality of removing the president, only that we didn't have an alternative that would be good . . .'

A wide smile suddenly crosses her face. 'When I try to remember anything from Maidan, I always see a very bright sunny day in my head; Khreshchatyk covered in snow, and people pulling up masonry from the road to throw at the police. It's a lovely feeling. It was such a sunny day . . . Somehow, I don't remember, or my brain is trying not to remember, all the bad things. The smell of corpses after the trade union house was burned . . . or the sight of the whole of Instytutska Street covered in blood . . . I just remember that sunny day, and the snow, and the people.'

In the bloody battle between the Berkut and the anti-government protesters, thirteen police officers and 108 protesters lost their lives. Since then, countless more Ukrainians have perished in the war in the Donbas and during the full-scale Russian invasion. It strikes me that the courage to face down riot police and snipers is the same courage being shown in the fields and streets to the east. But where does it come from – that courage to fight the regime, to fight off an invader, to stand up for your beliefs in a way that simply hasn't happened in Russia, in Azerbaijan, in Uzbekistan or in Belarus? And to stand up again and again, despite the revolution never reaching the shores of the promised land.

'Do you ever wonder why Ukraine has so many revolutions compared to other post-Soviet states?' I ask Julia.

She suddenly becomes very enthusiastic. 'OK, here I'm going to speak as a nationalist,' she grins. 'Firstly, we've always been fighting, ever since our first government a thousand years ago. I can't think of a time in history where we had a boring, peaceful time for more than twenty years! And then . . . well, we have this saying – "Freedom is our religion". Maybe it's because of the Cossacks, maybe it's in our blood to fight for what we want. Whether we *understand* what we want is a different matter, but if there is a reason to fight for something, we will! It's a good question actually, I haven't really thought about why . . .' She pauses for a second. 'Why not?' she says slowly. Before repeating it more strongly, 'Yeah, why not?'

Our walk has taken us to the top of Volodymyr's Hill as evening gathers and the mist begins to roll in from the river. On a clear summer's day back in 2016 you could see the Dnieper stretched out beneath you at this point, its tree-lined banks giving way to the eastern suburbs of the city, and finally to the flat, golden fields beyond. Back then, a huge stone monument had stood here – the Arch of the Friendship of Peoples, built in the 1980s to commemorate the sixtieth anniversary of the Soviet Union.[28] Under it had been a statue of two workers, a Russian and a Ukrainian, each raising the other's hand aloft. They took the figures down in April, beheading the Russian.

The arch still stands. It is now called The Arch of the Freedom of the Ukrainian People. Beneath it is nothing but empty space. A place to think about what was. Into that space the mist continues to creep up from the river, slithering over the city. Combined with the power-saving measures that the authorities have taken, there's almost nothing to be seen.

'I guess this fog makes for good anti-aircraft defence,' I mutter hopefully.

'Ha!' barks Julia. 'Nope. The Russians don't care what they hit as long as it terrifies someone. But it makes the anti-aircraft defence's job a hell of a lot harder.'

*

Kyiv station on that misty Sunday night is bathed in a strange greenish light. In the huge arched atrium, people mill in front of the departures board: young and old, civilians and soldiers. With no flights, the station has become the heart of the nation.

Next to the grand staircase there is another board. A list of train routes that, over the course of the last nine years, have been removed from the timetable: Kyiv–Simferopol; Kyiv–Donetsk; Kyiv–Mariupol . . . each terminus is now under enemy occupation. Nevertheless, next to each is a departure time. A statement of intent, that one day trains will ply these routes once more. One of the routes on this list has been coloured in brightly, signifying its restoration: Kyiv–Kherson. The city at the mouth of the Dnieper was recaptured three months previously.

On the way to the platform, I pass soldiers chewing on unlit cigarettes – out of stress or habit, I cannot tell. I notice how many of them are alone. I wonder if they are returning to their units or heading home on leave. These are not young men; some must be fifty at least. Fathers, grandfathers even. Eyes distant, rucksacks hitched resolutely onto their shoulders. That Kyiv still stands, that I've been able to float around bars and cafés, is down largely to these grim men.

The night train to the Polish border departs at 22.30. Despite my keenness to rid myself of the suffocating paranoia, it's hard to say goodbye. It's not just that I'm leaving people behind, it's the mere fact I can, while these fathers head out towards the front line, while Rustam must pay a bribe for the chance to see his son. I settle into my quarters, thinking of these grey heroes as we rumble into the night, away from the war, towards Poland. For us, the dawn is in Poland. We happy few who can leave.

EPILOGUE

Over the following years, I kept returning to Ukraine. Even in wartime, the Kyiv summer can be wonderful – the curfew had been shortened by one hour, the misty banks of the Dnieper were now in bloom. Smoke from the riverside barbecues mingled with the scent of sizzling *shashlik*, a dose of normality in a city under siege.

But the air raids continued. By 2024, the relentless punishment meted out to the power grid meant electricity had become a scarce commodity. Rolling blackouts saw Kyivans endure summer heatwaves with air conditioning strictly rationed. When the lifts were knocked out, I did the shopping for my eighty-year-old neighbour Olha, who was too old to use the stairs. Her food run became part of my daily routine – after all, what's the use of a fridge that only works for eight hours a day?

But Ukrainians are nothing if not adaptable: pizza places switched to wood-fired ovens, cash and QR payments replaced card machines, and the whole city would hum to the sound of diesel generators.

Harder to solve were the bombs themselves. Swarms of drones and missiles began to strike houses and hospitals in the city centre with increasing frequency. I soon took to drinking myself to sleep. But my suffering was slight in comparison: each visit has seen my friends further succumbing to exhaustion. 'Sometimes I'm relieved when we have nights of massive attacks,' Julia tells me. 'Because then I might die too. No more need to struggle.'

Mykola has left his sixteenth-floor flat for a place on the ninth, which he says is just about walkable. He stays busy, he and his wife have adopted a girl orphaned in Kharkiv.

On the Russian side, Steve has remained in Moscow, as, I presume, has Yegor, though I still haven't heard from him. Leo now works remotely from Bali, and Oksana, now in Germany, has a daughter.

'I always said I wouldn't be a traditional housewife,' she laughs. 'But I suppose we all had other plans once . . .'

She and Leo are among hundreds of thousands of Russians who have built a new life abroad, each trying to come to terms with what their country has done. They join an illustrious list of Russians in exile – Rachmaninoff, Stravinsky, Trotsky, Nabokov, even Lenin – sitting out the years, perhaps decades, until the winds of change blow again.

As for Ivan, the private jet no longer takes him to Mediterranean villas; the family now holiday in Dubai – his grandmother likes to stay in touch.

In the Caucasus, Arayik and his family fled the Karabakh in September 2023 when the Azerbaijani army moved in. He's now in a refugee camp in Germany, awaiting the outcome of his asylum application. The displacement of over 100,000 Karabakh Armenians marked the end of one of the three 'frozen conflicts' in the Caucasus, and in classic Caucasus fashion it resulted in a total victory for one side. Aliyev's *reconquista* has brought little improvement to the lot of the Azeri people, corruption continues unchecked and dissent is ever more harshly policed. A deal brokered by Donald Trump in August 2025 saw the two countries pencil their assent to a peace memorandum, but whether this leads to open borders and a full restoration of relations remains to be seen.

Across Eurasia, even in formerly liberal Georgia and Kyrgyzstan, authoritarians continue to throttle civil society, with journalists and activists frequently the subject of arbitrary arrest. Georgia fell from 89th in the World Press Freedom rankings in 2022 to 114th in 2025. Kyrgyzstan's fall in the same period, from 72nd to 144th, has been even more precipitous.[1] Many see the hand of the Kremlin at play, with both countries adopting strikingly similar laws on foreign agents to those passed in Russia.

In Central Asia, only one power is ascendent. Chinese cars drive on Chinese-paved roads; Chinese phones connect to Chinese-built 5G, Central Asian governments gorge on Beijing's easy credit and its students gratefully lap up Confucius Scholarships. This isn't necessarily a bad thing. China offers these countries a path to growth, while Russia, for all its thuggish officialdom, offers Central Asians a place to work. What do we in Europe offer apart from finger-wagging?

The trip has, I'm afraid to say, made me a little cynical, denuding me of moral certainties that my younger self may have had – although of course this may also be a consequence of turning thirty-five.

The question continues to nag at me: what was independence for?

Imagine, for a moment, that the USSR didn't collapse. The KGB coup plotters of August 1991 held their nerve, pro-democracy demonstrators in Moscow were massacred, the reformists purged, and the screws of authoritarian rule were tightened once more. The Party embraced capitalism, encouraged private entrepreneurship and tailored its five-year plans to attract foreign capital and focus on the new industries of the twenty-first century.

Unthinkable? In 1989, China faced its own democratic uprising and the Chinese Communist Party followed the playbook described above. Xi Jinping later warned his colleagues not to repeat Moscow's mistake: 'In the end, no one was a real man.'[2]

In the following three decades, China, despite also having restive regions and separatist movements, did not fragment. There have been no military conflicts. Its economy, 3.6 times smaller than that of the USSR in 1989, currently dwarfs it.

Now, am I saying that the Soviet Union would have had the same success as China if it had followed a similar path? Not necessarily.

Am I saying we should bring back the Soviet Union to find out? No, I am not.

But the Chinese case does show how history could have turned out differently, and it is always worth bearing in mind the alternative to collapsing a state. Recent history is full of warnings, from Iraq to Yugoslavia, Syria to Sudan, that the tale of dissolution is often written in blood.

What can future nations seeking independence learn from the Soviet republics' experience? Firstly, neighbours matter. Countries such as the Baltic States, blessed with a coastline and proximity to Scandinavia, have thrived, while countries like Tajikistan, stuck between Uzbekistan, Afghanistan and the Pamirs, have fared less well. This trend holds true across all fifteen countries, with the possible exception of Kazakhstan, whose oil and assiduous statecraft have seen it significantly outperform its geography.

Second, superpowers don't let go quietly. This applies pretty universally: look what happened to Cuba when they sought to break out of the USA's economic orbit, or Britain's scheming in Ireland, or modern-day China's increasingly menacing behaviour towards Taiwan. While Moscow's scant regard for human life is alarming, its continued desire for influence over its former territories is not unusual.

Third is that successful independence movements, like revolutions, often consolidate around their most extreme elements. Those who seek an accommodation with the old order are quickly accused of lacking sufficient revolutionary fervour and betraying the cause. This was as much the case after the British referendum on the EU as it was in the French Revolution. This has meant that, especially in the more democratic countries, the new republics rewrote their histories as liberation narratives, rushing to rename cities, to ennoble the local language and purge the imperial tongue.

Depending on your point of view, this might be necessary or rather sad. Personally, as someone rather conservative by nature, I find it a shame when old buildings or monuments are removed, usually at the whim of some populist. This year, the largest Lenin statue in Central Asia, the Osh Lenin, which had stood as one of the city's symbols for fifty years, was removed at a moment's notice, without pausing to consult its residents. A pointlessly tall Kyrgyz flag will stand in its place, lest anyone forget what country they are in.

And yet, modern Russia has given these new nationalists all the ammunition they could ever dream of. It could have played a leading role in guiding the whole region to a more positive future. There is enough wealth in Russia, enough talent in Russia, to feed and power half of Eurasia. Moscow might have offered scholarships and investment to support its neighbours; it might have trained a generation of teachers to send to rural areas; it might have used its immense engineering capabilities to help build the infrastructure projects that its neighbours desperately needed. The Soviet Union, for all its sins, did these things.

Today, the small, surly chap in the Kremlin offers his neighbours menace at best, destruction and ruin at worst. Perhaps the most consequential and damaging result of the Soviet collapse is Russia's reversion to a paranoid, angry country that jealously stymies any of its neighbours' attempts to strive for more and wilfully helps to entrench a venal, incompetent post-Soviet elite.

Even thirty-five years is short in the life of a nation. Ireland, for example, became independent in 1922. Fifty years later, in 1972, Ireland was still far poorer than its former imperial neighbour and thousands of Irish immigrants came to work on British construction sites. A hundred years on, however, and Ireland's courting of foreign multinationals has seen it shoot up the ranks of the world's richest countries, its living standards now rivalling those across the Irish Sea.[3]

This suggests that economically, some benefits may take a generation or two to emerge. But ultimately that may miss the point. Ask an Irishman today, or in 1970, whether they think Ireland should be independent, and I suspect you'd get a very similar answer. All this cost-benefit analysis must be weighed against the siren call of national emancipation, a freedom that is perhaps so seductive that no number of stunted GDP figures, setbacks in living standards, threats or even wars can convince people to abandon it.

And if this journey has taught me anything, it's that things can always get worse. As of the time of writing: Russia, Belarus, Azerbaijan, Uzbekistan, Tajikistan and Turkmenistan have all ended up living under regimes at least as repressive as during the late-Soviet period. Kazakhstan isn't much better, and Kyrgyzstan is heading the same way. Meanwhile, seven of the republics – Russia, Ukraine, Moldova, Georgia, Armenia, Azerbaijan and Tajikistan – have had full-scale wars, while Kyrgyzstan has suffered revolutions as well as ethnic pogroms in Osh in 2010.

Nevertheless, to a young, urban resident of Tallinn or Tashkent, Astana or even Moscow, it would be churlish to say that the Soviet collapse has been without its benefits. The brightest students now win scholarships to study in Europe or America. In most countries, private entrepreneurs have the freedom to pursue business ideas that their parents could never have contemplated. They no longer have to barter their life savings to buy a pair of jeans or to access their favourite music.

Such a mixed picture should not surprise us. It was a lot to expect these populations, in all their ethnic diversity, many of whom had no tradition of statehood and had lived under seventy years of Soviet propaganda, to throw it all off without breaking stride.

I've asked countless people on this trip about their personal experiences of the Soviet collapse. The general mood was perhaps best summed up by Dosym Satpayev back in Almaty. He was in his early twenties at the time and had been studying political science at university. He recalls the cultural flourishing during the period of *perestroika*: 'For young people throughout the Soviet Union, it was like a new page of our history. We only saw the possibilities, we didn't think about the difficulties, about the threats . . .'

Perhaps it must be so: no journey begins if doubts prevail. For these fifteen republics, the important thing is that the ice has been broken, the road is open, the way has been shown.

ACKNOWLEDGEMENTS

It's easy to say, 'I'd like to write a book one day.' Turning dreams into reality is the hard part. *Farewell to Russia* began with a conversation with Joey Brown in Seattle. To my whimsical musings that it would be great to do a travel project focused on the former USSR, his blunt 'Then do it' provided the initial impetus to get going. Everyone needs a friend to get their arse in gear.

The early encouragement from Will Fee, as well as Tom and Andy Stevens, was invaluable in getting the project off the ground. I'm also indebted to Ingrid Cranfield, Sarah Moore and Patrick Wright for their professional perspectives on how best to share my early scribblings with what, at the time, seemed a remote and distant publishing industry.

Key to opening those doors has been Tom Cull, my agent, who took a chance in championing a debut author, and Katie Bond, who was the first to pick up the book for E&T. I'd like to thank both for their enthusiasm in backing both the project and my idiosyncratic writing style from the outset.

The editorial process has immeasurably improved the work. Special thanks to Katie Bond and Celia Hayley, who managed to cut 30 per cent of the text while taking away little of substance – a lesson to us all on the art of not-babbling and staying on topic; to Jennie Condell, for steering me out of my bubble and making the book far more accessible to people unfamiliar with the region; and finally Linden Lawson and Pippa Crane for their diligent copy editing that has made me appear far less sloppy than I really am.

For the country specific read-throughs, I'm grateful for the time that Elina Turalyeva in Kyrgyzstan; Roman Lososovskij in the Baltic States; Ira Krushynska in Ukraine; Natallia Sadouskaya in Belarus; Saodat Umarova in Uzbekistan; and Asiya Abdraimova in Kazakhstan have spent helping to iron out errors and add much-needed nuance. Agnieszka Pikulica, David McArdle, Owen Prew and Sam Quicke's diligence in going through the text at large was also invaluable.

ACKNOWLEDGEMENTS

Travel writing, as a genre, likely has more debts than most to pay for the fruits of its labour. Almost every day on the road left me admiring the absurd generosity of strangers, people who stopped to give me a lift and then took me into their lives in the most unexpected places – from the Ferghana Valley to Transnistria, Armenia's valleys to Georgia's vineyards. Thank you to everyone who consented to be interviewed for this book. It is my greatest wish that your thoughts and experiences are reflected honestly and accurately in these pages.

I generally spent far longer in each country and there were far more stories than could possibly be counted here, so this is also an opportunity to thank all those who helped shape these pages behind the scenes: this includes Paolo Sorbello, Joanna Lillis, Sarah Bedford, Mariia Mazaeva, Meerim Abdikalikova, Vishal Sharma, Alexander Bachuwa, Anastasia Pustova, Michel Ghassibe, Vahan Tumasyan, Neil Hauer, Didara Rakhymzhanova, Asem Bolatbekova, Anar Burasheva, Aymen Huseynova, Tyler Green, David Smith, Dustin Gilbreath, Paulina Kanarek and Kacper Wańczyk. Much of the book's richness has come from your contributions.

I want to thank all my Russian language teachers over the years: Frida Gudim and Alya Latrigina in Moscow; Erica Rysulkova in Bishkek; I would have been incapable of having half of the conversations here without your teaching. Special thanks to Iryna Samchuk, who sat in a darkened room in Kharkiv during incessant air raids, patiently teaching me enough Ukrainian online so as not to offend half of Kyiv upon my arrival. Your professionalism and courage have left me in awe.

The same should be said for everyone I met in Ukraine, from the air defence crews monitoring the skies above my head, to the impeccable and immaculate staff on Ukrainian Railways, right through to the barmen and baristas, the hotel staff and taxistas. You expect many things from war, but poise, dignity, courtesy and humour are not always first on the list. 'Glory to the Heroes' is no understatement.

For all the travelling, this book was primarily written in London. The staff at the British Library and National Archives at Kew were fantastic – should anyone based in London plan on writing a book, there are no better places.

ACKNOWLEDGEMENTS

My last words should recognise four people without whom this work would have been impossible. To Yvonne Mould and Sam Quicke, who put up with the jaded presence of a frustrated author in their homes for so long, I hope this book goes some way to repaying your philanthropy. Finally, to my mother and father, for the unfailing support, constant encouragement, proofreading and willingness for this project to succeed, my eternal thanks and love.

A NOTE ON NAMES

When a character is referred to by first name and surname, their speech is based on the author's interviews with that individual, which were recorded with their consent.

When a character is referred to by first name only, their name has in some cases been changed to protect their anonymity.

For place names, I have generally used the names employed by the government of a country's internationally recognised territory. However, my overriding concern has been to make this book as accessible as possible to an English-speaking reader, and therefore for some places – Chernobyl, Lenin Peak, Moscow, Odessa, for instance – I have used the more common English spelling.

NOTES

Introduction

1. 'Economic Survey of Russia 1992', CIA, Directorate of Intelligence (1993), https://www.cia.gov/readingroom/docs/DOC_0000292328.pdf; 'Ot redaktsii: Oplata naturoy' ['From the editorial board: Payment in kind'], *Vedomosti*, 28 November 2008, https://www.vedomosti.ru/opinion/articles/2008/11/28/ot-redakcii-oplata-naturoj
2. Andrew Roth, 'Vladimir Putin says he resorted to driving a taxi after the fall of Soviet Union', *Guardian*, 13 December 2021, https://www.theguardian.com/world/2021/dec/13/vladimir-putin-says-he-resorted-to-taxi-driving-after-fall-of-soviet-union
3. 'Putin's approval rating reaches six-hear high – poll', Sputnik International, 15 May 2014, https://sputniknews.com/20140515/Putins-Approval-Rating-Reaches-Six-Year-High--Poll-189850984.html
4. 'Culture of Ukrainian borscht cooking inscribed on the List of Intangible Cultural Heritage in Need of Urgent Safeguarding', Press Release, UNESCO, 1 July 2022, https://www.unesco.org/en/articles/culture-ukrainian-borscht-cooking-inscribed-list-intangible-cultural-heritage-need-urgent
5. 'Ukraine: Lenin statue given Darth Vader makeover', BBC News, 23 October 2015, https://www.bbc.com/news/blogs-news-from-elsewhere-34594262

1. Russia: The Republic of Indifference

1. Shaun Walker, 'Russia retaliates against Western sanctions with ban on food imports,' *Guardian*, 7 August 2014, https://www.theguardian.com/world/2014/aug/07/russia-retaliates-western-sanctions-ban-food-imports
2. 'Russia classifies beer as alcoholic', BBC, 21 July 2011, https://www.bbc.co.uk/news/world-europe-14232970
3. 'Alcohol policy impact case study: The effects of alcohol control measures on mortality and life expectancy in the Russian Federation', World Health Organization, 30 September 2019
4. Andrew Roth, 'Russians ridicule Western media on "day of no invasion"', *Guardian*, 16 February 2022, https://www.theguardian.com/world/2022/feb/16/russians-ridicule-western-media-on-day-of-no-invasion
5. 'Russia: Police detain thousands at pro-Navalny protests,' *Human Rights Watch*, 25 January 2021, https://www.hrw.org/news/2021/01/25/russia-police-detain-thousands-pro-navalny-protests; OvD-Info, 'Spisok zaderzhannyh

na akciyah v podderzhku Alekseya Navalnogo 23 yanvarya 2021 goda' ['List of detainees during the protests in support of Alexey Navalny on 23 January 2021'], https://ovd.info/news/2021/01/23/spisok-zaderzhannyh-na-akciyah-v-podderzhku-alekseya-navalnogo-23-yanvarya-2021-goda; OvD-Info, 'Spisok zaderzhannyh na akcii v podderzhku Alekseya Navalnogo 31 yanvarya 2021 goda' ['List of detainees during the protests in support of Alexey Navalny on 31 January 2021'], https://ovd.info/news/2021/01/31/spisok-zaderzhannyh-na-akcii-v-podderzhku-alekseya-navalnogo-31-yanvarya-2021-goda
6. Sashko Shevchenko, '"Russian warship, go f*** yourself": Ex-POW describes "limitless violence" that followed defiant Ukrainian stand', Radio Free Europe/Radio Liberty, 21 June 2025, https://www.rferl.org/a/snake-island-pow-describes-russian-abuse-russian-warship/33449225.html
7. Natasha Turak, 'Russian stock analyst drinks to death of the stock market,' CNBC, 4 March 2022, https://www.cnbc.com/2022/03/04/russian-stock-analyst-drinks-to-death-of-the-stock-market.html
8. Russell Brandom, 'Russia has begun blocking Facebook and Twitter', *The Verge*, 26 February 2022, https://www.theverge.com/2022/2/26/22952006/russia-block-twitter-ukraine-invasion-censorship-putin
9. 'Russia to introduce jail terms for spreading fake information about army', Reuters, 4 March 2022, https://www.reuters.com/world/europe/russia-introduce-jail-terms-spreading-fake-information-about-army-2022-03-04/
10. 'Samoe strashnoe utro v zhizni' ['The most terrible morning of my life'], Meduza, 24 February 2022, https://meduza.io/feature/2022/02/24/samoe-strashnoe-utro-v-zhizni

2. Armenia: The Republic of Survival

1. Michael Wines, 'October 24–30; Assassination in Armenia,' *New York Times*, 31 October 1999, https://www.nytimes.com/1999/10/31/weekinreview/october-24-30-assassination-in-armenia.html
2. Liana Aghajanian, 'City of dust: how an ongoing construction boom is destroying Yerevan's architectural heritage', *Ianyan Magazine*, 19 March 2015, http://www.ianyanmag.com/city-of-dust-how-an-ongoing-construction-boom-is-destroying-yerevans-architectural-heritage/
3. George Gordon Byron, 'TO MR. MOORE', in *Letters and Journals of Lord Byron: With Notices of His Life*, edited by Thomas Moore (Cambridge: Cambridge University Press, 2012), pp. 565–67
4. Irina Marchesini, 'Russian (1917–1918) and Armenian (1922) orthographic reforms. Assessing the Russian influence on modern Armenian language', *Studi Slavistici*, vol. 14 (November 2017), pp. 171–90
5. Grant Mikaelyan, 'Skol'ko na samom dele pogiblo lyudey v rezul'tate Spitakskogo zemletryaseniya?' ['How many people really died as a result of

the Spitak earthquake?'], Kavkazskiy Uzel, 9 December 2017, https://www.kavkaz-uzel.eu/blogs/83781/posts/30990
6. 'Vsesoyuznaya perepis naseleniya 1926 goda' ['All-union population census of 1926'], Demoscope Weekly, https://www.demoscope.ru/weekly/ssp/ussr_nac_26.php
7. Yuri Slezkine, 'The USSR as a communal apartment, or how a socialist state promoted ethnic particularism', *Slavic Review*, vol. 53, no. 2 (Summer 1994), pp. 431–2
8. 'Vsesoyuznaya perepis naseleniya 1989 goda: raspredelenie gorodskogo i selskogho naseleniya Nagorno-Karabakhskoy AO po polu i natsional'nosti' ['All-union population census of 1989: Distribution of urban and rural population by sex and nationality in Nagorno-Karabakh Autonomous Oblast'], Demoscope Weekly, https://www.demoscope.ru/weekly/ssp/resp_nac_89.php?reg=71

3. Azerbaijan: The Republic of Oil and Gas

1. Faik Medzhid, 'Studenty Bakinskogo gosuniversiteta proveli aktsiyu protesta protiv uvol'neniya prepodavatelya Geyusheva' ['Students of Baku State University Held a Protest Against the Dismissal of Lecturer Geyushev'], Kavkazskiy Uzel, 14 November 2013, https://www.kavkaz-uzel.eu/articles/233444

4. Georgia: The Republic of Thorned Roses

1. John Steinbeck, *A Russian Journal* (New York: Viking Press, 1948), p. 150
2. 'Rankings', Doing Business, World Bank Group, May 2019, https://archive.doingbusiness.org/en/rankings
3. Maria Katamadze, 'The oligarch behind Georgia's pivot to Russia', *Deutsche Welle*, 7 March 2024, https://www.dw.com/en/the-oligarch-behind-georgias-pivot-to-russia/a-69165038
4. 'Public opinion on business in Georgia', Caucasus Barometer, 2019, https://caucasusbarometer.org/en/cb2019ge/BUSINGA/; and ibid., 2021, https://caucasusbarometer.org/en/cb2021ge/BUSINGA/
5. 'UNHCR Publication: CIS conference on displacement in the Caucasus', UNHCR, 1 May 1996, https://www.unhcr.org/uk/publications/unhcr-publication-cis-conference-displacement-cis-conflicts-caucasus

5. Kazakhstan: The Republic of Compromise

1. Aleksandr Solzhenitsyn, *The Gulag Archipelago*, translated by Thomas P. Whitney (New York: Harper & Row, 1973), p. 60

2. Steven A. Barnes, *Death and Redemption* (Princeton: Princeton University Press, 2011), p. 1
3. Ibid.
4. Aleksandr Solzhenitsyn, *Rebuilding Russia*, translated by Alexis Klimoff (New York: Farrar, Straus and Giroux, 1991), p. 15
5. Kathryn Jones, 'Kazakhstan and Chevron start venture', *New York Times*, 7 April 1993, https://www.nytimes.com/1993/04/07/business/kazakhstan-and-chevron-start-venture.html
6. 'Output at Kazakhstan's Tengiz oilfield to remain stable in 2024 – Energy Ministry', Reuters, 14 November 2023, https://www.reuters.com/business/energy/output-kazakhstans-tengiz-oilfield-remain-stable-2024-energy-ministry-2023-11-14/
7. Nicolas Bosetti, Tom Colthorpe, 'London identities', Centre for London, 18 April 2018, https://centreforlondon.org/reader/london-identities/the-changing-city/
8. Claire Bigg, 'Georgia: Tbilisi marks 30th anniversary of language protests', Radio Free Europe/Radio Liberty, 14 April 2008, https://www.rferl.org/a/1109567.html
9. Dosym Satpayev, 'Film Dosyma Satpayeva "Otkochevniki mertvoy stepi"' ['Film by Dosym Satpayev "Nomads of the Dead Steppe"'], YouTube, uploaded by AuditoriumQZ Досыма Сатпаева, 10 April 2019, https://www.youtube.com/watch?v=3yQCNRNB1OU

6. Kyrgyzstan: The Republic of Uprisings

1. Theo Merz, 'Ex-prisoner Sadyr Japarov confirmed as Kyrgyzstan president', *Guardian*, 16 October 2020, https://www.theguardian.com/world/2020/oct/16/kyrgyzstan-parliament-confirms-sadyr-japarov-new-president
2. Leila Nazgul Seitbek, 'V Kyrgyzstane novyj prezident: u nego kriminal'noe proshloe, a parlament on zakhvatyval siloy' ['In Kyrgyzstan a new president: he has a criminal past, and he captured the parliament by force'], *Zaborona*, 19 January 2021, https://zaborona.com/ru/v-kyrgyzstane-novyj-prezident-u-nego-kriminalnoe-proshloe-a-parlament-on-zahvatyval-siloj/
3. 'Personal remittances, received (% of GDP) – Kyrgyz Republic', World Bank, https://data.worldbank.org/indicator/BX.TRF.PWKR.DT.GD.ZS?locations=KG
4. Ivan Marchenko, 'Kosmicheskoe proshloe malen'koy respubliki' ['The cosmic past of a small republic'], 24.kg, 11 April 2011, https://24.kg/archive/ru/community/97421-kosmicheskoe-proshloe-malenkoj-respubliki.html/; Zoya Ismatulina, 'Zakrytyy kosmos' ['The closed cosmos'], MSN Kyrgyzstan, 10 August 2007, https://www.msn.kg/ru/news/19530/

5. Marek Dabrowski and Rafal Antczak, 'Economic reforms in Kyrgyzstan', CASE Network Studies and Analyses, No. 28 (1 September 1994), p. 3; http://dx.doi.org/10.2139/ssrn.1479566
6. Vladimir Paramonov and Aleksey Strokov, 'The evolution of Russia's Central Asia Policy', Advanced Research and Assessment Group, Defence Academy of the United Kingdom, June 2008, p. 2

7. Uzbekistan: The Republic of Islam

1. 'Uzbekistan: Recent economic developments', IMF Staff Country Report No. 1997/098, International Monetary Fund, 31 October 1997, footnote 49, https://www.imf.org/en/Publications/CR/Issues/2016/12/30/Uzbekistan-Recent-Economic-Developments-2399
2. Richard C. Paddock, 'A campaign of terror in the name of fighting it', *Los Angeles Times*, 14 June 2000, https://www.latimes.com/archives/la-xpm-2000-jun-14-mn-40863-story.html
3. Bruce Pannier, '"We Made Mistakes": In Uzbekistan, a rare admission over Andijon killings', Radio Free Europe/Radio Liberty, 18 February 2020
4. George N. Curzon, *Russia in Central Asia in 1889 and the Anglo-Russian Question* (London and New York: Longmans, Green, and Co, 1889), p. 220 (retrieved from the Library of Congress, www.loc.gov/item/03019109)
5. 'Uzbekistan: Export Profile', Observatory of Economic Complexity, https://oec.world/en/profile/country/uzb

8. Tajikistan: The Republic of Emigration

1. Alva Omarova, 'Inside the wardrobe: women's clothing increasingly policed in Tajikistan', Vlast, 11 September 2024, https://vlast.kz/english/61798-inside-the-wardrobe-womens-clothing-increasingly-policed-in-tajikistan.html
2. Kamelia Samoilenko, 'Tadzhikistan: V pervuyu ochered' zhena' ['Tajikistan: Wives in the first place'], Central Asian Bureau for Analytical Reporting, 2022, https://longreads.cabar.asia/femalebusinesstj
3. Bahodur Sheraliev, 'In search of Oxus Treasure – trip to Takhti Sangin', Foreign Commonwealth & Development Office, 25 March 2013, https://blogs.fcdo.gov.uk/ukintajikistan/2013/03/25/in-search-of-oxus-treasure-trip-to-takhti-sangin/
4. Shirin Akiner and Catherine Barnes, 'Tajik civil war: Causes and dynamics', Conciliation Resources Accord, Issue 10, April 2001, https://www.c-r.org/accord/tajikistan/tajik-civil-war-causes-and-dynamics
5. RFE/RL's Tajik Service, 'Rahmon urges Tajiks to eschew hijabs, beards', Radio Free Europe/Radio Liberty, 11 July 2017, https://www.rferl.org/a/tajikistan-rahmon-hijabs-beards/28610312.html

6. RFE/RL's Kyrgyz Service, 'Putin agrees to present archive maps to help solve border disputes between Kyrgyzstan, Tajikistan', Radio Free Europe/Radio Liberty, 17 October 2022, https://www.rferl.org/a/kyrgyzstan-tajikistan-borders-maps-russia/32088373.html
7. 'Kyrgyzstan evacuates over 136,000 from border conflict zone', AKIpress, 2022, https://akipress.com/news:679555:Kyrgyzstan_has_evacuated_over_136,000_from_border_conflict_zone/
8. 'CIAN bans "Slavs Only" ads for rental property', The Bell, 13 December 2021, https://en.thebell.io/cian-bans-slavs-only-ads-for-rental-property/

9. Turkmenistan: The Republic of the Great Leader

1. 'Profile: Kurbanguly Berdymukhamedov', BBC News, updated 21 December 2007, http://news.bbc.co.uk/1/hi/world/asia-pacific/6346185.stm

10. Belarus: The Remainer Republic

1. Andrew Roth, 'Belarus accused of "hijacking" Ryanair flight diverted to arrest blogger', *Guardian*, 23 May 2021, https://www.theguardian.com/world/2021/may/23/belarus-diverts-ryanair-plane-to-arrest-blogger-says-opposition
2. 'Urok diplomatii ot Aleksandra Lukashenko: on nazval geem nemetskogo ministra inostrannykh del' ['A lesson in diplomacy from Alexander Lukashenko: He called the German foreign minister gay'], Perviy Kanal (1TV), 6 March 2012, https://www.1tv.ru/news/2012-03-06/96203-urok_diplomatii_ot_aleksandra_lukashenko_on_nazval_geem_nemetskogo_ministra_inostrannyh_del
3. Andrew Wilson, *Belarus: The Last European Dictatorship* (New Haven: Yale University Press, 2011), p. 45
4. 'German–Soviet military parade in Brest-Litovsk, 1939', YouTube, uploaded by zarraza filmai 1, 8 April 2022, https://www.youtube.com/watch?v=__Ztie1-v7s
5. 'Natsional'nyy statisticheskiy komitet Respubliki Belarus', *Obshchaya chislennost' naseleniya, chislennost' naseleniya po vozrastu i polu, sostoyaniyu v brake, urovnyu obrazovaniya, natsional'nostyam, yazyku, istochnikam sredstv k sushchestvovaniyu po Respublike Belarus': statisticheskiy byulleten'* ['Total Population, Population by Age and Sex, Marital Status, Level of Education, Ethnicities, Language, Sources of Livelihood in the Republic of Belarus: Statistical Bulletin'], Minsk, 2020, pp. 36, 40, https://www.belstat.gov.by/upload/iblock/345/34515eeb3bb5f4ea5ca53b72290e9595.pdf
6. Wilson, *Belarus*, p. 45
7. Michael Specter, 'Belarus voters back populist in protest at the quality of life', *New York Times*, 25 June 1994, https://www.nytimes.com/1994/06/25/world/belarus-voters-back-populist-in-protest-at-the-quality-of-life.html

8. Sergei Kuznetsov, 'Prisoners tell horror stories of their detention in Belarus', Politico, May 5 2021, https://www.politico.eu/article/belarus-prisons-violence-alexander-lukashenko/; 'This Case Is Real', Meduza, 17 September 2020, https://meduza.io/en/feature/2020/09/17/this-case-is-real.
9. 'The potato eaters: Who loves spuds the most?' Radio Free Europe/Radio Liberty, May 11 2020, https://www.rferl.org/a/top-potato-eaters/30605403.html

11. The Baltic States: The Straight-A Republics

1. Zaiga Krisjane et al, 'Post-accession migration from the Baltic States: The case of Latvia', in *Mobility in Transition: Migration Patterns after EU Enlargement*, edited by Birgit Glorius et al. (Amsterdam University Press, 2013), p. 92
2. 'Corruption Perceptions Index 2023', Transparency International, https://www.transparency.org/en/cpi/2023
3. Aldis Purs, *Baltic Facades* (London: Reaktion Books, 2012), pp. 10–11
4. 'NATO expansion: What Gorbachev heard', National Security Archive, 12 December 2017, https://nsarchive.gwu.edu/briefing-book/russia-programs/2017-12-12/nato-expansion-what-gorbachev-heard-western-leaders-early
5. George W. Bush, 'Remarks to the citizens of Vilnius', US Department of State Archive, 23 November 2002, https://2001-2009.state.gov/p/eur/rls/rm/2002/15452.htm
6. Liz Sly, 'Russian military move into Belarus poses risks to more than Ukraine', *Washington Post*, 12 February 2022, https://www.washingtonpost.com/world/2022/02/12/russia-baltics-nato-suwalki-gap/; James Crisp, 'EU must stand firm in face of Vladimir Putin's plot to rebuild "Soviet Union 2.0", says Lithuania', *Telegraph*, 12 January 2022, https://www.telegraph.co.uk/world-news/2022/01/12/eu-must-stand-firm-face-vladimir-putins-plot-rebuild-soviet/
7. 'Allies enhance NATO air-policing duties in Baltic States, Poland, Romania', NATO, 29 April 2014, https://www.nato.int/cps/en/natohq/news_109354.htm
8. Jacek Tarociński and Justyna Gotkowska, 'Expectations versus reality: NATO brigades in the Baltic States', Ośrodek Studiów Wschodnich (Centre for Eastern Studies), 6 December 2022, https://www.osw.waw.pl/en/publikacje/analyses/2022-12-06/expectations-versus-reality-nato-brigades-baltic-states
9. Boriss Cilevičs, 'Access to nationality and the effective implementation of the European Convention on Nationality', Parliamentary Assembly of the Council of Europe, https://www.assembly.coe.int/LifeRay/JUR/pdf/TextesProvisoires/2013/20131002-NationalityAccess-EN.pdf

10. 'Latvia: UN experts concerned about severe curtailment of minority language', UN Office of the High Commissioner for Human Rights, 8 February 2023, https://www.ohchr.org/en/press-releases/2023/02/latvia-un-experts-concerned-about-severe-curtailment-minority-language
11. Ilya Koval, 'Narva: The EU's "Russian" city', *Deutsche Welle*, 26 May 2019, https://www.dw.com/en/narva-the-eus-russian-city/a-48878744

12. Moldova: The Republic of Reunions

1. Liam Gilliver, 'Inside tiny country frozen in time', *Mirror*, 23 June 2025, https://www.mirror.co.uk/travel/news/inside-tiny-country-frozen-time-35425499
2. Tony Wesolowsky, 'The shadowy business empire behind the meteoric rise of Sheriff Tiraspol', Radio Free Europe/Radio Liberty, 18 October 2021, https://www.rferl.org/a/moldova-sheriff-tiraspol-murky-business/31516518.html

13. Ukraine: The Republic of Resistance

1. Yuri Shvets, 'Staryy zheleznodorozhnyy vokzal kishinyova' ['Old Pictures of Chișinău Station',] Old Chisinau, http://oldchisinau.com/transport-kishinyova/staryy-zheleznodorozhnyy-vokzal-kishin/
2. 'Population of Ukraine', World Population Review, https://worldpopulationreview.com/countries/ukraine-population
3. 'Ukraine GDP', Macrotrends, https://www.macrotrends.net/countries/UKR/ukraine/gdp-gross-domestic-product
4. 'Ukraine Inflation, 1993', Statbureau, https://www.statbureau.org/en/ukraine/inflation/1993
5. Luke McGee, 'Here's what we know about the 40-mile-long Russian convoy outside Ukraine's capital', CNN, 3 March 2022, https://edition.cnn.com/2022/03/03/europe/russian-convoy-stalled-outside-kyiv-intl/index.html
6. Courtney Kube and Rhoda Kwan, 'Russia has massed 70 percent of forces needed to invade Ukraine, source says', NBC News, 6 February 2022, https://www.nbcnews.com/news/world/russia-massed-70-percent-forces-needed-invade-ukraine-source-says-rcna15060
7. Dmitriy Bavyrin, '"General Moroz" pytalsya voyevat' za gitlera', 'General Frost tried to fight for Hitler', Vzglyad, 12 November 2021, https://vz.ru/society/2021/11/12/1128604.html
8. Mikhail Kizilov, 'Polish slaves and captives in the Crimea in the seventeenth century', *Acta Orientalia Academiae Scientiarum Hungaricae*, vol. 73, no. 2 (June 2020), pp. 253–67, https://doi.org/10.1556/062.2020.00011

9. Mark Kramer, 'Why did Russia give away Crimea sixty years ago?', Wilson Center, 19 March 2014, https://www.wilsoncenter.org/publication/why-did-russia-give-away-crimea-sixty-years-ago; Brian Glyn Williams, *The Crimean Tatars: From Soviet Genocide to Putin's Conquest* (London: Hurst & Company, 2015), p. 89
10. Gleb Golod, 'Otpravlyayut na voynu protiv rodnoy strany' ['They are being sent to war against their native country'], Meduza, 20 February 2023, https://meduza.io/feature/2023/02/20/otpravlyayut-na-voynu-protiv-rodnoy-strany
11. Taras Shevchenko, 'The Caucasus', translated by John Weir, https://taras-shevchenko.storinka.org/taras-shevchenko-the-caucasus%E2%80%8B%E2%80%8B-poem-english-translation-by-john-weir.html
12. Yulia Zhukova, 'Two years later, massacre of Ukrainian civilians in Bucha is "impossible to forget"', Radio Free Europe/Radio Liberty, March 30 2024, https://www.rferl.org/a/anniversary-bucha-ukraine-mass-killings-civilians/32883760.html
13. 'The second session of the Verkhovna Rada of Ukraine of the seventh convocation has opened', Verkhovna Rada of Ukraine, 22 February 2013, https://www.rada.gov.ua/en/news/News/News%202/73173.html (315 out of 349 deputies voted in favour of the Association Agreement with the European Union)
14. 'Yakym shlyakhom ity ukrayini — do yakoho soyuzu pryyednuvatys'?' ['Which path should Ukraine take — which union should it join?'], КIIS (Kyiv International Institute of Sociology), 3 October 2013, https://www.kiis.com.ua/?lang=ukr&cat=reports&id=196&page=1
15. 'Fist fight in Ukrainian parliament over language law', Radio Free Europe/Radio Liberty, 24 May 2012, https://www.rferl.org/a/ukraine/24592293.html
16. Adrian Karatnycky, 'Ukraine's Orange Revolution', *Foreign Affairs*, vol. 84, no. 2 (2005), pp. 35–52, https://doi.org/10.2307/20034274
17. 'Ukraine police disperse EU-deal protesters', BBC, 30 November 2013, https://www.bbc.com/news/world-europe-25164990
18. Mark Rachkevych, 'Survey: Euromaidan is grassroots movement in danger of being radicalized', *Kyiv Post*, 10 December 2013, https://archive.kyivpost.com/article/content/ukraine-politics/survey-euromaidan-is-grassroots-movement-in-danger-of-being-radicalized-333391.html
19. 'Беркут роздягнув і облив двох хлопців водою, змусив бігти голими на Майдан' ['Berkut stripped and doused two boys with water, forced them to run naked on Maidan'], *I*, 20 January 2014, https://web.archive.org/web/20140125141337/http://www.theinsider.com.ua/politics/52dc881707d14/
20. 'Rocks, sticks and AK-47s: the weapons of Ukraine's protests', France24 Observers, 20 February 2014, observers.france24.com/en/20140220-ukraine-maidan-protesters-snipers-weapons

21. 'МОЗ: З початку сутичок померло 28 людей' ['Ministry of Health: 28 People Have Died Since the Start of Clashes'], *Ukrayinska Pravda*, 20 February 2014, https://www.pravda.com.ua/news/2014/02/20/7015026/; Ian Traynor, 'Ukraine's bloodiest day: Dozens Dead as Kiev protesters regain territory from police', *Guardian*, 20 February 2014, https://www.theguardian.com/world/2014/feb/20/ukraine-dead-protesters-police
22. Andrew Higgins and Andrew E. Kramer, 'Ukraine leader was defeated even before he was ousted', *New York Times*, 3 January 2015, https://www.nytimes.com/2015/01/04/world/europe/ukraine-leader-was-defeated-even-before-he-was-ousted.html
23. Interfax-Ukraine, 'More Ukrainians disapprove of Euromaidan protests than approve of it', *Kyiv Post*, 7 February 2014, https://archive.kyivpost.com/article/content/ukraine-politics/more-ukrainians-disapprove-of-euromaidan-protests-than-approve-of-it-poll-336461.html
24. Daisy Sindelar, 'Was Yanukovych's ouster constitutional?', Radio Free Europe/Radio Liberty, 23 February 2014, https://www.rferl.org/a/was-yanukovychs-ouster-constitutional/25274346.html
25. 'Ukraine crisis: Putin adviser accuses US of meddling', BBC News, 6 February 2014, https://www.bbc.co.uk/news/world-europe-26068994
26. 'МЗС Росії: В Україні ‹коричнева› революція, ми застосуємо весь вплив' ['Russian Foreign Ministry: "brown" revolution in Ukraine, we will use all our Influence'], *Ukrayinska Pravda*, 19 February 2014, https://www.pravda.com.ua/news/2014/02/19/7014748/
27. David Stern, 'Ukraine's far-right Svoboda Party hold torch-lit Kiev march', BBC News, 1 January 2014, https://www.bbc.com/news/world-europe-25571805
28. Asya Zolnikova, 'No one feels sorry for them', Meduza, 14 June 2022, https://meduza.io/en/feature/2022/06/14/no-one-feels-sorry-for-them

Epilogue

1. 'World Press Freedom Index 2025', Reporters Without Borders, https://rsf.org/en/index?year=2025
2. Chu Bailiang, 习近平警告中共记取前苏联教训 ['Xi Jinping warns the CCP to learn from the Soviet Union's lessons'], *New York Times Chinese Edition*, 15 February 2013, https://cn.nytimes.com/world/20130215/c15xi/dual/
3. John Campbell, 'Living standards in UK and Ireland compared in new research', BBC, 27 June 2023, https://www.bbc.com/news/uk-northern-ireland-66029416

INDEX

A

alcoholism 3–4, 67, 149–50, 241
Aliyev, Heydar 49–53, 59
Aliyev, Ilham 53–54, 66
Arab-Islamic influence 24–25, 31–32, 48, 64, 86, 115, 146, 150–51, 179, 183, 224, 255
    Uzbekistan 121–140
Armenia 21–46
    Azerbaijan, relationship with 32–33, 35, 38–39, 55, 56–58, 62
Atatürk, Mustafa Kemal 26, 73
authoritarianism 30, 44–45, 49, 54, 107–8, 113, 137, 140, 147, 161, 192, 240, 274–75
Azerbaijan, 47–62
    Armenia, relationship with 32–33, 35, 38–39, 55, 56–58, 62

B

Baku 39, 40–41, 44–45, 47–49, 52, 54, 55, 57, 58–59, 66, 101, 145
Baltic States 211–32
    see also Estonia: Latvia; Lithuania
Belarus 189–210
Belt and Road Initiative 118–19
Bolshevik Revolution (1917) *see* Russian Civil War
border conflicts 50, 57, 71, 152, 156
    Azerbaijan–Armenia conflicts 32–33, 36–38, 50, 55, 57
    Georgia–Ukraine conflicts 71
    Kyrgyzstan–Tajikistan conflicts 152, 156
Brezhnev, Leonid 49–50

C

Chernobyl Nuclear Disaster (1986) xiv, 198, 230
chess 26–27, 32, 52
China 86, 114–15, 122, 158, 159–60, 183, 174–75
    Belt and Road Initiative 118–19
    China Road and Bridge Corporation 118–19, 154
    gas imports 176
    infrastructure projects 118–19
    Kazakh migrants 90, 97, 100–1
    Silk Road 154–55
    Taiwan 276
China Road and Bridge Corporation 118–19, 154
Christianity 25, 28, 35–36, 140, 194–95
climate change 139–40
coastal states 275
construction 30, 124–25, 149, 160, 174, 277
coronavirus 47, 160, 165
corruption 30, 38, 43–44, 50–51, 66, 79, 93, 105, 157, 162–63, 199, 215–16, 225, 239–40, 247–48, 257, 260, 268–69, 274
Crimea *see* Ukraine
cuisine and culinary heritage xvii, 28–29, 39–40, 64, 249, 256, 262
cultural heritage 29–30, 65, 120, 178

D

dictatorships 54, 62, 99, 135, 150–51, 170, 189–90, 210, 211
    corruption 50–51, 66, 105, 162–63, 216

dictatorships (continued)
    dynastic dictatorship 50–51
    ethnic hatred and militarism
        57–58
    oligarchic dictatorship 66
drug smuggling 142, 143
drug use and addiction 10, 239–40

E
economy and economics 14, 54, 87, 102, 126, 184, 251, 277
    China, influence of 275
    drugs 143
    EU alignment 215–16, 225, 234–35, 237–38
    Eurasian Economic Union 44, 267
    GDP 44, 99, 112, 116–17, 142, 159, 211, 240, 251, 277
    Gorbachev's reforms 38
    immigrant workers 142, 160–61
    independence impact of 123, 140, 223, 230–31
    inflation x, 198–99, 251
    oil and gas sector 62, 176
    perestroika 38, 114
    planned economy 136–37
    Soviet collapse 116–18, 149
    subsidies 116
    war 210
    Yeltsin 116
    see also corruption
Engels, Friedrich xiv, 90
environment
    climate change 139–40
    environmental mismanagement 38
    pollution 118
Estonia 78, 198, 211, 216
    Estonia–Russia border 229–32
    history 217–18
    Latvia–Estonia frontier 219–24
    Narva 227–29
    NATO 225–26

ethnic cleansing 38–39, 57–58, 71, 77, 88, 97–98, 101, 183, 223, 231, 277–78
    First Nagorno-Karabakh War 39–41, 56–57
    Medz Yeghern (Great Crime/Armenian Genocide) 25–26, 27, 58
ethnic minorities xvi, 14, 80, 104, 150, 267–68
ethnic nationalism
    Azeri nationalism 38–39, 41–42, 50, 53–54, 59
    Belarus nationalism 209–10
    ethnic hatred and militarism 57–58
    First Nagorno-Karabakh War 39–41, 56–57
    Georgian nationalism 71, 74, 80
    Kazakh nationalism 92, 98
    Medz Yeghern (Great Crime/Armenian Genocide) 25–26, 27, 58
    Moldavian nationalism 236
    Romanian nationalism 236, 241
    Russian nationalism 92, 116, 161, 276
    Turkish nationalism 25–26
    Turkmenistan nationalism 183
    Ukrainian nationalism 252–53
EU alignment support and influence 65–69, 190–91, 200, 215–16, 219, 225, 229–30, 231–32, 237–38
Eurasian Economic Union 44, 267

F
Filat, Vlad 240
financial sector ix–x, 7, 38, 67
    digital banking 13
    financial sanctions 13–14
First World War 25, 36–37, 205, 253
five-year plans 2, 90, 159, 275
flag burning 24, 25, 57–58
flight sanctions 13, 67
Formula One 47–49
frozen conflicts 39, 274

G

Ganja 58–61
GDP 44, 99, 112, 116–17, 142, 159, 211, 240, 251, 277
genocide xvi, 5, 35
    Khojaly genocide 56–57
    Medz Yeghern (Great Crime/Armenian Genocide) 25, 27, 29, 58
geography 25, 33–34, 67, 86, 100, 117, 149, 153–54, 162–63, 182, 252, 275
Georgia 63–80
glasnost 38
Gorbachev, Mikhail x, xiv, 38, 50, 113, 225
Goris 33–34, 36, 39
Great Patriotic War (1941–45) xii, 196
Gulags 64, 86, 88, 90, 96, 116, 119, 203
Gyumri 35

H

heritage *see* cultural heritage

I

identity xvi, 90–91, 107–8, 114–15, 137, 172, 196, 202, 218–19, 236
identity cards 75–76, 220
immigration 27–29
    immigrant workers 142, 160–61
imperial influences 25, 80, 114–15, 171
    Achaemenid Empire 148
    Austrian Empire 236
    modern Yerevan 29–30
    Ottoman Empire 25–26, 236
    Russian Empire 36–37, 48, 129, 223, 236, 261
    Seljuk Empire 179
    Soviet Empire xiv, 44–45, 88, 116
independence 62, 71–73, 99, 100, 176, 183, 198, 209–10, 219, 230–31, 241, 251
    border conflicts 32–33, 36–39, 44, 48–49, 50, 57, 71, 152, 156

civil war 50, 102, 121, 136, 142, 148, 149–50, 153, 162–63, 246
economic impact of 123, 140, 223–24, 225, 230–31
independence movements 72, 275–76
Soviet collapse xiv, xvi–xvii, 53–54, 86–87, 107–8, 113–14, 116–18, 140, 149, 199–200, 227
inequalities 104–5, 130–31, 132, 211
inflation x, 198–99, 251
infrastructure 211, 276
    Baku–Tbilisi–Ceyhan pipeline 52
    Belt and Road Initiative 118–19
    bridges 229–30
    China Road and Bridge Corporation 118–19, 154
    pipelines 52
    power stations 118
    railways 33, 41, 44–45, 117, 181, 239
    roads 30–31, 33–34, 36, 41–42, 156, 229–30, 239
    Tallinn–Saint Petersburg highway 229–30
international aid 112
International Labour Organization 138–39
international relations xi, 8, 51–53, 148, 228–29
Iranian influence 25, 27, 28, 42, 44, 86, 147, 153
Islamic religion 24, 49, 86, 115, 121, 126–28, 130–31, 134–36, 139–40, 146, 150–51, 179, 183, 255
Ivanishvili, Bidzina 67

J

Japarov, Sadyr 111–13, 247–48
Jewish populations 73, 196, 213, 231, 251

K

Karaganda 86–91
Karimov, Islam 135–37, 139–40, 171

Kazakhstan 85–105
KGB xvi–xvii, 38, 51, 52, 199, 206–8, 212–13, 275
khans and khanates xv, 114–15, 122, 128, 171, 174
Khojaly genocide (1992) 56–57
Khrushchev, Nikita xi, 7, 77–78, 136, 177
Kuchma, Leonid 266
Kyiv/Kiev 253–54, 257–59, 262, 263–65, 268, 272
Kyrgyzstan 107–120

L
landlocked nature of states 25, 116, 122, 149, 233
Latvia 211, 217–19
  falling population 224
  immigrants 231–32
    Russian immigrants 227–28, 229
  Latvia–Estonia frontier 219–24
  NATO forces 226
  Lithuania, relationship with 217–18, 222–23
Lenin, Vladimir 7, 73, 90, 175, 269, 274
LGBTQ+ rights xvi, 67–68, 69–71
life expectancy x, 3–4, 80
Lithuania 189, 212, 252, 255
  border 229
  Christianity 194–95, 218
  falling population 224
  Jewish population 231
  language 217–18
  Latvia, relationship with 217–18, 222–23
  NATO forces 226–27
  Polish population 231
  Polish-Lithuanian Commonwealth 194–95, 218
  Vilnius 212–14
  World Corruption Perception Index 216
literary culture 31, 57, 109, 183

M
Marx, Karl 90, 120, 135
media xii–xiii, 10, 14, 33, 112–13, 169
  social media 54, 103, 142, 169
  state media 50, 69–70, 270
  see also propaganda
Medz Yeghern (Great Crime/Armenian Genocide) 25–26, 27, 29, 58
migration xvi, 86, 102, 114–15, 161
Mirziyoyev, Shavkat 139–40
Moldova 233–48
Molotov-Ribbentrop Pact 195, 217, 236
multiculturalism 37–38, 101
musical culture 28–29, 34, 40, 56, 103, 259, 277

N
Nagorno-Karabakh Wars
  Autonomous Oblast status 37–38
  Azerbaijani offensive in Nagorno-Karabakh (2023) 41, 274
  First Nagorno-Karabakh War (1988–94) 32, 39–41, 56–57
  Nagorno-Karabakh/Artsakh 32–36
  Second Nagorno-Karabakh War (2020) 28, 32–33, 57
national anthems x, 24, 28, 66, 195–96, 205
national security xiii, 231
  see also NATO; security forces
NATO xii, 4–5, 12, 65–66, 104, 151, 190–91, 219, 225–27, 231–32
natural resources 25, 47–48
  European dependence on 49
Nazarbayev, Nursultan 91–94, 97, 98–99
Nazi death camps 88, 96
9/11 attacks 150–51
Niyazov, Saparmurat 136, 170, 171–73
nuclear tests 86
nuclear weapons xvi, 196

O
October Revolutions 36–37, 102, 128

oil and gas sector 62, 116–19, 165, 171–72, 176, 182, 200, 233–35, 242, 248
oligarchic dictatorship 66–67, 99, 235, 239–40, 258
Olympics (1980) 53–54
Operation Barbarossa (1941) 195
Ottoman empire 25, 56–58, 234, 236

P

Paksas, Rolandas 216
patriotism xii, 125, 201
perestroika x, 38, 114, 205, 278
Persian influence 25, 31–32, 41, 48, 64, 86, 147–49, 171
Plahotniuc, Vlad 240
pogroms
    Medz Yeghern (Great Crime/Armenian Genocide) 25
    Osh pogrom 277
    Sumgait pogrom 38–39, 57
Polish-Lithuanian Commonwealth 194–95, 218
populism 199, 240, 276
propaganda 12, 70, 100, 189–90, 195, 236, 278
    see also media
Putin, Vladimir xii, 7, 52, 69–70, 72, 103, 137, 230
    Chechnya 150–51
    Crimea 200, 256
    NATO 225–26
    Ukraine 252–53
    see also Ukraine

R

Rahmon, Emomali 142, 144, 150–51, 199, 200
Red Army xiv, 73, 90, 108, 220, 223, 225, 236
Riga 218–19, 222
Russia 1–15
Russian Federation x, 92, 116–17, 191, 225
Russophobia 225–26, 227–28
Russian Civil War (1917–22) 37, 74, 212, 243
Russian peacekeeping 39–41
Rose Revolution (2003) 66, 72

S

Saakashvili, Mikheil 66–67, 72, 79–80, 215
sanctions xi, 2, 13–14, 113, 233, 267
Sandu, Maia 234
Sargsyan, Vazgen 30
Second World War xii, 48, 51, 88, 96, 100, 148, 171, 199–201, 211, 213, 231, 236, 243
    Molotov-Ribbentrop Pact 195, 217, 236
    Nazi invasion of the Soviet Union 134–36, 195–96, 223, 253, 255–56
secret police 73, 190, 202–3, 206
security forces 51, 73, 268–69
    see also national security; NATO
Shevardnadze, Eduard 66, 73
Siberia 115
social media 54, 103, 142, 169
Soviet Union's collapse xiv, xvi–xvii, 53–54, 57, 113–14, 80, 86–87, 107–8, 113–14, 140, 199–200, 227
    economic impact 116–18, 149
Stalin, Joseph 128
    Baltic States 217
    Crimea 255–56
    five-year plans 2, 90–91
    Georgia 73–75, 77–80, 135
    Kazakhstan 90–91
    Molotov-Ribbentrop Pact 195, 217, 236
    Operation Barbarossa 195
    Tajikistan 144
    Ukraine xiv, 7
state media 50, 69–70, 270
subsidies 116, 200, 242, 248, 267
Sumgait pogrom 38–39, 57
Silk Road xv, xvii, 86, 122–23, 140, 147

T

Tajikistan 141–163
Tallinn 217–19, 224, 226–28, 246, 277
    Tallinn–Saint Petersburg highway 229–30
Tbilisi 65–72, 74–75, 77–79, 101, 202–3
    Baku–Tbilisi–Ceyhan pipeline 52
Ter-Petrosyan, Levon 31
Timur, Amir 133–35, 136
Tokayev, Kassym-Jomart 97, 99, 103
Treaty of Kars (1921) 26
Turkey and Turkish influence 33
    Armenian Question 24–25, 25–26, 44, 45–46
    Turkish nationalism 25–26
    see also Ottoman empire
Turkmenistan 165–184
Transnistria 241–48, 251, 254, 280

U

Ukraine 249–72
    Russian invasion of Ukraine 1–7, 270–72
    demonstrations against 9–13
    financial markets 7–8
    migration and refugees 15
    propaganda 12–13
    Security Council 7
USSR xiv, 36–37, 77
    China, relationship with 275
    emigration from 97–98
    Gorbachev 38–39
    Great Patriotic War 196
    identity destruction of 90–91
    military service 161–62
    nuclear testing sites 86
    Rose Revolution 66
    Soviet collapse xiv, xvi–xvii, 32, 53–54, 57, 113–14, 80, 86–87, 107–8, 113–14, 116–18, 140, 149, 199–200, 227
Uzbekistan 121–140
UNESCO
    culinary traditions and food xiii, 39
    heritage sites 178

V

Vilnius 189, 210, 212–19, 224

W

wealth and prosperity ix–x, 30, 47–48, 58–59, 125, 132, 179–80, 224, 276
    corruption 239–40
    oil and gas 48–49, 116–17, 184
writing systems 31–32
World Corruption Perception Index 216

Y

Yanukovych, Viktor 265–66, 267–70
Yeltsin, Boris 116
Yerevan 22, 24, 26–34